Tarantino

A to Zed

Alan Barnes & Marcus Hearn

Tarantino

A to Zed
The films of Quentin Tarantino

B T Batsford Ltd, London

© Alan Barnes and Marcus Hearn 1996
First published 1996
Printed and bound by BPC Consumer Books Ltd
a member of the British Printing Company.

for the publishers
B T Batsford Ltd
4 Fitzhardinge Street
London W1H 0AH

ISBN 0 7134 7990 6

A CIP catalogue record for this book is available
from the British Library

Thanks to:
The British Film Institute, Claire and Chris
Coulthard, Max Decharne, Chris Gavin, Warwick
Gray, David Hanks, Joe McIntyre,
Simon Middleton and Adrian Rigelsford.

Special thanks to Richard Reynolds for
having faith.

For Jane, who won't watch *Reservoir Dogs* - AB

For Samantha, who will - MH

Photographic credits:
BFI Stills, Posters and Designs; Ixtlan/New
Regency/Warner Bros; Live Entertainment Inc;
Morgan Creek/Warner Bros; Miramax/Buena Vista;
Miramax/Dimension Films; Miramax/Rank; Rysher
Entertainment/Savoy Pictures/Jim Sheldon. The
publisher will be happy to correct any uninten-
tional omissions or oversights in future editions
of this book.

CONTENTS

INTRODUCTION: SHOTS IN THE DARK

It's somewhat naive to assume that writer/director Quentin Tarantino is fundamentally artless, and that his major works - *True Romance, Natural Born Killers, Reservoir Dogs, Pulp Fiction* and *From Dusk Till Dawn* - function solely on a similarly unsophisticated level.

The story - and it's been told many times before - goes something like this: goofy kid from Knoxville, Tennessee comes to represent the spirit of the age via sensational and nihilistic screenplays which place inverted commas around contemporary media. He writes from the heart; he writes all he knows. Ageing, obscure films, syndicated reruns of creaky TV shows, fast food, fast death, fast talk, quick fixes: all are grist to his mill. From humble beginnings, this MTV messiah of a generation equally crass, equally empty-headed - and wannabees all - comes to incarnate the zeitgeist; his is the apotheosis of the banal.

It's an old story; it's the story of George Washington, Kurt Cobain, and a thousand more besides. It's a crass story, a Hollywood story, and we've seen and heard it all before. Quentin Tarantino is last year's news; the King is dead.

There is, however, a story as yet untold. It's the story of a cunning and clever film-maker, a wily teller of devious and deviant tales; a man who has revitalized the art of film dialogue, rejected linear narrative style and, indeed, conventional narrative exposition. It's the story, too, of his films; of their content, not just their context, not just their style. This, too, is the story of Quentin Tarantino; long live the King.

This book attempts to reclaim Quentin Tarantino and his films from the clutches of the smartass and the cynical; from the devoted and the devotional, the fucked-off and the fucked-over. We seek to identify the primary concerns of Tarantino's many texts, and key elements within their discourse; we seek, also, recurrent images and motifs. We seek to identify Tarantino's purpose and reason; in interviews, he is often reluctant to enter into precise explanation and examination of aspects of his work. His honest evasiveness hints at some subconscious cinematic mojo which he can't quite pin down; the hellhound at his heels. And where his biography casts light on his filmography, that, too, is documented.

We seek to contextualise Tarantino's films in terms of cinema history, and theory; we seek to identify his influences. We seek to place his films within genres, fragmented and blurred as their borders may be; we analyse his writing through his characters. We tell the stories, too, of his significant collaborators, divorced from the larger Tarantino myth. In short, we seek to present Quentin Tarantino as a fully-fledged auteur, not merely as chancer, stylist, generation hero, passing phenomenon or idiot savant.

To this end, *Tarantino A to Zed* exhaustively catalogues all things Tarantino: meaningful, apocryphal, ephemeral, trivial and debatable alike. Duly cross-referenced, this book attempts to echo in form the poetic jumble of diverse and arcane references which doubtless reverberates throughout the mind of Quentin Tarantino.

You may be none the wiser, but you'll be better informed.

Alan Barnes and Marcus Hearn
London 1996

AUTHORS' NOTE

Tarantino: A to Zed traces the development of Quentin Tarantino's work through his screenwriting and direction above all other aspects of his career. Unless otherwise specified, quotes or reported script dialogue belong to the final drafts completed by Tarantino and/or his chosen collaborators. The major scripts are considered in order of their completion:

My Best Friend's Birthday

Initially written by Craig Hamann and Quentin Tarantino in 1985, the protracted production of the film saw its screenplay constantly revised over the following three years.

True Romance

Written by Quentin Tarantino in 1987, drawing upon elements of a Roger Avary script entitled *The Open Road* (1985). From 1992 to 1993, director Tony Scott undertook minor revisions which were completed when Roger Avary rewrote the beginning and end of the screenplay. The *True Romance* referred to in this book is the final draft screenplay filmed by Tony Scott.

Natural Born Killers

Completed by Quentin Tarantino in 1989, once again drawing upon Avary's *The Open Road*. The script was supplemented by Roger Avary in 1990, and radically rewritten by David Veloz, Richard Rotowski and Oliver Stone in 1993. The 1990 version of the script is the version concentrated on in this book.

Reservoir Dogs

Completed in 1991, following initial work in 1990.

Pulp Fiction

Completed in early 1993, after nearly a year's work. Storyline input was contributed by Roger Avary in 1992.

Four Rooms

Penthouse: The Man From Hollywood, Quentin Tarantino's segment of this anthology, was written in 1994.

From Dusk Till Dawn

Initially written by Quentin Tarantino in 1990 from a storyline by Robert Kurtzman. The script was extensively overhauled by Tarantino in 1995 to form the screenplay for Robert Rodriguez's film.

NB: Films of the above screenplays are considered in order of their release. For further details see appendix.

The spelling of character names Dr Emil Reinghold and Wayne Gayle differ in Tarantino's script of *Natural Born Killers* and Oliver Stone's screenplay. Depending on which version of *Natural Born Killers* is under consideration, spelling alters accordingly.

'I ALWAYS HOPE THAT IF ONE MILLION PEOPLE SEE MY MOVIE, THEY SEE A MILLION DIFFERENT MOVIES'

QUENTIN TARANTINO

TARANTINO: A to ZED

a

A BAND APART PRODUCTIONS

The production company part-responsible for *Pulp Fiction*, *Four Rooms* and *From Dusk Till Dawn* was founded late in 1991 by Tarantino and producer Lawrence Bender (qv), and named after Jean-Luc Godard's 1964 movie *Bande a Part*, aka *Band of Outsiders*. Start-up finance came from Danny De Vito's Jersey Films, impressed enough by *Reservoir Dogs*'s script to involve themselves in a loose, co-operative development arrangement. Later, the company's overheads were paid by Miramax Pictures as part of a deal which granted Miramax first refusal on their projects for two years. A second company, A Band Apart Commercials, was formed in 1995: this, overseen by Bender, produces advertisements and promos. The company's *Reservoir Dogs*-inspired logo was first seen opening the *Pulp Fiction* title sequence, and was later cheekily corrupted in *Four Rooms*'s animated introduction.

ALABAMA WHITMAN

Although the original script of *True Romance* had Alabama wetting herself in a moment of weakness, she remains the strongest, and most resourceful, female character Tarantino has yet devised.

Alabama claims to have acquired her curious Christian name following an amusing incident when her mother went into labour. Her father was so shocked that he crashed the car taking her to hospital. As Mrs Whitman's contractions started, a passing bus stopped and the driver picked up the couple, going out of his way to drive them to hospital. The proud parents were so grateful to the driver that they offered to name their baby girl after him. Unfortunately his name was Waldo, so they instead opted for the driver's place of birth - Alabama. The baby girl grows up and grows out of Tallahassee, moving to Detroit and finding a job as a call-girl for drug-pushing pimp Drexl Spivey. It is when she is hired as a birthday present for comic shop clerk Clarence Worley that she finds true romance.

Clarence is Alabama's third, and last, 'trick'. The two fall in love and marry. 'Is she a four alarm fire or what?' Clarence proudly asks his father, who is similarly impressed. 'Son of a bitch was right', he exclaims after receiving a lingering goodbye kiss. 'She tastes like a peach.' If, as Tarantino has claimed, Alabama was a 'dream girlfriend', then she proves to be Clarence's wet dream of a wife - such favourites as X-rated martial arts movies, fast food, and sex in phone boxes are all on the menu. Following Clarence's murder of Drexl, Alabama is similarly devoted.

Whereas Clarence learns his streetwise behaviour from the movies he devours, it is Alabama's bitter experience that has ingrained certain instincts for survival. She is an accomplished liar, initially deceiving Clarence into thinking theirs was a chance meeting and later fooling Dick into thinking that her facial injuries are the result of a basketball mishap. At one point, she even fools herself into thinking a call girl is different from a whore, and that the whole sordid experience would lead to something better.

Her resourcefulness also manifests itself in her brutal self-defence against murderous hitman Virgil. Her corkscrew attack was heavily censored from director Tony Scott's film, but Tarantino's script revealed much of the passionate hatred behind her animalistic retaliation: 'The ferocity in women that comes out at certain times, and is just under the surface in every woman all of the time, is unleashed.'

Four Rooms: The Man From Hollywood, based on *Alfred Hitchcock Presents: Man From the South.*

In the original script of *True Romance* Alabama is widowed, with only her memories and a *Sgt Fury* comic to remind her of Clarence. She contemplates suicide, then drifts into a life of crime, teaming up with *Reservoir Dogs*'s Larry Dimick before once more going solo. The ending devised by Roger Avary for the film is far more satisfying - Alabama and Clarence raise a family in paradise and finally achieve their dream. After all she's been through, she deserves it.

(See also: Arquette, Patricia; Clarence Worley; Women; X-rated)

ALFRED HITCHCOCK PRESENTS: MAN FROM THE SOUTH

An episode of the US TV anthology series invoked in, and inspiring, Tarantino's *Four Rooms* segment, *The Man from Hollywood.* Incorrectly recalled in *Four Rooms* as 'The Man From Rio', *Man From the South* - first broadcast on 13 March 1960, directed by Norman Lloyd, teleplay by William Fay from a short story by Roald Dahl - starred Steve McQueen and Peter Lorre as the participants in an ill-fated bet concerning a Zippo lighter. (Other parts were played by Neile Adams, Tyler McVey, Katherine Squire, Marc Cavell and Phil Gordon.) The segment has been remade twice: in 1979, as the first instalment of Anglia Television's long-running British anthology series, *Tales of the Unexpected* (first broadcast 24 March 1979, directed by Michael Tuchner, teleplay by Kevin Goldstein-Jackson, and starring Jose Ferrer, Michael Ontkean, Katy Jurado, Cyril Luckham, and Pamela Stephenson); and in 1985, as the second part of a one-off two-hour NBC TV movie which re-created four *Alfred HItchcock Presents* segments in all (first broadcast 5 May 1985, directed by Steve De Jarnatt, teleplay by Steve De Jarnatt from William Fay's 1960 script, and starring John Huston, Steven Bauer, Melanie Griffith, Tippi Hedren, Kim Novak, Jack Thibeau and Danny de la Paz). The original Dahl story can be found in the anthology *Someone Like You.*

(See also: Fingers; Lighters)

ALTER EGOS

A curious discrepancy emerges in Tarantino's accounts of his characters' inspiration. He often justifies their controversial dialogue by claiming they seem to take on lives of their own. He explained the process of self-discovery to *Time Out's* Geoff Andrew: 'When Jules has his epiphany, there was no big dictation on my part he'd end up that way; it was his decision, that's how he had to end up. I never force that moral stuff on my characters.' However, he also told *Sky* magazine's Karen Krizanovich: 'The thing is, there are all these different characters, but they're all ultimately me.'

Early on in his writing career, pragmatism dictated that Tarantino wrote a role for himself as rockabilly Clarence Pool in *My Best Friend's Birthday*. Another early effort, *Natural Born Killers*, featured an intended part for Tarantino in the obnoxious television anchorman Wayne Gayle. The most interesting script from this period was ultimately produced without an appearance from its author, although it is now regarded as his most autobiographical work. *True Romance* is a thinly disguised catalogue of key times and places from Tarantino's life. Prior to his reinvention as a small-time drug baron, Clarence Worley provides a revealing insight into the lifestyle of Tarantino circa 1987, when *True Romance* was written. The similarities between the character and its creator are clear: Clarence lives next to an airport - Tarantino lived by Los Angeles Airport; Clarence has worked in a comic shop for nearly four years - Tarantino was a comics fan who, by 1987, had been working at a video rental store for just that time; Clarence has a benevolent boss called Lance - Tarantino enjoyed a relaxed relationship with Video Archives's *laissez faire* manager Lance Lawson; Clarence watches three *Streetfighter* films as a birthday treat - Tarantino's birthday treats also included triple bills of Sonny Chiba's *Terry Surki* movies; Clarence spoons excessive heaps of sugar into his coffee - Tarantino has a sweet tooth when it comes to the same tasty beverage

(in *Pulp Fiction*, Winston Wolf similarly prefers 'lotsa cream, lotsa sugar'). A scripted reference by Clarence to 'that Merchant-Ivory claptrap' never made it into Tony Scott's finished film, although Tarantino has since echoed similar sentiments: 'I don't want to do a Merchant-Ivory film at all', he once claimed. 'I don't even want to see one.'

True Romance first crosses over into fantasy when Alabama's fairy tale love for Clarence is affirmed when the couple marry. Even here, however, an element of wishful thinking inspired the script. 'He meets this girl and becomes this romantic fool', recalled Tarantino. 'I had never had a girlfriend when I wrote that script.'

Tarantino wrote a role for himself in *Reservoir Dogs*, originally as the reprehensible Mr Pink, but the script generally borrows more from cinema than real life. The influence of its author's personal experience is most obvious in the pre-credit sequence, where Mr White refuses to tip the pancake house waitress out of principle. Lance Lawson recalls the young Tarantino sharing a similar aversion to tipping, although he concedes this was probably a long abandoned by-product of having no money. In the finished screenplay, it is Mr Pink, and not Mr White, who keeps his wallet in his pocket. Elsewhere, Freddy Newendyke lies about how his friend's brother is serving a sentence in the county jail because his 'traffic ticket's gone to warrant'. The same fate befell Tarantino when, unable to pay $7000 worth of amassed traffic tickets, he served ten days in prison.

One of the key self-referential elements the author builds into both *True Romance* and *Reservoir Dogs* is the dysfunctional father-son relationship. (Although he has long since adopted his surname, Tarantino is yet to meet his own father.) Both films take an optimistic stance on such painful separation - Clarence is reunited with Cliff after three years of non-communication and, following some initial hostility, his father soon agrees to take a risk on behalf his son and new daughter-in-law. The strength of their hurriedly resumed relationship is overwhelming. In *Reservoir Dogs*, the paternal attitude Joe takes towards his most trusted 'soldiers' is eclipsed by the father-son relationship that develops between Mr White and Mr Orange. The closeness between the two men develops from friendly advice to close physical contact. 'Will you please hold me?' pleads the dying Mr Orange, and Mr White cradles the younger man like a baby. The revelation of the deceit behind that trust proved taxing for both actors. 'Harvey [Keitel] is one of those actors who, when he's performing, always looks for something personal from his own experience to get the emotions', Tim Roth told *The Face* magazine. 'So we had to go to some very dark places to do that scene at the end, which is about betrayal, the father-son relationship between us.'

If Clarence Worley is a veiled representation of Quentin Tarantino as he was in 1987, then Chester Rush is a more obvious parody of Quentin Tarantino in 1995. The script of *Four Rooms: Penthouse: The Man From Hollywood* included a character description of the man many detractors were all to eager to believe was the real Quentin Tarantino: 'And standing in the middle of the biggest room in the hotel is the hottest, newest comedy star to burst onto the Hollywood scene in nearly a decade; Chester Rush. At this moment in time he's the king, and he has the swagger of a new king. After only one movie, he pulled the sword out of the stone.'

'I just got through reading three, count 'em, three, biographies of my life', Tarantino told *Premiere*'s Peter Biskind, prior to the release of *Four Rooms*. 'They're questioning my character - I'm a really bad person, I've fucked all the Video Archives guys, Roger Avary is the true genius behind all my work. All these questions about what an asshole I've become, what do I

do? I come out with a movie where I play an asshole!'

Whereas *True Romance* stands as an affectionate memoir, *The Man From Hollywood* is perhaps best seen as a satire on the world Tarantino now finds himself in. Although the two scripts have different aspirations, they are both informed by the same observational style. 'The things that Clarence says, they're the things that I and the rest of us said,' claimed Tarantino, recalling *True Romance*. 'The conversations he has are the conversations we had.'

(See also: Chester Rush; Clarence Worley; Tarantino, Quentin [as actor]; Yuppie scum)

AMOS 'N' ANDY

Immortalised in *Pulp Fiction* as a $5.00 Jack Rabbit Slim's milkshake, Amos 'n' Andy were the lead characters in *The Amos 'n' Andy Show*, a long-running and massively popular US radio comedy series which began in 1925. White actors Charles Correll and Freeman F Gosden played black NYC residents Amos Jones and Andrew Halt Brown: Correll and Gosden later produced the TV version, which debuted on CBS on 28 June 1951. Despite the two leads being given to black actors Alvin Childress and Spencer Williams Jr, the small screen version proved racially controversial, and the last episode aired on 11 June 1953. (Although unspecified, the Amos 'n' Andy shake is presumably chocolate-flavoured, as opposed to the vanilla Martin and Lewis.)

(See also: Jack Rabbit Slim's; Martin and Lewis)

ANDERS, ALLISON (1954 -)
Writer/director, *Four Rooms: Honeymoon Suite: The Missing Ingredient*

Following a traumatic adolescence which led to her being temporarily committed to a mental asylum, Kentucky-born Anders graduated from UCLA's prestigious film course and first worked as a production assistant on Wim Wenders's *Paris, Texas*. After co-directing (with Kurt Voss) 1988's *Border Radio*, her debut solo project was 1992's *Gas Food Lodging*, which was entered into competition at that year's Sundance Film Festival. There, she first met Tarantino, who'd noticed the *Charlie's Angels* board game in the background of a scene in Anders's film. One year later, Anders was engaged in post-production on her follow-up, *Mi Vida Loca* ('My Crazy Life', which, pre-*Pulp Fiction*, used three separate narratives concerning an interconnected set of characters), when they met up again at a screening of Alexandre Rockwell's *In The Soup*. Anders and Tarantino dated occasionally, and indulged his passion for board games - including the aforementioned *Charlie's Angels* game, the Mr T game, and a game called Mystery Date - and also guested together on a phone-in radio show, *Love Lines*. Late in 1994, Anders helmed the *The Missing Ingredient* segment of *Four Rooms*, each part of which was directed by an attendee at Sundance in 1992: originally, Anders scripted references to *Reservoir Dogs*'s Mr Pink, which were cut

when Steve Buscemi (qv) passed on the role of the bellhop. *Grace of My Heart*, Anders's third solo film, was shot during 1995. Produced by Martin Scorsese, it starred Patsy Kensit (whom Anders had wanted for *The Missing Ingredient*), John Turturro, Matt Dillon, and Eric Stoltz (qv).

(See also: Sundance institute; Trust and betrayal)

ARQUETTE, ALEXIS (1970 -)
Fourth Man, *Pulp Fiction*

Brother to Rosanna and Patricia (both qv), Alexis played the Fourth Man, whose panicked shooting at Jules and Vincent - 'Die, you motherfuckers! Die!' - becomes subject to 'divine intervention'. Other credits include: *Letzte Ausfahrt Brooklyn* (Last Exit to Brooklyn) (1989) and *Jumpin' at the Boneyard* [with Tim Roth, qv] (1991).

ARQUETTE, PATRICIA (1968 -)
Alabama Whitman, *True Romance*

Patricia Arquette was born in Chicago, Illinois into a well-practised clan of actors: grandfather Cliff was best known for playing the mill owner in *The Waltons*, parents Lewis and Brenda were hippy performers, and her various siblings - Rosanna (qv), Richmond, Alexis (qv) and David - later acted in features to varying degrees of success. First married young, her son, Enzo, was named after the baker in *The Godfather* - and appeared as Elvis, the son of Clarence and Alabama, in the closing shots of *True Romance*. Her initial brush with Tarantino came when she was auditioned sometime in 1991 for a part in the twenty-minute *American Maniacs* segment of *Natural Born Killers* which the then-attached producer Rand Vossler was planning to direct in order to attract potential investors to the project; nothing came of it (see Stone, Oliver). Arquette was cast as *True Romance*'s Alabama in the late summer of 1992 (Jennifer Jason Leigh's name having been briefly attached to

Alexis Arquette, the Fourth Man in *Pulp Fiction*, is about to miss from very close range . . .

Patricia Arquette stars in
True Romance.

now owns *True Romance*'s purple Cadillac, a present from director Tony Scott. Other credits include: *A Nightmare on Elm Street 3* (1987), *The Indian Runner* (1991), *Trouble Bound* [with Michael Madsen, qv] (1992), *Ethan Frome* (1993), *Beyond Rangoon* (1994) and *Ed Wood* (1994).

(See also: Alabama Whitman; X-rated)

ARQUETTE, ROSANNA (1959 -)
Jody, *Pulp Fiction*

Elder sister to Patricia (qv), Rosanna Arquette plays *Pulp Fiction*'s Jody, wife to drug dealer Lance, whose obsession with body-piercing results in her proudly sporting five holes in each ear, and one apiece in her left nipple, her left eyebrow, her right nostril, her lip, her clitoris, and a stud in her tongue - this latter 'a sex thing' (it helps fellatio, apparently). As a teenager, Arquette claims to have had 'a huge crush' on later *Pulp* co-star John Travolta; Travolta's sister, Ellen, was a friend of the family. Arquette was originally auditioned by Tarantino for the part of Mia Wallace; she was inspired to have her nose pierced after playing Jody. Other credits include: *Baby, It's You* [with Robert Downey Jr, qv] (1982), *Desperately Seeking Susan* [with Madonna and Steven Wright, both qv] (1985), *Silverado* (1985), *After Hours* [with Dick Miller and Bronson Pinchot, both qv] (1985), *8 Million Ways To Die* [with Randy Brooks, part-written by Oliver Stone, both qv] (1986) and *New York Stories* [with Steve Buscemi, qv] (1989).

the role). 'I loved Alabama', she says, 'What a terrible childhood she had - always saying, "I've got to get noticed, I'll put on a pretty dress".' Arquette played Alabama's Southern accent as an affectation. *True Romance*'s standout scene - wherein Alabama is tormented by, and later executes, the sadistic Mafia hitman Virgil - caused her to delve deep into the character's psyche. She told America's *Interview* magazine: 'I wanted Alabama to get to a point where - although she wasn't enjoying being beaten by Virgil - it would be emotionally painful to her to kill him. As Alabama, I know one of us is gonna end up dead, and it's not gonna be me . . . I have no doubt about the strength of women. I have no doubt what we're capable of . . . Of course, Alabama ends up being victorious in the end, but I wanted to show emotionally how much more of a weight it is for a woman to get there.' Arquette

AUSTEN, JANE (1775 - 1817)

English novelist (*Pride and Prejudice*, etc); in 1995, a resurgence of popular interest in her work following a number of high-profile television adaptations led Charles Denton, head of BBC drama, to describe her as 'the Quentin Tarantino of the middle classes'.

(See also: Spoofs)

AVARY, ROGER (1965 -)
Co-writer, *True Romance*
Co-writer, *Natural Born Killers*
Co-writer, *Reservoir Dogs*
Co-writer, *Pulp Fiction*

Collaborator with and former writing partner to Tarantino, Roger Roberts Avary, a one-time would-be animator, began his film career at 13 by making a number of 8mm shorts: three years later, one of these garnered him first prize at the Los Angeles Student Film Expo. He enrolled at, but later dropped out of, Pasadena's Art Center College of Design's Film Program. Having met frequent customer Tarantino while clerking at Video Archives (qv) in 1984, it was Avary who inviegled his fellow cinephile into a job there. They struck up a close friendship, and devised the *Top Gun* 'go the gay way' routine which Tarantino would later recite as part of his cameo appearance in 1994's *Sleep With Me* (see Tarantino, Quentin [as actor]).

Avary's ambition to work in the film industry was part-satisfied when he took time off to work briefly for schlock straight-to-video impresario Charles Band; he'd also made shorts with best friend Scott McGill, who later worked with Tarantino on the aborted *Lovebirds in Bondage*. Avary mucked in, too, as a crew member on Tarantino's ill-fated *My Best Friend's Birthday*. Tarantino and Avary's first formal collaboration came when elements of Avary's spec screenplay, *The Open Road* (qv) were reworked, with Avary's blessing, by Tarantino: this project mutated into an early composite of *True Romance* and *Natural Born Killers*. Avary had intended to produce both of these projects at an early stage, but would be sidelined during their development. Later, it was Avary who was called upon to make minor trims to, and rewrite the ending of, the Tony Scott-directed version of *True Romance*, altering Tarantino's bleak climax in which Clarence is killed to one in which Clarence and Alabama live happily ever after in Mexico. Avary also authored the 'bodybuilders' scene

in Tarantino's draft of *Natural Born Killers*, wherein the dismembered Brothers Hun, stars of *Conquering Huns of Neptune*, discuss - amongst other things - 1977's *Pumping Iron* and its stars Arnold Schwarzenegger and later Incredible Hulk, Lou Ferrigno. (This scene, cut from the cinema version, is retained on the US laserdisc edition of *NBK*.) By proxy, Avary also appears in *NBK*, Tarantino having created the character of Roger the soundman in tribute: described as wearing 'wild Hawaiian shirts and Bermuda shorts', 'Roger' suggests that interviewing Mickey Knox is on a par with 'Raymond Burr witnessing the destruction of Tokyo by Godzilla'.

Avary quit Video Archives at roughly the same time as Tarantino: in 1986 they worked as production assistants on the Dolph Lundgren exercise video *Maximum Potential*. They were paid $20 per day, and once had to pick a lawn clean of dog crap for the privilege. Together, they devised the basic notion of *Black Mask*, the three-part crime anthology which would evolve into *Pulp Fiction*. Avary wrote his segment up as a screenplay: *Pandemonium Reigns* concerned a boxer who doesn't throw a fight as planned and goes on the run from a bunch of gangsters. It included a McGuffin in the shape of a watch and an encounter with sexually sadistic rednecks - and everyone died in the finale. In the summer of 1992, with *Pulp Fiction* in pre-production, Tarantino bought the rights to *Pandemonium Reigns*, and Avary went to Amsterdam, where Tarantino was writing *Pulp*, to assist in weaving his story into *Pulp*'s complex fabric: it became *The Gold Watch*. Tarantino later claimed that the bathroom scene between Butch and Fabienne was the only part of the eventual screenplay to be entirely Avary's; Avary, however, disputed this, claiming that other parts of the segment remained distinctly his. (The two would stage a public reconciliation at the Academy Awards.)

Having also written the radio voices barely heard under the *Reservoir Dogs* soundtrack,

Avary had, by now, established a career as a
writer/director independent of his, if you
will, comrade-in-arms: he'd worked for LA ad
agency D'Arcy Masius Benton & Bowles as a
copywriter, authored several scripts, and completed rewrites on a screenplay of *Godfather*
novelist Mario Puzo's *The Lorch Team*. In the
spring of 1993 he shot his debut solo feature,
Killing Zoe (qv), starring Eric Stoltz (also qv).
Future projects include the science-fiction TV
movie *Mr Stitch*, with Rutger Hauer and Tom
Savini (qv); also mooted is a vampire flick
entitled *99 Days*, to be filmed in France starring *Zoe*'s Jean-Hugues Anglade. And
semi-legendary Hong Kong chopsocky maestro John Woo has been linked to an Avary
screenplay, *Hatchetman* (a draft of which featured a scene concerning *Top Gun* that has
since, unsurprisingly, been excised).

(See also: Awards; Europe; Pulp; Stoltz, Eric)

AWARDS

Pulp Fiction won the highly-regarded Palme
D'Or at the 1994 Cannes Film Festival; this
win would be followed by seven Oscar nomi-
nations - for best picture, best director, best
actor (John Travolta, qv), best original screenplay (Tarantino and Roger Avary, qv), best
supporting actor (Samuel L Jackson, qv), best
supporting actress (Uma Thurman, qv) and
best film editing (Sally Menke, qv) - at the
67th annual Academy Awards. Only one stat-
uette would go in the *Pulp* club's direction on
27 March 1995, their film losing out largely
to the Mom's apple pie-flavoured *Forrest
Gump*: Tarantino and Avary staged a very public
reconciliation in receiving jointly the award
for best original screenplay (but one week
previous, Tarantino had taken the equivalent
Golden Globe solo, a source of some dispute).
Neither of the recipients made any attempt at

Cannes, 1994:
Travolta, Thurman,
Tarantino and Willis.

a meaningful acceptance speech; seen
mouthing 'Shit!' on live TV when he lost out
to Martin Landau for his role as Bela Lugosi in
Ed Wood, Samuel L Jackson summed up his
feelings in a more succinct manner. *Pulp* was
also garlanded at the LA Critics' Awards (best
picture, best director, best screenplay, and best
actor to Travolta), at the New York Film Critics'
Circle (best director, best screenplay), at the
National Board of Review (best picture, best
director), at the BAFTA ceremony (best screenplay, best supporting actor to Jackson), and at
the Independent Spirit Awards (best feature,
best director, best screenplay, and best male
lead, again to Jackson). In 1995, *Pulp* was also
voted onto the top of the list of Britain's
well-respected *Empire* magazine's Readers' 100
Favourite Films of All Time. Places 2-5 were
taken by *Star Wars*, *Reservoir Dogs*, *Raging Bull*
and *Schindler's List* respectively, a listing which
led *The Observer*'s Philip French to bemoan,
'So much for film education'.

b

BADLANDS
(US, 1973, dir. Terrence Malick)

Key to both *True Romance* and *Natural Born Killers* is Malick's seminal love-on-the-run tale, *Badlands*. Indeed, both Alabama's voiceover and the chiming, childlike theme repeated throughout *True Romance* were added by director Tony Scott in post-production in explicit imitation of, respectively, Sissy Spacek's spaced-out Southern Belle 'teen romance' narration, and portions of Erik Satie's *Badlands* score.

In *Badlands*, loosely based on the Starkweather-Fugate killings of 1958, Kit Carruthers (Martin Sheen) and Holly Sargis (Sissy Spacek) flee justice after Kit coolly murders Holly's possessive father. After a long spell hiding out in woodlands, a paranoid Kit - with an increasingly reluctant Holly in tow - goes on an apparently motiveless killing spree across Dakota; their ever-spiralling notoriety inspires Kit to build up their 'legend'. Textual elements reprised in *True Romance* include: Kit himself, who, like Clarence, is an idol-worshipping obsessive (in this case, of James Dean. It would be convenient, despite the discrepancy between dates, to claim that Kit's insistence that Holly adopt the pseudonym

'Priscilla' might indicate a well-hidden Elvis Presley fixation on his part. It certainly could be claimed that Tarantino picked up on this, despite the error: *Badlands* is set in 1958-9, whereas Elvis didn't marry Priscilla until 1967. A fully intertextual reading might also note that Christian Slater, who played Clarence, was previously well-identified with Dean via the character of 'JD' in 1989's *Heathers*); the Cadillac (black in *Badlands*, purple in *True Romance*); and the lovers' desire to escape to 'a magical land beyond the reach of the law' (Satskatchewan and Cancun respectively). In *NBK*, Mickey and Mallory's killing spree begins with the murder of Mallory's father; the family bed is consumed with fire, again after *Badlands*; Mickey and Mallory enjoy a spell in the wilderness; and the star-crossed lovers share a common dialogue through Fifties American pop ephemera. More significantly, both Kit and Holly and Mickey and Mallory are consumed by their own infamy: lionised and demonised in their respective mass medias, both pairs desire to mythologise themselves, as seen in Kit's cynical commemoration of his declared last stand, and in Mickey and Mallory's leaving of one sole survivor in the diner to tell the world that they'd been there. After his capture, Kit is

asked why he committed the killings, and responds, 'I don't know . . . I always wanted to be a criminal, I guess' (he sees himself, perhaps, as a natural born killer): he even hands out his personal effects as mementoes to his arresting officers.

All three films share a common bond in their repudiation of liberal denials of media causality: if Kit murders to be identified with James Dean, then Mickey desires to see himself in the pantheon of legendary mass-murderers alongside such as Starkweather/Kit, and, in turn, movie geek Clarence might well seek to be identified with Martin Sheen as Starkweather/Kit (certainly, James Dean acts as Kit's mentor - albeit silently -in much the same way as Elvis eggs on Clarence). It should be noted that *Badlands* itself followed in a long-established line of 'love-on-the-run'

pictures: notorious couples who might count themselves as distant ancestors to Kit and Holly, Clarence and Alabama, and Mickey and Mallory would include Eddie and Jo Taylor in *You Only Live Once* (1937); 'Gunner' Martin and Dorothy Bronson in *Persons in Hiding* (1938); Bowie and Keechie in both *They Live By Night* (1948) and Robert Altman's 1974 re-make, *Thieves Like Us*; Bart Tare and Annie Laurie Starr in *Gun Crazy* (1949); and Bonnie Parker and Clyde Barrow in *Guns Don't Argue* (1957), *The Bonnie Parker Story* (1958), and *Bonnie and Clyde* (1967). Post-*Badlands*, such as Sailor and Lula in 1990's *Wild at Heart*, the killers in 1993's *Kalifornia* - plus, of course, *Pulp Fiction*'s Pumpkin and Honey Bunny - have upheld the tradition.

(See also: Causality and imitation; *The Open Road*)

Badlands, Terrence Malick's seminal love-on-the-run tale. Novelist and critic Will Self believes the film 'foreshadows *Natural Born Killers* in almost every respect'.

BALTZ, KIRK
Marvin Nash, *Reservoir Dogs*
Roger, *Natural Born Killers*

Aka Marvin the Cop, the hapless Baltz - the subject of perhaps the contemporary cinema's single most notorious act of violence - was scarcely treated better off-screen than on. Tied to a chair and muffled with tape during the ear scene ('sweaty and near to tears', recalled a crew member), Baltz had earlier requested that Michael Madsen (qv) lock him in the boot of his car, allegedly to 'get into character', to see what it felt like to be Mr Blonde's hostage. (Madsen actually took off with the incarcerated Baltz for a full half-hour, far more than the quick drive round the block Baltz had anticipated, and even stopped off for a Coke on the way.) Baltz later appeared in *NBK* as TV presenter Wayne Gale's cameraman, Roger, and - apparently - shot some scenes as live himself. Other credits include: *On the Make* (1989), *Dances With Wolves* (1991), *Probable Cause* (TVM, 1994) and *Kingfish* (TVM, 1995).

(See also: Stone, Oliver)

Kirk Baltz (seated) as Officer Marvin Nash in *Reservoir Dogs*. Mr Blonde (Michael Madsen) waits for his opportunity to speak with Nash in private - on the roof of a hearse . . .

BATHROOMS

'It's small, it's private, and you have a mirror in front of you. What more could you want?' asks Tarantino, who has employed the bathroom as the location for some of the most crucial character development in his scripts. In *True Romance*, Clarence's two on-screen bathroom visits are shared by the ghost of Elvis Presley (qv), half-glimpsed in the background or as a blurred reflection in the mirror. In *Pulp Fiction*, Vincent wrestles with his conscience and his feelings for Mia while alone in her bathroom.

Mirrors are an effective, if obvious, metaphor for the process of self-reflection. Clarence's self-image is so closely modelled on Elvis Presley that the ruminations of his conscience are voiced by Elvis himself. Alabama is clearly aware of her husband's fixation with The King (she names their son after him) but Clarence saves his most spiritual communions for the privacy of the smallest room.

In *Pulp*, Vincent addresses Mia's bathroom mirror in much the same way, except he doesn't benefit from Elvis's advice. 'You see, this is a moral test of oneself', he tells the mirror, pondering whether to make a pass at his boss's wife. The recent memory of Tony Rocky Horror's grisly fate is probably as strong an influence as any in Vincent's desicion to go home and jerk off instead. (Mia's imminent overdose is about to make her a distinctly unattractive proposition anyway.)

Freddy Newendyke addresses a mirror to boost his confidence prior to the *Reservoir Dogs* robbery, and bathrooms are employed elsewhere simply because they offer discreet hideaways. In *Dogs*, Mr White and Mr Pink argue over the botched heist in a tiled area towards the back of the warehouse, away from the dying Mr Orange. (Although the script states this to be a bathroom, the coffins and hearse outside would suggest it is actually a mortuary. When Mr Pink wants to go to the toilet, Mr White directs him all the way to the first floor.)

In *Pulp*, the bathroom at Jack Rabbit Slim's is hardly a discreet location for Mia to snort cocaine, but nobody seems to mind anyway. On the other hand, Brett's bathroom comes in very useful for the Fourth Man to launch his surprise attack on Jules and Vincent. As he privately rallies himself, summoning up the courage to assassinate the hitmen, his concentration is only broken by the sound of Jules quoting Ezekiel 25:17. He doesn't regain it in time to shoot straight.

BANDE A PART
(See: Godard, Jean-Luc)

BENDER, LAWRENCE
Producer, *Reservoir Dogs*
Producer/Long Hair Yuppie Scum,
Pulp Fiction
Producer/Long Hair Yuppie Scum,
Four Rooms
Co-executive producer, *From Dusk*
Till Dawn

Perhaps the least likely, but certainly the most significant, of Tarantino's many accredited Svengalis, Lawrence Bender was the man who effectively launched Tarantino's directorial career. A graduate in civil engineering from the University of Maine, Bender - bizarrely - took up a scholarship at Louis Falco's dance academy in New York; his planned Terpsichorean career was ended by a series of injuries. Plotting a shift into acting, he studied under drama coach Sandra Seacat; in the early Eighties, he took a number of very small film and television roles. (These included an episode of TV series *General Hospital*; once, he acted in an impromptu staging of *A Midsummer Night's Dream* with Christopher Walken, later cast in *Pulp*.) Acting wasn't working out; he crewed for free on an American Film Institute picture, enjoyed it, and did some more in various lowly capacities. His sights were now set on production. A mutual friend, Boaz Yakim, introduced

Bender to writer Scott Spiegel. Spiegel had devised an el cheapo schlock horror flick set in a supermarket; Bender saw his way in, learning producing skills on the hoof. The film, *Intruder* (aka *Night Crew - The Final Checkout*) found backing in October 1987, and was shot in the spring of 1988; it cost a meagre $125,000. Shortly thereafter, writer/director Spiegel met fellow film geek Tarantino; Tarantino and Bender were introduced at a Spiegel barbecue in 1990. Somewhat jaded, Bender had been unable to get any more projects off the ground since *Intruder*. Off-the-cuff, Tarantino pitched Bender the core notion of the as-yet-unwritten *Reservoir Dogs*; later, he gave Bender a full screenplay. An impressed Bender, having been warned that Tarantino was planning to shoot *Dogs* himself for next-to-nothing, asked for six months to find formal financial backing; he was given two, but promised a part in the Tarantino version, playing Nice Guy Eddie to Tarantino's Pink. Through a mutual acquaintance, Bender involved eventual executive producer Monte Hellman (qv) in the pre-production process (it was Hellman who would lead *Dogs* to financiers Live Entertainment); simultaneously, Bender drew Harvey Keitel (qv) into the circle through one of his former acting coaches, Lily Parker. After passing on several hopeless deals - one to do the film in a slapstick vein, one in which Mr Blonde would be a Ms - the Live Entertainment deal came good to the tune of $1.5 million. Bender attended the *Dogs* casting sessions - including those in New York - with Tarantino and Keitel. Bender drew up the film's schedule to protect its fledgling director: 'Quentin's big worry was being fired', he told *FilmMaker*, 'so we weren't going to schedule the more unconventional stuff upfront. There's a scene [between White and Pink] that's designed for very little coverage and we scheduled that in the middle of the shoot. And we scheduled some of the more conventional stuff in the beginning. So by the time [Live] saw it, they were already feeling good about the movie. It's not about lying or fooling people but about building confidence.'

Bender formed A Band Apart Productions (qv) with Tarantino, and devised the uniform per-week salary formula that kept *Pulp Fiction*'s budget down to a manageable $8.5 million. During *Pulp*'s pre-production process, Bender produced the drama *Fresh*, featuring Samuel L Jackson, for director Boaz Yakim; he also, with Tarantino, co-executive produced Roger Avary's *Killing Zoe* (qv). He attended the *Pulp* auditions, and was cast as 'Long Hair Yuppie Scum', a minor character in the film's climax (Bender reprised the role between *Four Rooms*'s first and second sections). He sees no need for over-inflated budgets: 'Make every dollar count . . . We could make *Reservoir Dogs* now for $15 million but we wouldn't. We would make it for $3 million . . .' Of his ongoing partnership with Tarantino, and their working relationship, Bender says, 'I'll be on the set and people will mistake me for the director because Quentin will be saying, "We don't have the time and money for that shot", and I'll be saying, "C'mon Quentin, I'll find the money for you. It's a great shot!"'

(See also: Yuppie scum)

BIG STORY, THE
(UK, 1994, dir. Tim Watts and David Stoten)
Tarantino was so impressed by this piece of stop-motion animation that he personally insisted it be added to the *Pulp Fiction* bill as a support feature. *The Big Story* fills its 2 minutes 5 seconds with a slice of black and white melodrama which parodies Billy Wilder's mordantly satirical 1951 movie *Ace in the Hole* (aka *The Big Carnival*). A newspaper editor's office is the scene of a bitter row between a disgruntled young reporter (Kirk Douglas) and his brash editor. The reporter is tired of being fobbed off with second-rate assignments and longs to cover front page stories. His boss, however, has other ideas.

The Big Story was shot on 35mm film by writers/directors Tim Watts and David Stoten for Spitting Image Productions. The two had first met while working on the satirical puppet show *Spitting Image* in 1984 and had intermittently worked on sculptures and animation for television title sequences ever since. *The Big Story* was their first film together. Frank Gorshin, famous for his portrayal of The Riddler in the Sixties television series *Batman*, provided the uncanny Kirk Douglas impression.

BLAXPLOITATION
Pulp Fiction's Jules Winnfield (qv) might have grooved straight outta any frame from any blaxploitation picture of the early Seventies; indeed, taken in tandem with the release of pictures such as Keenan Ivory Wayans's *I'm Gonna Git You, Sucka* and *A Low Down Dirty Shame*, he may yet be seen to have reinvigorated the entire genre. Hollywood's racist streak was first explicitly demonstrated in 1915's *The Birth of a Nation*; prior to the blaxploitation boom, cinema's black characters had only rarely been seen on an equal footing with whites, and scarcely, if ever, independent of the white man's philosophy and dress codes.

Post-Sydney Poitier, and kicked into gear by the growth of Black Power, Ossie Davis's Sam Goldwyn-financed *Cotton Comes to Harlem* (1970) attempted to redress the balance in its representation of genuine and unapologetic black heroes; however, Mario Van Peebles's independently-produced *Sweet Sweetback's Badasssss Song* (1971) took a bolder step forward. Bearing a dedication 'to all the Brothers and Sisters who have had enough of the Man', *Sweet Sweetback's* was the angry and polemicised tale of a young black man on the run from white urban (in)justice. That same year, Gordon Parks's *Shaft* formally identified the genre. Richard Roundtree's private eye John Shaft, a Bond in black leather, pits his wits against Harlem racketeers, pausing only to talk back to cops and bed his *lay-deez* (includingly

- incredibly - white chicks), all to the pulsing beat of Isaac Hayes's Oscar-winning soundtrack. *Shaft*'s huge success begat two MGM sequels (*Shaft's Big Score* and *Shaft in Africa*) and a TV series which lasted a mere eight instalments. But *Shaft*'s influence endured: blaxploitation boomed. Four major subgenres are identifiable: pimp movies (*Sweet Sweetback's*, *The Candy Tangerine Man*), pusher movies (*Superfly*, *Coffy*), prison movies (*The Slams*), and violent gangster epics (*Black Caesar*, *Detroit 9000*). And black women, led by Pam Grier (qv) and Tamara Dobson (as 'the

Hottest Super Agent Ever', *Cleopatra Jones*), began to get in on the act, too. The genre was all but dead by the mid-Seventies, swamped in a welter of cliche and silly horror movies such as *Blackenstein* and *Scream, Blacula, Scream!*. Blaxploitation did, nevertheless, pave the way for the reclaiming by the black community of former insults such as 'nigger' (amply demonstrated by Jules), and the early Nineties wave of political 'hood' movies, such as *New Jack City*, directed by Melvin Van Peebles's son, Mario. (Melvin would also script Mario's 1995

Max Julien (left) and Richard Pryor star in *The Mack*.

27

documentary-drama, *Panther*.) Scenes from 1974's *The Mack* - a popular and violent variation on the pimp movie - can be glimpsed in *True Romance*, where Clarence doesn't even have to spare the 'titties' showing on Drexl's TV a second glance to know what film is airing, because he saw it seven years previously: 'It's *The Mack* with Max Julian, Carol Speed, and Richard Pryor . . .' Cult blaxploitation/straight-to-video hero Fred Williamson (*The Legend of Nigger Charley*, *Black Caesar*, *Boss Nigger* etc) made a barely-credible cameo in *From Dusk Till Dawn* as harder-than hard Vietnam vet Frost; Williamson went on to star alongside the aforementioned Pam Grier - plus Jim Brown (*Black Gunn*), Ron O'Neal (*Superfly*) and Richard Roundtree - in Larry Cohen's celebratory 1995 homage, *Original Gangstas*.

(See also: Drexl Spivey; Jackson, Samuel L; Pulp; Race)

BLONDE ('TOOTHPICK' VIC VEGA)

'Hey Joe, want me to shoot this guy?' asks Mr Blonde during the pre-credit sequence of *Reservoir Dogs*. Such is his devotion to the gang leader that one could believe he is capable of murdering a colleague at the drop of a hat. His typically subdued threat typifies a man whose well-mannered air makes such callous immorality all the more alarming.

The man Joe and Eddie know as 'Toothpick' Vic Vega has a long history with 'the company' - he has already been arrested with stolen goods inside one of Joe's warehouses and resolutely refused to name his boss throughout a four year jail sentence. His loyalty is repaid with a cover job at a dockyard in Long Beach - legitimate enough to satisfy curious parole officers and sufficiently watertight an arrangement to free Vic for the diamond heist. Although Joe is initially reluctant to use one of his 'boys' on the job (a term of endearment applied either to those he has known since childhood, or those who are readily identified as being suspected accomplices), Eddie convinces him that Vic belongs in the gang. 'The guy's a fuckin' rabbit's foot', Nice Guy argues. 'We know he can handle himself and you damn sure know you can trust him.'

But prison has changed Vic more than anyone realises. During the robbery, Mr Blonde is assigned the task of controlling employees and customers, a role he tackles somewhat over enthusiastically. When an alarm is triggered, Blonde apparently starts firing indiscriminately, killing a young black girl and possibly injuring others. 'Fuck 'em', he later sneers. 'They set off the alarm. They deserve what they got.' His shooting almost kills Mr White and attracts the attention of the police, one of whom he kidnaps in order to make his escape from the chaotic scene. He bundles the hapless Officer Nash into the boot of his car and drives to the warehouse rendezvous, pausing only to call Eddie and pick up some fast food on the way. It is only when Mr Blonde begins torturing the policeman that we witness first hand why the others regard him as a 'psycho'. The sadistic maiming of the cop is clearly a well-versed practice Blonde takes great pleasure from: 'you can say anything you want - I've heard it all before', he claims. Prison has not only given him a taste for torture, but an incentive for revenge against the people who put him there. It is only Mr Orange, revealing his true personality beneath his disguise for the first time, who prevents Mr Blonde from burning the cop alive.

Eddie greets Mr Blonde's murder with obvious dismay - his blind loyalty towards the man he once knew speeds *Reservoir Dogs* to its bloody climax. In actual fact, the man Eddie once knew was obviously long dead before Freddy killed him.

(See also: Ears; Madsen, Michael; Morality; Vincent Vega)

BLOOD

'All this blood scares the shit out of me, Larry' - Mr Orange, *Reservoir Dogs*.

Buckets of the stuff are spilled throughout Tarantino's *oeuvre*. The ever-growing pool of Orange's blood that spreads during the course of *Reservoir Dogs* is a constant reminder of the director's responsible and realistic approach to depicting brutality. We are never allowed to forget that if you get shot in the gut you will slowly and painfully bleed to death.

Blood is also a feature of two recurring devices. In Tony Scott and Roger Avary's reworked ending to *True Romance*, Alabama crawls over to the 'dead' Clarence, believing him to have been shot in the head. When he finally stirs, she realises that 'Honey, you have blood in your eye.' (Had Tarantino had his way, Clarence would have had a bullet in his head as well.) In *Dogs*, Mr Brown succeeds in driving the car back to the warehouse after the robbery, even though he actually has been shot in the head. As death approaches, his senses begin to fail. A shell-shocked Mr Orange reassures him with, 'You're not blind, there's just blood in your eyes.' He's mistaken.

Whoever originated the idea, Roger Avary recalled the possible inspiration - a nuisance visitor to Video Archives. Tarantino was forced to manhandle the person from the shop, and in doing so slammed his head against the counter. The hapless customer started bleeding, the blood covering one of his eyes and collecting into a small pool.

Tarantino is also fond of spilling blood all over the insides of Chevy Novas, causing widespread staining to upholstery. The Nova Mr White commandeers after the *Dogs* robbery is considerably bloodied by Mr Orange's wounds. Having said that, the injured cop's writhing can't touch the mess made when Vincent accidentally shoots Marvin in *Pulp Fiction*. In a scene originally intended for

inclusion in *True Romance*, an accidental pistol shot covers the inside of the Nova, and its two surviving occupants, with blood and brain tissue. As originally scripted, Vincent shot Marvin in the neck and was then forced to put the gurgling victim out of his misery by shooting him in the head. John Travolta told Tarantino he felt the scene to be gratuitous; it was abridged so that Marvin was killed outright with the first shot. Despite this last minute re-think, Marvin's corpse appears to have a bloody neck wound when briefly glimpsed in the Nova's boot.

The man *The Face* magazine once described as having 'fake blood on his hands and the world at his feet' surpassed himself with the screenplay of *From Dusk Till Dawn*. From Seth Gecko's threat to turn Benny's World of Liquor into 'Benny's World of Blood' up to the bloodbath at the Titty Twister, contemporary horror cinema is graced with a film stained red from beginning to end.

(See also: Ears; Fingers; Orange [Freddy Newendyke]; Violence)

BLUE

The lowest-profile member of the *Reservoir Dogs* gang is Mr Blue. This grizzled old pro is assigned to handle crowd control at Karina's Wholesale Diamonds with the trigger-happy Mr Blonde. Back at the warehouse, Joe reveals that Mr Blue has been shot, and is 'dead as Dillinger'.

(See also: Bunker, Eddie)

BOARD GAMES

'Well, we sell other things too . . . *Green Hornet* board games. Shit like that' - Clarence, *True Romance*.

Tarantino has long been a board game enthusiast and collector. Fond of cementing important relationships over some plastic counters and the roll of a dice, such pivotal personalities as Allison Anders and John Travolta (both qv) have found themselves the bemused opponents in some of Quentin's tackier film and TV spin-off games. Oliver Stone (qv) has expressed an interest in playing the *Platoon* board game with Quentin, but a rendezvous remains unlikely.

Diligent viewers of *Pulp Fiction* will have noted two of the classier games from Tarantino's extensive collection making a brief appearance. When Vincent brings the comatose Mia Wallace to Lance's house, his attempt to revive her is played out while the classic board games *Operation* and *Life* sit metaphorically in the corner. Although overdosing isn't one of the obstacles presented in *Life*, and piercing one's sternum with a syringe isn't one of the surgical procedures in *Operation*, Mrs Wallace nevertheless gets the point.

BONNIE

This largely unseen character is only gradually revealed to us over the course of three Tarantino films. Towards the end of *True Romance*, negotiations between the drug-dealing Clarence and film producer Lee Donowitz are briefly interrupted when Elliot, Donowitz's personal assistant, hands him a piece of paper to sign. Donowitz duly autographs the note, mumbling, 'Whatever Bonnie wants . . .'

We learn something of Bonnie's profession in a sequence of *Reservoir Dogs* cut from the finished film. Mr Pink is driving Mr White and Nice Guy Eddie, who is going through the stolen satchel of diamonds. Eddie estimates that there are $2 million worth of diamonds in the bag, and declares the robbery a qualified success. An incredulous Mr White is more concerned about the dying Mr Orange. 'Bonnie'll take care of him', Eddie insists. 'I called three doctors and couldn't get through to shit. Now, time being a

factor, I called Bonnie. Sweet broad, helluva broad, and a registered nurse. Told her a bullshit story, upside; she said bring him to her apartment.' This compromise for looking after Mr Orange until Joe can arrange a doctor clearly carries its own risks. Eddie later snaps at Mr White: 'I am personally leaving myself vulnerable with this Bonnie situation.'

Bonnie finally made her screen debut in a segment of *Pulp Fiction* which took its title from that piece of discarded *Reservoir Dogs* dialogue. *The Bonnie Situation* sees Jules visit his old colleague Jimmie, who is not best pleased at seeing his friend arrive with a bloody hitman and a headless corpse in tow. Although not explicit in the screenplay, Tarantino has explained that Jimmie gave up his work for Marsellus under pressure from his new wife Bonnie. Her imminent return from the hospital night shift naturally causes concern all round. 'You got to appreciate what an explosive element this Bonnie situation is', Jules tells Marsellus on the phone. 'She comes home from a hard day's work, finds a bunch of gangsters in the kitchen doing a bunch of gangster shit, there ain't no telling what she's liable to do.' The nightmare scenario is played before us - Bonnie returns from work to find Jimmie, Jules and Vincent manhandling Marvin's corpse across the dining room.

The Wolf is called and disaster is averted. Whether the cream of the LA underworld is mobilised out of respect to Jimmie or fear of Bonnie is never made clear, but Bonnie (who is only ever glimpsed from behind, wearing a white nurse's uniform) leaves her mark as perhaps the most influential woman yet seen in Tarantino's world.

(See also: Grier, Pam; Names)

BRIEFCASE

The contents of the briefcase that Jules and Vincent are dispatched to retrieve from Brett

'Gabrielle, listen to me as if I were Cerberus with all his heads barking at the gates of Hell . . . don't, don't open the box': Gaby Rodgers in *Kiss Me Deadly*.

contents, and that it was simply written into the screenplay as an intriguing McGuffin. The resulting open season amongst enthusiasts threw up such polarised suggestions that the case concealed the diamonds from the *Reservoir Dogs* jewellery heist and 'the evil that men do'.

Although Tarantino claims not to have made the connection until after he completed the script, many critics have drawn parallels between *Pulp Fiction*'s briefcase sub-plot and the storyline of the Robert Aldrich film *Kiss Me Deadly* (qv). In Aldrich's 1955 *noir* classic, private detective Mike Hammer (Ralph Meeker) is searching for a case full of radioactive material. There is a more obvious precedent in *True Romance*, where a suitcase of stolen cocaine offers Clarence and Alabama the possibility of a new life. Similarly, a suitcase of stolen money is jealously guarded by the Gecko brothers in *From Dusk Till Dawn*.

The only categorical look we've ever been granted inside *Pulp Fiction*'s case was in the television commercial announcing the film's sell-thru video release in September 1995. After a selection of clips which included Pumpkin's 'Is that what I think it is?' the closing shot revealed the coveted contents to be . . . a copy of the video cassette.

and his friends is an unresolved mystery that underpins the beginning and end of *Pulp Fiction*. By watching closely, we can establish that the combination numbers on its lock are 666, and that whatever is inside bathes onlookers in a bright golden light. Marsellus clearly wants the briefcase badly enough to plant a mole (Marvin) in Brett's midst. Jules clearly has no intention of parting with it, even when threatened with death when the Hawthorne Grill is held up by Pumpkin and Honey Bunny. It is therefore probably safe to assume that it doesn't actually contain, as Jules suggests, 'My boss's dirty laundry.'

Tarantino has admitted that there is no 'official' explanation behind the briefcase's

BROOKS, RANDY
Holdaway, *Reservoir Dogs*

Randy Brooks won his role as Freddy Newendyke's undercover contact over actors including Samuel L Jackson and Ving Rhames (both qv). His other film credits include: *8 Million Ways to Die* [with Rosanna Arquette, part-written by Oliver Stone, both qv] (1986), *Assassination* (1987) and *Colors* [director Dennis Hopper, qv] (1988).

BROWN

Reservoir Dogs's supposed authority on Madonna's mid-Eighties hits dominates conversation with a forceful self-assurance. He certainly isn't afraid to assert himself before Joe Cabot when he is allocated his code name: 'Mr Brown - that's a little too close to Mr Shit.'

The little-seen Mr Brown holds the vital role of getaway driver in the diamond store raid. He is entrusted to park on the other side of the street from Karina's, waiting for the signal from Mr Orange to pull up outside the store and put his foot down. Things don't go well for Mr Brown - he only succeeds in picking up Mr Orange and Mr White before being shot in the head by a policeman. His injury leads to the erratic driving which crashes the getaway car. As Mr White fends off the advancing police, the dazed Mr Brown's senses begin to fail as he sits at the wheel. By the time Mr White has seen off their pursuers, Mr Brown is dead.

(See also: Blood; Tarantino, Quentin)

BULLWINKLE PART II

'Mind if I shoot up here?' Vincent asks Lance in *Pulp Fiction*. Time seems to slow down as Vincent carefully prepares the Choco heroin before injecting it into his veins. The pumping bass of *Bullwinkle Part II* by The Centurians kicks in and the precisely executed ritual begins.

'In *Reservoir Dogs*, every piece of music in the movie was source music - you know, somebody turned on the radio and heard something. In the case of *Pulp*, I actually use score', explained Tarantino at the time of *Pulp Fiction*'s release. 'In this case a lot of the surf music in the movie I actually used as score. I always really dug surf music a lot, but the thing is I never really understood what the hell it had to do with surfing. To me it sounded like rock and roll spaghetti western music - rock and roll Ennio Morricone. Which made it perfect for this movie, because this movie kinda is a rock and roll

spaghetti western. The trick was finding these instrumental pieces that actually could function as a score. The *Bullwinkle Part II* one is great - I love that.'

BUNKER, EDDIE (1938 -)
Mr Blue, *Reservoir Dogs*

Once (among his many felonies) a notorious armed robber, ex-con Bunker has - since going straight in 1975 - carved himself a niche as a novelist, screenwriter, and occasional actor, latterly becoming Hollywood's 'technical adviser' on all matters criminal. He began writing his first novel, the semi-autobiographical *No Beast So Fierce*, while incarcerated; the film rights were eventually sold to Dustin Hoffman in the mid-Seventies, and, with Alvin Sargent, Bunker co-authored the screenplay during visiting hours in his final stretch for safe-cracking. Released just prior to shooting, Bunker took the small role of Mickey in the film, which, re-titled *Straight Time*, directed by Ulu Grosbard, and starring Hoffman, Theresa Russell and Harry Dean Stanton, was critically panned upon its release in 1978. Nevertheless, Bunker's dual careers flourished: he later penned the novels *The Animal Factory* (1977) and *Little Boy Blue* (1981), and had a hand in the screenplay of 1985's *Runaway Train*, in which he also played Jonah. Bunker took the part of *Reservoir Dogs*'s Mr Blue after Tarantino had studied *Straight Time* during his time at the Sundance Institute (qv); he was friends, also, with Chris Penn (qv). Bunker made a small cameo appearance in *Somebody to Love* (1994); directed by Alexandre Rockwell (qv), the film also featured Steve Buscemi, Harvey Keitel, and Tarantino (all qv). His first three novels were re-issued by No Exit Press in 1994-5, resplendent in jackets aping *Dogs*'s distinctive poster design and carrying a eulogistic soundbite courtesy Tarantino; his fourth, entitled *Dog Eat Dog*, was published in July 1996. The film rights have since been purchased by *Badlands* producer Edward R

Pressman. Other acting credits include: *The Long Riders* (1980), *Shy People* (1987).

(See also: Blue)

BUSCEMI, STEVE (1958 -)
Mr Pink, *Reservoir Dogs*
Buddy Holly, *Pulp Fiction*

A champion of the latter-day American independent cinema, Buscemi, once the hardest-working supporting actor in the contemporary low-budget scene, has progressed to directing; his first feature, *Trees Lounge*, was scheduled for release in 1996. Inspired to take up acting by the 'intensity' of John Cazale's and Al Pacino's performances in Sidney Lumet's 1975 *Dog Day Afternoon*, and citing among his influences similarly unconventional actor/director John Cassavetes, Buscemi endured several years working for the New York Fire Department, sometimes making a part-time living as a would-be stand-up comic. He took acting classes, and made his feature debut in 1985's *Parting Glances*, one of the earliest American films to address the subject of AIDS.

Buscemi first came to Tarantino's attention after the latter, in the process of casting *Reservoir Dogs*, had seen his unsuccessful audition tape for a comedy, *The Marrying Man* (UK title: *Too Hot To Handle*), in which Buscemi, with slicked-back hair and wearing a Fifties-style shirt, 'looked like a criminal'. Initially considered as a Mr Orange or a Nice Guy Eddie, Buscemi held out for the part of Mr Pink, which, after auditions in New York, duly became his when Tarantino grudgingly dropped plans to play the character himself (Dennis Hopper, qv - a much older actor - had also been mooted for the role). Shortly after, in June 1991, Buscemi went to Utah's Sundance Institute (qv) with Tarantino, where they shot two try-out scenes in the lead-up to shooting *Dogs* proper; the first being the bathroom scene between Pink and White

(Tarantino played White), the second being the hastily-conceived *Bell Jar* scene between Joe Cabot (qv) and Pink which was cut from the finished film (see Tierney, Lawrence). During principal photography, Buscemi and company would embellish the dialogue: 'I added a line when [White] says, "Have a smoke", and I say, "I quit!". That came out of the situation, but 95 per cent of the film was scripted', he told Australia's *Cinema Papers*. 'We had a two-week rehearsal period where we

'We're supposed to be fuckin' professionals!' Steve Buscemi as Mr Pink.

talked about a lot of things . . . It was very thorough and we really explored every aspect of the script. We even rehearsed scenes that weren't written. We just made up situations that these characters might be in; little improvisations.'

Post-Pink, Buscemi was offered the roles of both uptight Hollywood PA Elliot Blitzer and detective Nicky Dimes in *True Romance*, but declined both (the parts went, respectively, to Bronson Pinchot and Chris Penn, both qv); and out of loyalty to Tarantino he nixed a mooted role in Oliver Stone's (qv) *Natural Born Killers*. His next major appearance was as Adolpho Rollo, the lead of Alexandre Rockwell's (qv) *In The Soup*; playing a low-rent would-be arthouse director; he managed to persuade Rockwell to let him shoot for real the short which his character makes during the course of the movie (which also starred Cassavetes mainstay Seymour Cassel). Shortly after came a second short, *What Happened To Pete?*, this time wholly his own.

Unable to take a major role in *Pulp Fiction* due to other commitments, he nevertheless managed a cameo appearance as 'Buddy Holly', Jack Rabbit Slim's in-character waiter ('How 'bout you, Peggy Sue?'). Slated to play the bellboy linking *Four Rooms*, Buscemi reluctantly backed out of the anthology project, having felt he'd taken too similar a part in the earlier *Barton Fink*. He appeared in drag alongside Tarantino, Harvey Keitel, and Eddie Bunker (all qv) in Rockwell's follow-up to *In The Soup*, *Somebody to Love*, and was once more reunited with Tarantino when he took a small role in Robert Rodriguez's (qv) *Desperado*. After several years of trying, he finally directed his own full feature, *Trees Lounge*, during the late summer of 1995. Funded by Live Entertainment - *Dogs*'s financiers - Buscemi's script drew upon his time growing up in Valley Stream, a suburb of Long Island, where it was also shot. The cast, led by himself, included Seymour Cassel and Samuel L Jackson (qv). Other acting credits include: *New York Stories* [with Rosanna Arquette, qv] (1989), *Mystery Train* (1989), *Miller's Crossing* (1990), *Living in Oblivion* (1995), *Things To Do In Denver When You're Dead* [with Christopher Walken, qv] (1996).

(See also: Pink)

BUTCH COOLIDGE

Boxer Butch smokes unathletic Red Apples; he plays with fire likewise when he decides to take on kingpin Marsellus Wallace (*Pulp Fiction*'s script has Butch remark that his ill-fated opponent Floyd Willis's death is 'what he gets for fuckin' up my sport', which might well be Marsellus's rationale for wanting Butch dead). After his last fight, Butch hopes to return - albeit temporarily - to (presumably) the family home: Knoxville, Tennessee, where his grandfather's gold watch was bought. Butch is prepared to stake his life on this family heirloom; remembering the circumstances of the watch's ancestry, and Captain Koons's testimony that two men who are in the 'pit of hell' together take on certain responsibilities of each other, he returns to Zed and Maynard's backroom Sodom to rescue Marsellus, redeeming himself, reacquiring his freedom, and perhaps growing up in the process.

For what else is Butch but a big baby? His wide eyes and shaven head mark him thus physically; he shares an exclusive childish language with his babydoll cutie paramour Fabienne (qv); piqued, he's prone to fearsome outbursts of temparament, reducing Fabienne to tears; he dreams of himself as a child before the big fight; he keeps less-than-mature souvenirs in his home (his 'little kangaroo' beside the table drawer, for example); hell, he even eats Pop Tarts. His ordeal in *The Gold Watch* is surely no more than a rite-of-passage: from the boy to the man.

(See also: *Deliverance*; De Medeiros, Maria; Inferno; *Kiss Me Deadly*; Redemption; Willis, Bruce)

C

CAUSALITY AND IMITATION

In media studies, the so-called 'hypodermic needle' theory of cause-and-effect, supposedly proven by the mass hysteria resulting from Orson Welles's 1938 *War of the Worlds* radio broadcast, has been passed over in later years in favour of more liberal, consiliatory, reasoned notions of received and mediated cognition. However, particularly with reference to the brouhaha surrounding *Reservoir Dogs* and *Natural Born Killers*, right-wing, 'common sense' commentators, especially in the British press, have sought to re-establish a direct link between criminality and film imagery.

These commentators found themselves surfing a fresh wave of condemnation after a supposed connection was made between the murder of toddler Jamie Bulger in 1993 and incidents in the film *Child's Play 3*. The *Daily Mail* ran a hate campaign - 'This Film Must Be Banned in Britain!' - against *NBK* which contributed to the delay of its theatrical release. Throughout the autumn of 1994, newspapers had linked 10 'copycat' killings in total - 6 in America - to the film. A double murder in Salt Lake City by a disturbed teenager, Nathan Martinez, of his step-mother and half-sister would be repeatedly invoked, most notably

on a BBC *Panorama* broadcast, *The Killing Screens*: allegedly, Martinez had viewed *NBK* and subsequently shaved his head and taken to wearing tinted glasses after Mickey Knox. In Dallas, a 14-year-old boy decapitated a girl one year his junior, apparently telling friends that he wanted to be famous 'like the *Natural Born Killers*'. In October, a Frenchwoman, Florence Rey, and her boyfriend, went on a killing spree in the eastern districts of Paris which resulted in the deaths of three policemen, a taxi driver and the boyfriend himself; again, the incident was linked to the film. (It should be noted that in all bar one of the American incidents, the perpetrators had a either a history of mental illness or one of criminal detention.) On 2 August 1995, London's *Evening Standard* reported the case of 14-year-old Scott Richards, who, together with a friend, 'terrorised two shopkeepers with a replica 9mm gun . . . Before the incidents they had sniffed amyl nitrate and watched a pirate copy of *Reservoir Dogs*'. The boy's father, Chris Richards, was quoted as saying: 'I know my son was influenced by that film. He even told the police afterwards that he did what he did because he had watched *Reservoir Dogs* and decided he wanted "see what it would be like to be a gangster" [sic]

. . . It is the baddies in *Reservoir Dogs* who are the heroes. And kids who see that film are going to relate to them as heroes.' (Mr Richards's comments - if any - on the mind-altering properties of amyl nitrate were not reported.)

Rather more seriously, *NBK*'s director and co-writer Oliver Stone (qv) was, at time of writing, facing a $20 million lawsuit brought against himself and studio Warner Brothers by one Patsy Ann Byers, a shop assistant from Tangipahoa Parish, Louisiana. Allegedly, Byers was left paralysed after being shot in the throat by 18 year-old bandit Sarah Edmondson; Edmondson, a judge's daughter, claimed to have viewed *NBK* with boyfriend Benjamin Durrus prior to setting off on a crime spree which culminated in Byers's maiming and the murder of businessman William Savage. Byers's case, brought under US product liability law, seeks to prove that Stone and Warner Bros 'knew or should have known *Natural Born Killers* would cause and inspire people such as the defendants to commit crimes'. Byers's claims were supported by millionaire novelist John Grisham (*The Firm*, etc); according to Byers's lawyer, *NBK* 'glorifies violence. It gives confused, tortured young people something to emulate.' For his part, Stone remains bullish, calling the case 'ridiculous' and 'without merit': 'It is only a small step from silencing art to silencing artists and then to silence those who support them . . .'

Despite such instances, certain sequences in Tarantino's films themselves can be seen as vindicating his and Stone's detractors' very viewpoint: in *True Romance*, the impressionable Clarence's behaviour is modelled explicitly after pop culture influence -his murder of Drexl, according to the hapless dealer himself, results from Clarence confronting Drexl in the manner of Charles Bronson in *Mr Majestyk*. (See *Badlands*, qv, for a fuller examination of Clarence and *NBK*'s Mickey and Mallory Knox.) In *Reservoir Dogs*, the ill-fated

Freddie Newendyke psyches himself up by imagining himself as TV cop Baretta; in *Pulp Fiction*, hitmen Jules and Vincent have to 'get into character' prior to killing Brett and 'Flock of Seagulls' (see Role playing, qv); even in *Four Rooms*, the luckless Norman would not have wagered his finger were it not for the *Alfred Hitchcock Presents* episode, *Man From the South* (qv).

(See also: Slater, Christian; Violence; X-rated)

CENSORSHIP
(See: X-rated)

CHESTER RUSH
The loudmouth renting the penthouse suite at the Mon Signor Hotel on New Year's Eve doesn't let his hangers-on forget he's a movie star. Although Ted the bellhop hasn't seen Chester's comedy hit, *The Wacky Detective*, he soon learns that it grossed $72.1 million on domestic ticket sales alone. Its follow-up, *The Dog Catcher*, is expected to make over a $100 million. This donut-munching egomaniac seems relieved he won't have to rely on video sales to turn a buck. 'Fuck video!' he exclaims. 'Fuck it! Did *Jaws* make it back on fucking video? No sir. You know why? Because there wasn't any fucking video when *Jaws* came out. We're talking fuckin' asses on fuckin' seats.'

Clearly something of a film buff, Chester compares Ted to Jerry Lewis in *The Bellboy*, and launches into a drunken appreciation of the comedian's masterful technique in the movie. In Tarantino's original script for *Four Rooms: Penthouse: The Man from Hollywood*, Chester again dominates conversation by reeling off a list of famous Teds from history, all drawn from a brain as addled by pop culture as it is by alcohol.

Despite his success, life holds few thrills for Chester. Now he's at the top of the Hollywood tree, his decadence must be all the more dangerous and daring. He spends all night planning a recreation of a bizarre bet seen in an old episode of *Alfred Hitchcock Presents* (qv). He wagers that his friend Norman can't light his Zippo ten times in a row - if Norman succeeds, he wins Chester's red, 1964, mint condition Chevy Chevelle. If Norman fails, he has his little finger sliced off. Although enthusiastic about the wager, Chester lacks the fortitude to wield the punishing cleaver himself, so he skilfully convinces Ted to shoulder the responsibility for a thousand dollars.

Ultimately, Norman loses his finger, Ted takes the cash, and Chester keeps his car. It is unlikely that Chester is repentant. After all, he claims, 'When has America ever been fair?'

(See also: Alter egos; Tarantino, Quentin [as actor]; Wayne Gayle; Yuppie scum)

CITY ON FIRE
(Hong Kong, 1987, dir. Ringo Lam)

Let's go to wok. The heist movie perhaps most directly influential upon *Reservoir Dogs*'s narrative, *City On Fire* - an otherwise unremarkable Eastern gangster thriller - was exposed as hitherto unacknowledged source material after mini-features in both *Film Threat* and *Empire* magazines; at a New York film festival in March 1995, a short entitled *Who Do You Think You're Fooling?* was exhibited. Edited by a film student, Mike White, the film cut together scenes from *City On Fire* with those allegedly plagiarised by Tarantino for *Reservoir Dogs*. Tarantino has since owned up to its influence, but downplays the extent of it. Certainly, *Dogs* - and arguably *City On Fire* itself - is clearly affected by the entire catalogue of Hollywood caper movies (see Heist movies, qv).

In *City On Fire* (a Cinema Co Ltd picture produced and directed by Ringo Lam; screenplay by Tommy Sham from a story by Lam), renegade undercover cop Ko Chow (Chow Yun Fat) is ordered by his uncle, the shortly-to-be-retired Inspector Lau, to infiltrate a murderous gang of six jewel thieves headed by one Brother Nam. Posing as an arms dealer, he strikes up a friendship with Nam's lieutenant, Fu, and is eventually asked to participate in the gang's next heist; meanwhile, a rival police division has lost faith in Chow, believing him to have gone native. At the heist, the cops are waiting; in the ensuing gunfight, Chow is shot in the stomach. The surviving gang members reassemble at a deserted out-of-town warehouse, where Nam accuses Chow of being an undercover cop, and levels a gun to Chow's head. Fu, in turn, points his gun at Nam, refusing to believe that friend Chow has betrayed him. Another gangster, Song, aims at Fu. The stand-off is broken when the cops arrive outside; all bar Chow and Fu are killed. Mortally wounded, Chow confesses his true identity to Fu, but dies of his injuries before Fu can execute him.

The textual similarities to *Dogs*, therefore, are obvious; it should be noted, however, that the main heist and subsequent falling-out only occupies the movie's third and final act, the greater part of its length concerning Chow's infiltration of the gang, intercut with scenes of bureaucratic police in-fighting. Chow could be Mr Orange; Fu, Mr White; Brother Nam, Joe Cabot; Inspector Lau, Holdaway; and Song, Mr Blonde (the latter, a previously placid individual, is the first to start shooting during the heist). The remaining gang members - Bill, Bony, and Joe - are of no real interest; two are killed during the course of the getaway (one of these writhes, wounded, on the back seat of a fleeing car). Other particular scenes might be said to be reprised, albeit partially, in *Dogs*: immediately before the first robbery, the gang strut, *Wild Bunch*-style, towards the camera (this immediately preceded by Nam's line, 'Let's go to work'). Chow first sets up a meeting with Fu in a coffee-shop; later, clutching a bag *à la* Mr Pink, he is pursued by rival cops down a shopping street in a series of long, flat-on tracking shots (this sequence ends when Chow, still bag-laden, falls heavily to the ground immediately before a moving car). Our Orange progenitor also faces a rites-of-passage ordeal in a bathroom, where he confronts - and is badly beaten by - a horde of policemen. Immediately before the second, and final, robbery, a brief conversation between two of the gang might be said to be echoed in Pink and White's 'just cops' routine (asked if he hates cops, one replies: 'They kill us, we kill them . . . it's the fortunes of war'). At the robbery of the Tai Kong Gold Company - like that of Karina's - the gang don Ray-Bans; in the escape, Fu - uncannily like White - empties the barrels of two handguns into the windscreen of an oncoming police van, killing its occupants. At the rendezvous, Nam talks of there being 'a rat amongst us'. And finally, Chow is bloodied and dying when he croaks his confession to Fu: 'I'm a cop.'

It might also be pertinent to note some of the substantial *City* plot material that Tarantino quite definitely excluded from *Dogs*. Throughout Lam's film, Chow's motivation is considerably more credible - or at least better fleshed-out - than Orange's. Chow is initally reluctant to go undercover after a previous operation resulted in his betrayal of Shing who, like White/Fu, was a man he befriended who wound up being killed because of Chow. Nam's gang, meanwhile, are seemingly plagued by undercover cops, which explains Nam's paranoia and immediate suspicion of Chow. And Chow goes native when his fiancee, Hung, leaves him and jets to Hawaii; women, of course, are conspicuous by their absence from the *Dogs* narrative.

CLARENCE WORLEY

The young 'hipster hepcat' of *True Romance* is an Elvis-fixated rockabilly who kicks away from the cloistered life of a comic store clerk

into the heady world of gangsters, cocaine, and murder.

Clarence's transformation is triggered by falling in love for the first time and his accidental acquisition of a suitcase packed with hot snow. These events mark a turning point - he always had a taste for the finer things in life, but whereas before this extended to quality fast food, imported beer and uncut martial arts movies, the new Clarence indulges in sex on the road, gun play and dangerous drug deals with Hollywood producers.

Clarence lives his life according to his hero - Elvis Presley. Dressed as The King since an early age, Clarence continues the tradition by sporting ultra cool aviator shades. His admiration knows no bounds: 'I always said if I had to fuck a guy . . . I mean *had* to 'cause my life depended on it . . . I'd fuck Elvis.' It could be argued that the ghost of Elvis returns the compliment by goading Clarence into murdering Alabama's former pimp and later overseeing the cocaine deal that ultimately gets the rockabilly boy killed.

Ultimately, although he also takes his inspiration from the movies and comics he devours, everything Clarence does is for his beloved Alabama, and he remains a true romantic at heart. The revised screenplay of Tony Scott's film delivers a welcome reprieve for Alabama's sweetheart - Clarence keeps his head (or most of it) while all about are having theirs blown away, and retires to an idyllic paradise with his adoring wife and son, Elvis.

'Clarence, I like you', compliments his mentor. 'Always have, always will.'

(See also: Alter egos; *Badlands*; Causality and imitation; Slater, Christian)

CLIFFORD WORLEY

In *True Romance*, Clarence's father is a 45-year-old ex-cop with a broken marriage

'I just need help, and you can fuckin' help me, alright?': father and son in *True Romance*.

of drinking and absenteeism are redeemed with a heartfelt, if belated, sacrifice.

(See also: Alter egos; Hopper, Dennis)

CLOONEY, GEORGE
Seth Gecko, *From Dusk Till Dawn*

From a family well-acquainted with stage and screen - singing aunt Rosemary (*Red Garters, White Christmas*, etc) was married to Jose Ferrer, father Nick was a sometime TV presenter - erstwhile television star Clooney is no stranger to the horror genre: having appeared in the low-rent *Return To Horror High* (1987) and *Return of the Killer Tomatoes* (1988), he played alongside Charlie Sheen and Laura Dern in *The Predator: Grizzly II* - a film allegedly considered so bad that it languishes as yet unreleased. Clooney began his TV career under contract to ABC, and appeared in shows such as *Roseanne*, *Facts of Life* and *Sisters*; he'd be Emmy-nominated as Dr Ross in hospital drama *ER* (qv). Clooney had earlier auditioned for a part in *Reservoir Dogs*, but was unsuccessful; the role of *From Dusk Till Dawn*'s Seth Gecko had apparently been earmarked for veteran actor Robert Blake (*Baretta*, etc).

(See also: Seth Gecko)

COCONUT

The lyrics to Harry Nilsson's *Coconut* bring a poignancy to the close of *Reservoir Dogs*. 'Doctor . . . Is there nothing I can take to relieve this belly ache?' plays over the credits just moments after the pain of Mr Orange's gut injury is finally silenced by a bullet from Mr White.

and a history of alcoholism. Now working as a security guard, he proves invaluable when he confirms that Clarence is free of police suspicion over the murder of Alabama's former pimp, Drexl Spivey.

Cliff is reunited with his son after three years of non-communication when Clarence visits the trailer park where his father lives to introduce Alabama and ask a favour. Guilty about the drinking and long absences that drove his wife and son away, Cliff takes little persuading to ring around his police contacts. He soon discovers that the police suspect gangster Blue Lou Boyle of Drexl's murder. Clarence and Alabama move on to sell the cocaine that will finance their honeymoon, but not before Clarence leaves a contact address and Alabama leaves a peach-flavoured kiss.

Unfortunately, Clarence's visit to his father doesn't go unnoticed by Blue Lou Boyle's consul, Vincent Coccotti - a man so evil that even Cliff's dog won't go near the trailer when he lurks inside. Cliff is tortured by Coccotti for his son's destination, and dies attempting to keep Clarence's whereabouts a secret. The years

Harry Nilsson (born Harry Edward Nelson III) gave up his job at the Bank of America in 1967 when his burgeoning songwriting income was given a boost by The Yardbirds's version of *Ten Little Indians* and The

Monkees's cover of *Cuddly Toy*. As the decade progressed his work earned the admiration of The Beatles - during a 1968 press conference both Paul McCartney and John Lennon named the singer/songwriter as their favourite artist. Nilsson's career went from strength to strength - his version of *Everybody's Talkin* (written by influential folk singer Fred Neil) charted three times in the UK between 1969 and 1970, popularised by its selection as the theme to John Schlesinger's 1969 film *Midnight Cowboy*. Nilsson's other big single success was his heartfelt cover of Badfinger's *Without You*, which went to number 1 in the UK in February 1972. The follow up, *Coconut*, went top ten in the US and reached number 42 in the UK that summer. Typical of a man whose music remained unpredictable and unconventional, Nilsson also dabbled in movies, joining Ringo Starr in the bizarre horror musical *Son of Dracula*. The cast's high living excesses were typified by some extremely eccentric behaviour - director Freddie Francis recalls Nilsson surprising everyone by pulling his teeth out simply to make his vampire fangs fit better.

Nilsson largely turned his back on recording in the Eighties, releasing only one album, *A Touch More Schmilsson In The Night*, in 1988. The Nineties saw a number of financial difficulties, and after he conquered his alcoholism he went on to develop diabetes and suffer a series of heart attacks. The use of his music in both *The Fisher King* (1991) and *Reservoir Dogs* brought prominence to his work for the last time before his death, at the age of 53, on 15 January 1994. 'I have no doubt he was one of the great American figures of international popular music', recalled The Beatles's former publicist Derek Taylor, 'and a powerful life-force in the second half of the century'.

COMANCHE

During one of the most tense sequences in *Pulp Fiction*, Marsellus's rape ordeal is played

out against the musical backdrop of this driving sax instrumental by The Revels.

Originally scripted as being played out to a Judds record, Tarantino's later intention had been to score the sequence with *My Sharona*, a 1979 US chart-topper for Sixties-influenced The Knack. '*My Sharona* has a really good sodomy beat to it', he jokes. 'I could set the time by that. It just seemed so funny to me - too funny not to use. And so we tried to get them, and apparently part of the band was for it but one of the band has become a born-again Christian and he just wasn't interested: "The guy who did *Reservoir Dogs*? Oh yeah, please, let me give you my song. That's what we got and you're gonna screw it up in everybody's minds." Ultimately, I'm glad. It would have been too cutely comic.'

'*Comanche* still works the same, it's kind of funny actually, but it doesn't break the scene. I think *Comanche* and sodomy are married from here on out. I dare somebody to try to use it and not bring up connotations.'

CONTINUITY ERRORS

While not containing cock-ups of the magnitude of the legendary Mini in 1959's *Ben Hur*, or the wristwatch in 1967's *The Viking Queen*, Tarantino's films nevertheless include their fair share of goofs. In *Reservoir Dogs*'s opening scene, Mr Blue's cigar mysteriously lengthens between shots; later, the film crew can be glimpsed reflected in a shop window as Mr Pink runs past. Likewise, the cops in pursuit of Pink run by certain stores before the professional perpetrator. And when Pink pulls the woman from the car he hijacks, his bag is on the ground; there is no bag in the car with him, but he has reacquired it later. In *Pulp Fiction*, young Butch has blue eyes, old Butch brown; when Captain Koons first shows young Butch the gold watch, it clearly shows 12.15, but in close-up it reads 12 noon; in the scene where Butch realises that Fabienne has left the watch in their apartment, the arrangement of the coathangers on the rail in the background changes from shot to shot; in the reprise of the killing of Brett, Jules's gun does not retract as before; later in the same scene, there are bullet-holes in the wall behind Jules and Vincent before the Fourth Man shoots at the pair; and when Mr Wolf rings Jimmie's doorbell, sound and vision don't quite tie. The difference between Honey Bunny's threat in the prologue and in *The Bonnie Situation* - from 'Any of you fuckin' pricks move and I'll execute every mother-fuckin' last one of you!' to 'Any of you fuckin' pricks move and I'll execute every one of you motherfuckers!' - was deliberate. The alteration appears in later drafts of the script.

CRIMSON TIDE
(US, 1995, dir. Tony Scott)

Tarantino was called upon by *True Romance*'s director Tony Scott to doctor some of the dialogue in Michael Schiffer's screenplay for *Crimson Tide*; Scott's successful drama starred Gene Hackman and Denzel Washington as in-fighting officers aboard a nuclear subma-rine ordered to carry out a a pre-emptive missile strike upon Russia. Although others would perform rewrites, too - notably Robert Towne (*Chinatown*, etc) - some obvi-ous Tarantinoisms remain. The characters Weps and Zimmer had 'served together on the *Baton Rouge*'; another sub here, but in *Pulp Fiction* it's the name of the show Mia Wallace's *Fox Force Five* co-star Sommerset O'Neal had appeared in. Immediately prior to embarking on their mission, certain crewmembers discuss the stars of submarine movies *The Enemy Below* (1957, with Robert Mitchum and Curt Jurgens) and *Run Silent Run Deep* (1958, with Clark Gable and Burt Lancaster). A fight breaks out in the crew mess: it concerns which artist drew Marvel Comics's *Silver Surfer* the best, Jack Kirby or Moebius. ('Everybody who reads comic books knows that Kirby's Silver Surfer is the only true Silver Surfer', says Hunter; note that in Jim McBride's 1983 remake of Jean-Luc Godard's *A Bout de Souffle*, *Breathless*, Richard Gere's character has a *Silver Surfer* obsession, as does *Reservoir Dogs*'s Freddy Newendyke.)

There are characters named Russell Vossler and Lawson; the first presumably in tribute to Tarantino's Video Archives (qv) cohort of the same name, the second in tribute to the Archives's owner, Lance Lawson. Vossler and Hunter model their on-screen relationship after that shared between *Star Trek*'s Captain Kirk and Mr Scott ('Vossler, this is Captain Kirk. I need warp speed on that radio'). The final confrontation between Hackman's Ramsey and Washington's Hunter includes a dialogue concerning the true line of descent of a certain breed of Portuguese stallion; it bears remarkable similarities to Clifford Worley's 'Sicilians' speech in *True Romance*.

And the name of the sub? The USS *Alabama* . . .

(See also: Dialogue; Names)

Sub plot: Denzel Washington and Gene Hackman in *Crimson Tide*.

d

DELIVERANCE
(US, 1972, dir. John Boorman)

Consciously alluded to in *Pulp Fiction*'s central *The Gold Watch* segment, John Boorman's classic of rural-urban antagonism was first seen by Tarantino at a very tender age as part of a double-bill with *The Wild Bunch* (see Peckinpah, Sam). In Boorman's film, four city-dwellers go canoeing in the backwoods of the American South and fall foul of local men: in one sequence, two of the city types - Bobby and Ed - are apprehended by two of the hicks, who

Maynard calls Zed: 'The spider just caught a coupla flies'.

tie Ed to a tree while they sodomise Bobby. (This encounter develops into a bloody struggle between the separate parties: the film has been identified by writer Carol J Clover as spawning the 'urbanoia' sub-genre, which finds later expression in films such as *Hunter's Blood*, *The Hills Have Eyes*, *The Texas Chainsaw Massacre* - also fleetingly referred to in *The Gold Watch* - and *I Spit On Your Grave*.) Tellingly, in *Pulp*, Butch encounters hillbilly Maynard in the 'Mason-Dixon Pawnshop'; the Mason-Dixon line, of course, dividing America's North and South. Inside the pawnshop, therefore, is another country, clearly signposted by Maynard's backwoods lumber dress and inflection. (Note, however, that the iconography of Butch and Marsellus's three assailants might also be interpreted as a clear signal of their sexual proclivities: the uniformed cop, the lumberjack, and the leather boy all being Village People-style gay archetypes. It's worth pointing out that, beyond his costume, there is no other textual indication to suggest that Zed is actually a policeman; his chopper is hardly federal issue.) Zed and Maynard's transgression is heightened by the script's indication that they are brothers, and that Zed is married: *Village Voice* critic Devon Jackson has observed that the rednecks are portrayed as 'deviants of the worst kind: queers who pass themselves off as he-men. They are thus more fearsome, hence, vengeance taken upon them for their grotesque sins shall be meted out twice as harsh.'

(See also: Avary, Roger; Inferno; Men)

DE MEDEIROS, MARIA (1965 -)
Fabienne, *Pulp Fiction*

Portuguese-French, sister of actress Ines, and alleged one-time date of Lawrence Bender (qv). After a number of parts in French pictures from 1984 on, De Medeiros landed her first English-speaking role - alongside Uma Thurman (qv) - as writer Anais Nin in the 1990 biopic *Henry and June*. De Medeiros was apparently cast in *Pulp Fiction* after meeting Tarantino and Bender at several film festivals around the time of *Dogs*: it is thought that Fabienne was tailored specifically for her. As Fabienne, she was required to share 'the secret language of lovers' with Bruce Willis's Butch: she told *Premiere*, 'People who are in love say a lot of nonsense. You don't often see that in films because everything is choreographed to look glamorous on camera. Quentin wanted to catch this intimacy of talking nonsense for hours and hours . . .' Other credits include: *Paris Vu Par . . . 20 Ans Apres* (1984), *Meeting Venus* (1990), *Bois Transparents* (1994) and *Adam Y Eva* (1995).

(See also: Dialogue; Fabienne)

DESTINY TURNS ON THE RADIO
(US, 1996, dir. Jack Baran)

Tarantino's first major acting role away from movies he scripted and/or directed was in this 1995 US box-office flop. Tarantino plays the eponymous Johnny Destiny, a mysterious Las Vegas gambler with seemingly supernormal powers. However, the film is not designed to appeal to fans of Tarantino's auteur work, resembling instead a rather languid episode

Another country: a back-woodsman prepares to mete out *Deliverance*.

of *The X Files* directed in the style of an off-colour David Lynch. Talky and lacking in suspense, the film was panned by the critics on its release - it is, nevertheless, not quite as contemptible as is sometimes asserted by those who haven't seen it (most people haven't!).

There are one or two touches especially for the fans crammed into Tarantino's fleeting on-screen moments. Johnny Destiny's 1968 (or is it '69?) Chevy belongs in the best tradition of classic Tarantino gas guzzlers. Some of Johnny Destiny's dialogue seems consciously to recall *Pulp Fiction*: 'Las Vegas - that's an explosive situation.' And it is possible to infer that Johnny Destiny's red pack of cigarettes constitute another appearance for the fictional Red Apple brand. 'Good choice' says Johnny.

(See: Tarantino, Quentin [as actor])

DIALOGUE

'Did you kill anybody?'
'A few cops.'
'No real people?'
'Just cops.' - Mr Pink and Mr White,
Reservoir Dogs

Although he regards himself primarily as a director, Tarantino's greatest contribution to contemporary cinema has undoubtedly been his astonishing style, and deployment, of dialogue. Tarantino takes the lyrical street rap from his favourite pulp authors and the snarling dialogue from Brian De Palma's archetypal *Scarface* (1983) to develop a striking dictionary of naturalistic phrasing which cloaks his characters' often amoral attitudes towards violence. This approach, perhaps best witnessed in the 'just cops' exchange between Mr Pink and Mr White, frees violence for use as a purely aesthetic tool, disinheriting the judgmental implications and moral consequences that dog Oliver Stone's (qv) *Natural Born Killers*.

More tangible benefits have included *Pulp Fiction* becoming the best-selling script book of all time, soundtrack albums which carry speech extracts as well as music and, of course, a 1995 Academy Award.

The recurrence of certain phrases and expressions throughout Tarantino's work reinforce an underlying instinct that, however varied his characters may be, they all speak with the same voice. 'We've got everything here from a diddle-eyed Joe to a damned-if-I-know', Drexl tells Clarence in *True Romance*, illustrating the variety of his Chinese take-away. In *Reservoir Dogs*, Holdaway's hunch about Mr White's origin is expressed thus: 'I'll bet you everything from a diddle-eyed Joe to a damned-if-I-know that in Milwaukee they got a sheet on this Mr White motherfucker's ass.'

Natural Born Killers and *Pulp Fiction* share similar scenes where the selection of victims is undertaken in the same way. At the climax of Mickey and Mallory's diner massacre, the serial killers leave one person alive to tell their story to the media. There is only the 'Pinball Cowboy' and waitress Mabel left. 'Eanie, meanie, minie, mo, catch a redneck by the toe', Mallory chants. 'If he hollers, let him go. Eanie, meanie, minie, mo.' Mabel draws the short straw. In *Pulp Fiction*, Zed selects the first person to be dragged into 'Russell's old room' by whispering the same rhyme while pointing between Marsellus and Butch.

Other recurring phrases include *True Romance's* 'Honey, you have blood in your eye', which is redolent of *Reservoir Dogs'* 'You're not blind, there's just blood in your eyes.' In *True Romance* Clarence says 'No problem, Elliot. I'm just fuckin' wit ya, that's all', and Drexl tells Floyd 'We jus' fuckin' with ya.' The phrase is reused in *Pulp Fiction* when Marsellus gives Butch the bribe for throwing the boxing match. 'You may feel a slight sting. That's pride fuckin' wit ya. Fuck pride.' Butch reminds his former boss of the phrase when he beats him up in the pawn shop. 'Feel that sting, big boy?' he asks as he punches Marsellus in the face. 'That's pride fuckin' wit ya, see.' *Four Rooms: Penthouse: The Man From Hollywood* yet again made use of the same phrase. 'Pay no attention to Norman here', Chester tells Ted, 'he's just fuckin' wit ya, that's all'. Finally, 'OK ramblers, let's get rambling' is the call to arms from Joe Cabot in *Reservoir Dogs* and Seth Gecko in *From Dusk to Dawn*.

Elsewhere, Tarantino is unafraid to recycle dialogue that he feels hasn't been given adequate exposure. Examples include Clarence's 'test of oneself' soliloquy, cut from *True Romance* but rewritten for Vincent in *Pulp*

Fiction. Mickey's Little Red Riding Hood joke ('I'm gonna just rip off your dress and squeeze your titties' threatens the Big Bad Wolf), absent from Oliver Stone's *Natural Born Killers*, similarly reappears in *From Dusk Till Dawn*, told by Seth at The Titty Twister and again to Carlos at the end of the script.

Perhaps the most distinctive recurring phrase is the one accorded most relish. 'You mind if I have some of your tasty beverage to wash this down with?' Jules asks Brett in *Pulp Fiction* after he's taken a bite of his burger. Chester similarly refers to the Cristal Champagne he offers Ted as 'a tasty beverage', repeating the recommendation in flamboyant style.

There are, however, more serious disadvantages to Tarantino's naturalistic dialogue than characters that rely on a limited library of expressions. Tarantino the director is perhaps not as strict as he could be on Tarantino the writer. His screenplays are characteristically dialogue-intensive, but this intensity can leaden the pace of sequences such as Butch (qv) and Fabienne's stay in the motel. The period in *Pulp Fiction* between Butch escaping from the theatre and his discovery that Fabienne has forgotten his watch seems to labour over the establishment of the couple's child-like rapport. Elsewhere, however, Tarantino uses this intensity to good effect in emphasising the banality of Vincent and Mia's conversation during their 'date' at Jack Rabbit Slim's. The sequence as seen had already undergone some trimming by the film's editor, Sally Menke (qv). 'There's a lot of dialogue that's been taken out', she explained. 'I actually lobbied pretty hard to take out even more dialogue and Quentin really stuck by his guns and really wanted it to remain as long as it is.' Tarantino countered the scene's detractors by describing his reasons for investing time in dialogue and character establishment: 'You get totally more involved with them, and so after that, when the story takes off, it means so much more and actually it moves even faster. My point of view is, if you're afraid of talking you shouldn't be watching one of my movies.' Tarantino's talent for humanising characters with naturalistic dialogue was recognised early on in his career. One of his earliest commissions was to enhance Frank Norwood's script for the 1991 film *Past Midnight*. He received an associate producer's credit and $7000 for his trouble. While his fee has significantly increased, his work as a dialogue doctor has continued on the films *It's Pat* and *Crimson Tide* (both 1995). His contribution to both goes uncredited.

(See also: Alter egos; *Crimson Tide*; *It's Pat*; *Past Midnight*; Violence)

DIE HARD WITH A VENGEANCE
(US, 1995, dir. John McTiernan)

With his career revitalised following *Pulp Fiction*, Bruce Willis (qv) rejoined his *Pulp* co-star Samuel L Jackson (qv) for the third movie in the *Die Hard* series. Director John McTiernan couldn't resist the opportunity of accordingly slipping in a few Tarantino-related in-jokes. Early on during the uneasy alliance between Zeus (Jackson) and John McClane (Willis), Zeus asks the reinstated cop what he was doing during his recent suspension of duties. 'Smokin' cigarettes and watching *Captain Kangaroo*', is McClane's wry reply, quoting a lyric from The Statler Brothers' *Flowers on the Wall* (qv), the song heard while Willis's Butch is driving away from his apartment having retrieved his watch. Towards the end of the film, Germanic villain 'Simon' (Jeremy Irons) rallies his troops with the cry 'Let's go to work!'

DOWN IN MEXICO

The star attraction at the Titty Twister's cabaret night is the Mexican goddess Razor Charlie describes as 'The Mistress of the Macabre. The Epitome of Evil. The most sinister woman to dance on the face of the Earth . . . Santanico Pandemonium!'. The lights dim and the incredible woman begins her act as the sound of The Coasters' *Down in Mexico* fills the air. *From Dusk Till Dawn* is about to take an astonishing turn . . .

Down in Mexico was the only song Tarantino's script specified for inclusion in *From Dusk Till Dawn*, although it never made the finished film. The song's lyrics continued the story begun in their 1955 single *Smokey Joe's Cafe*, and set the pace for the wry social observance that would typify their most successful work. The group had greater success with *Yakety Yak* (1958) and *Charlie Brown* (1959), both of which were typically light-hearted rock 'n' roll vocal numbers which made the pop charts on both sides of the Atlantic.

Following the acknowledged influence of The Coasters (and their songwriters/producers Leiber and Stoller) on the developing sound of rock 'n' roll, they began to sound dated in the early Sixties. A tendency towards self-parody precipitated their fade from the charts. The group ultimately divided into two and, despite the deaths of key members Bobby Nunn and Cornell Gunther, an 'official' version of The Coasters continues to play live.

DOWNEY JR, ROBERT (1965 -)
Wayne Gale, *Natural Born Killers*

The son of independent writer/director Robert Downey, Downey Jr made his acting debut at five years of age in his father's film, *Pound*, and has appeared in several other of Downey *père*'s features (including *Greaser's Palace*, *Rented Lips* and *Too Much Sun*). Having played in several minor mid-Eighties 'brat pack' movies, he won his first lead role in *The Pick-Up Artist* opposite Molly Ringwald, Dennis Hopper and Harvey Keitel (both qv). A one-time *Saturday Night Live* regular, Downey Jr was hired by director Richard Attenborough to play the title role in the

1992 biopic *Chaplin*. Obnoxious *American Maniacs* host Wayne Gayle had been very much a key figure in Tarantino's draft of *Natural Born Killers*; rewritten and cast by Oliver Stone, Downey Jr's character Gale (without the 'y') underwent a shift of emphasis. 'Like I was what [Stone] was mad at', says the actor. 'I was the devil . . . There was no way he was going to let me live through this film.' Described in Tarantino's draft as an ersatz Geraldo Rivera, the character was made Antipodean after Downey Jr had researched and trailed Steve Dunleavy, Aussie presenter of the US show *A Current Affair*. (It's been reported that Rivera was in the running to play the Gale role as himself.) Other credits include: *Baby, It's You* [with Rosanna Arquette, qv] (1982), *Weird Science* (1985), *Less Than Zero* (1987), *Air America* (1990), *Soapdish* (1991), *Heart and Souls* [with Tom Sizemore, qv] (1993) and *Only You* (1994).

(See also: Wayne Gayle)

DREXL SPIVEY

True Romance's Drexl Spivey's claim that he is half-Apache is a half-hearted justification for his incongruent personality: Alabama's pimp is a white man whose speech and behaviour projects a bizarre caricature of a fast-talking black dude.

There is nothing to commend the horribly scarred Drexl; his place in the Cass Quarter of Detroit is crawling with stoned hookers and murderous hoods. Drexl himself is traitorous to his own colleagues, murdering Floyd and Big D in cold blood to steal Blue Lou Boyle's suitcase of cocaine. His attitude to women is similarly reprehensible, categorising them simply as different types of 'pussy' and violently abusing the girls who work for him.

The thought of Drexl even breathing the same air brings out the vigilante in comic shop clerk Clarence. The ghost of Elvis tells him to

'Shoot him in the face - put him down like a dog.' A shared enthusiasm for early Seventies films (Drexl is watching *The Mack* and compares Clarence to *Mr Majestyk* on his visit) can't save the sadistic pimp from having his balls, and later his head, blown to bits.

'I think he was a fuckin' freeloadin', parasitic scumbag', Clarence tells his friend Dick in the original script, 'and he got exactly what he deserved.'

(See also: Blaxploitation; Dialogue; Oldman, Gary; Race; Role playing)

DRUGS

Tarantino's reliance on the criminal underworld to inform his favoured *milieu* has naturally seen the introduction of drug abuse into his storylines. Like Freddy Newendyke in *Reservoir Dogs*, he perhaps feels the introduction of a well-spun narcotics yarn adds a little authenticity to proceedings.

In *True Romance*, Tarantino uses drugs as a satirical tool and moral barometer. In Detroit, Clarence murders drug-dealing pimp Drexl Spivey and mistakenly takes his suitcase packed with $1,000,000 worth of cocaine. Together

True Romance.
The culturally confused Drexl Spivey settles down to a Chinese take-away.

with his new bride, Drexl's former 'call girl' Alabama, he is quick to realise the case's potential to earn them a vast sum of money. Not conversant with drug sub-culture in his home town (and murdering one of its principal exponents clearly isn't going to open any doors) he takes the case, and Alabama, to Hollywood where he hopes his old friend and fellow film buff Dick will be able to help him 'offload' the coke now he's an actor. Tarantino uses Clarence's efforts to sell the coke to film producer Lee Donowitz (producer of hit Vietnam flick *Comin' Home in a Body Bag*) as an opportunity to satirise the movie community's drug-fuelled decadence. In keeping with the script's romantic aspirations for its 'good' characters, neither Clarence, Alabama, or Dick ever express any interest in taking any of the readily available cocaine for themselves. The morally deficient characters such as Coccoti, Donowitz and Elliot (who steals a 'sample bag' of the stuff from under his boss Donowitz's nose) are left scrabbling around to secure the drugs by any means necessary.

Reservoir Dogs's Joe Cabot seems to inhabit a more gentlemanly world of organised crime where diamond heists and drugs busts just don't mix. In that film's follow-up, however, drugs are employed as a key to characters' strata in the criminal underworld. *Pulp Fiction* begins with the now legendary conversation between hitmen Jules and Vincent ('OK, so tell me about the hash bars . . .') which illustrates that both use soft drugs. Vincent's later visit to his dealer Lance ('That was the best damn shooting up scene in the history of cinema!' - Tarantino) portrays him as something of a connoisseur of heroin. In common with *True Romance*, cocaine is seen as the exclusive indulgence of the wealthy and powerful. Marsellus Wallace's wife, Mia, is seen using cocaine in the bathroom at Jack Rabbit Slim's (the script features an extra sequence of her snorting lines in her own house) and is obviously unfamiliar with heroin - her mistaking of Vincent's stash for cocaine leads to her near fatal overdose.

Elsewhere, Tarantino is unafraid to use the depiction of drug-taking to his own ends, much as the depiction of violence is used to manipulate our emotions. Floyd, Dick's flatmate in *True Romance*, is a character who seems to exist purely to elicit laughs from his constant druggy stupor. Dick is left unsure about the time of Clarence's arrival because Floyd has apparently smoked the second page of his friend's letter. Later, Floyd cheerfully invites Virgil to join him watching television, genuinely believing the hitman to be a hallucination.

Tarantino added the heroin references in *Pulp Fiction*'s script after being inspired by a rough cut of Roger Avary's *Killing Zoe* (qv), which he saw when his friend and collaborator joined him in Amsterdam while he was writing. While by no means the most important element in the multi-faceted film, the heroin abuse scenes nevertheless caused problems. John Travolta originally considered Vincent Vega's behaviour so morally defunct that he harboured serious doubts about whether he should take the role, and it was the explicit abuse of the substance which gave TriStar cold feet over distributing *Pulp Fiction*. The company had already warned Jersey Films's Danny De Vito that they felt the film too graphic, and the heroin factor proved the final straw. 'They had big problems with the scene where John Travolta's character shoots up heroin', recalled Tarantino. 'I'm going, "Look, guys, relax, it's going to be funny", and they're saying, "No, Quentin, heroin is not funny. A guy sticking a needle in his arm does not make for big laughs." In the end I just said. "You're gonna have to trust me on this one, guys." They didn't. I guess they just couldn't make the leap.'

(See also: Mia Wallace; Vincent Vega)

e

EARS

Taken hostage during the getaway from *Reservoir Dogs*'s jewellery raid, policeman Marvin Nash is bound and left under the supervision of Mr Blonde. While Mr Orange slowly bleeds to death in a corner of the warehouse, Blonde tortures the cop, slashing his face and severing his ear. His sadistic mockery of the victimised policeman continues with him addressing the detached ear before casually tossing it aside. The disfigured Nash is only narrowly saved from a gasoline torching by the last-minute intervention of Mr Orange, who shoots Blonde.

The removal of Marvin Nash's ear provided *Dogs* with its most notorious talking point. Played out against the easy-listening backdrop of *Stuck In The Middle With You* (qv) by Stealer's Wheel this scene balances its more immediate dichotomies with consummate ease - at no point do we ever share a joke Mr Blonde clearly finds hilarious. The scene remains one of the most sickening depictions of psychotic sadism in modern cinema. Reportedly, at Spain's Sitges horror film festival, at which Tarantino guested, fifteen attendees, including slash auteur Wes Craven (*The Hills Have Eyes, A Nightmare on Elm*

Street, etc) and gore SFX maestro Rick Baker (*An American Werewolf in London*), walked out while the scene was playing. Baker is alleged to have told Tarantino: 'You're dealing with real-life violence, and I can't deal with that.'

The actual slicing itself takes place off-screen. 'In a way, it makes it more powerful', mused Tarantino, reflecting on his favourite sequence from the film. 'If you saw him actually cutting the ear, you'd think, OK, it's a movie, and that's a fake ear, but with the camera going off it, it makes it more real, stops it from being a movie. At the time I was doing it, I felt that maybe it was like an old Roger Corman monster movie, where they just talk about the monster most of the time and have, like, three shots of a guy in a rubber suit.'

On 15 November 1994, London's *Evening Standard* confirmed the cult status the ear scene had earned amongst the film's devotees. 'The Prince Charles cinema has screened *Reservoir Dogs* for the past two years. Every week passionate groupies turn up wearing the wicked suits and carrying plastic guns. They have become known as the Doggies . . . Later this month the Doggies are holding a convention at which they will each receive a fake

severed ear, complete with dripping 'blood'.
A hundred ears will be given away as a tribute
to the dedicated Doggies who have made it
the cinema's most successful film.'

Surprisingly, considering the controversy it
engendered, the scene merely continued a tradition from previous cinematic lobal
detachments. Ear slicings have been a feature
of such diverse films as *Blue Velvet* (1986) and
Carry On Columbus (1992), and remain a
favourite means of traumatising an audience.
Aural separation was an inevitable feature of

Van Gogh biopics *Lust For Life* (1956), *Vincent*
(1987) and *Vincent et Theo* (1990). The latter
starred Tim Roth (qv) as the mentally tortured
artist who famously did away with his own ear
before doing away with himself.

More significantly, Martin Scorsese's *The Last
Temptation of Christ* (1988) followed St Luke's
version of Christ's arrest by showing the
Messiah's miraculous reattachment of a severed ear. The ear in question is sliced off by a
belligerent disciple in the presence of Harvey
Keitel's (qv) Judas.

'Was that as good for you
as it was for me?' asks
Mr Blonde.

Perhaps the most notable detached ear film is David Lynch's metaphorical nightmare *Blue Velvet* (1986). It is the discovery of a scissored human ear by Jeffrey Beaumont (Kyle MacLachlan) that triggers his investigation into the depraved sub-culture of suburban Lumberton. The decapitator responsible is rapist Frank Booth (Dennis Hopper, qv) who warns the ear's widow to 'stay alive baby . . . do it for Van Gogh.' Hopper would later get to work on someone's ear in *Speed* (1994), a film Tarantino was offered but turned down.

If, however, we were to attempt to pinpoint one film most likely to have influenced Tarantino's choice of torture, then it would be unwise to overlook Sergio Corbucci's seminal spaghetti western *Django* (1966). During the course of the film, the town preacher is accused of being a spy by a visiting Mexican general. The general duly cuts off one of the preacher's ears and forces the man to eat it. The general, clearly a man with a penchant for such pruning, later threatens a hotel whore with the same treatment. *Django*, a film so violent it was originally refused a certificate by the BBFC, surely wins the award for featuring the most graphic lug-dismemberment pre-*Reservoir Dogs*.

The tradition continues - in 1993, John Woo's *Hard Target* and Sydney Pollack's *The Firm* both featured hapless characters who developed hearing difficulties. Incredibly, Oliver Stone's *Natural Born Killers* featured a scene where Mallory zooms a video camera in on Wayne Gale's mutilated ear. 'Oh my God, that is so gross!' she exclaims. While the influence *Reservoir Dogs* had on at least two of those films is debatable, it remains that no-one has yet to match the hysterical potency Tarantino elicited from perhaps his most infamous moment.

(See also: Violence)

ELLIOT BLITZER
(See: Pinchot, Bronson; Role playing; Yuppie scum)

ELVIS PRESLEY
'Man, you were cooler than cool' - Mentor, *True Romance*.

The King of Rock and Roll, and the man who undoubtedly sits at the top of the American pop culture tree, has made a significant impact on Tarantino's acting and writing. 'When I was young, I used to think Elvis was the voice of truth', he told *Melody Maker*. 'I don't know what that means, but his voice . . . shit, man, it sounded so fucking pure, y'know?'

Aside from some limited theatre work, the only legitimate acting job Tarantino earned before becoming a director was playing an Elvis impersonator in an episode of *The Golden Girls* sit-com first transmitted on 19 November 1988. The episode, in which Tarantino joined a group of twelve Elvis impersonators singing the *Hawaiian Love Chant*, later reappeared in a 'best of' compilation episode, boosting his salary. 'It was real fun', he recalled, 'and I made $3,000 from royalties. Easiest money I've ever earned.' Significantly, Tarantino was the only member of the troupe not dressed in a Las Vegas style jump-suit, opting instead for the 'cooler' Fifties look.

In *True Romance*, the ghost of a 'cool' Elvis Presley appears to Clarence during his visits to the bathroom. (It is fitting that Elvis should restrict his spectral appearances to the smallest room, seeing as he met his end while on the toilet). The King directs Clarence's destiny during *True Romance*, and clearly influences his style and taste as well. Clarence's Elvis memorabilia include the postcard stuck on his wall, his shades and the souvenir decanter that Alabama ends up crashing over Virgil's head. (In Tony Scott's film, it is a brand-new plaster bust of The King that Alabama reaches for.) Although Clarence murders Drexl upon Elvis's recommendation, he still regards his actions as perfectly reasonable. When he later comes across the burger bar customer reading a *Newsweek* article on Elvis he flicks through the magazine telling the stranger that 'the fanatics . . . give me the creeps'. The irony of his statement clearly eludes him. Director Tony Scott was nervous about the Presley estate's reaction to the film so omitted Clarence's scripted comment about one of these so-called 'fanatics' ('Elvis wouldn't fuck her with Pat Boone's dick') from the film. For the same reason, Val Kilmer's Elvis was credited simply as 'Mentor' on the film's closing credits.

True Romance's ultimate tribute to The King was, however, actually scripted by Roger Avary (qv). Having survived the hotel shoot-out in Avary's rewrite, Clarence uses the cocaine money to take his wife to Mexico. In her closing narration, Alabama describes how she named their first son Elvis.

Aside from a fleeting mention in *Natural Born Killers*, the only other significant reference to Elvis was cut prior to filming on *Pulp Fiction*. When Vincent Vega arrives at Mia Wallace's house, a question/answer session ensues during which Mia attempts to learn quickly about Vincent through a series of questions about his pop culture preferences. As she explains, 'Beatles people can like Elvis. And Elvis people can like the Beatles. But nobody likes them both equally. Somewhere you have to make a choice. And that choice tells me who you are.' Although this sequence never made it into the finished film, Mia's telling Vincent that 'This is Jack Rabbit Slim's. An Elvis man should love it' remains.

There are several likely sources for Tarantino's Elvis predilection, the likeliest being a genuine enthusiasm for the man and his music inherited from his mother, Connie. *Viva Las Vegas* (1964) remains a film they both share a special fondness for. Another source of inspiration may have been the hotel-based comedy anthology *Mystery Train* (1989). Jim Jarmush's film features such locations as the Sun Records building and Graceland, and even includes a scene where the ghost of Elvis appears to a recently widowed woman.

(See also: *Badlands*; Causality and imitation; Clarence Worley; Hotels; Tarantino, Quentin [as actor]; Vincent Vega)

'Cooler than cool': The King.

ER: MOTHERHOOD

The penultimate episode in the first season of NBC's Michael Crichton-created medical TV series, Tarantino came to direct *Motherhood* after he'd - apparently - called the production office to request a cassette of an instalment he'd missed; the producers insisted he directed an episode in return. In the episode, set on Mother's Day, Dr Lewis (Sherry Stringfield) delivers her sister's child (coincidentally, a minor plot strand concerned a gang member admitted to the hospital having had her ear ripped off). First transmitted in the US on 11 May 1995, the show also featured George Clooney (qv) as Dr Ross, and Anthony Edwards as Dr Mark Greene, who said of the instalment's director: 'On the show we are really having to tell the story visually because most of America doesn't understand the jargon we're using. The dialogue's important, but if you watched *ER* with just the music and movement, you would still know what was going on. Tarantino likes that.' Principal production credits: Director Quentin Tarantino; Producer Dennis Murphy; Written by Lydia Woodward, Robert Nathan and Paul Manning; Photography Thomas Del Ruth; Editor Randy Jon Morgan; Production Designer Michael Helmy. Other cast members include: Kathleen Wilhoite as Chloe, Noah Wyle as John Carter, and Angela Jones (qv).

ESMARELDA VILLALOBOS

When Butch needs to make a quick getaway, it is another of *Pulp Fiction*'s barefoot beauties that comes to his rescue. The sultry Colombian Esmarelda Villalobos ('It means "Esmarelda of the wolves"' she tells Butch in the original script) succeeds in looking sophisticated with nothing more than an old-fashioned radio and a Thermos flask at her disposal.

The journey to the River Glen Motel sees Esmarelda attempt to satisfy her curiosity about Butch's manslaughter of his opponent. The thought of Butch having beaten a man to death with his bare hands, or possibly just the thought of Butch, clearly excites her,

although she learns little from her inquisitive psychoanalysis. At the end of the evening, the Big Jerry Cab Co is $45.60 richer, Esmarelda receives a little something for remaining tight-lipped about her passenger, and the couple's burgeoning sexual chemistry remains unresolved. *Bon soir*, Esmarelda Villalobos.

(See also: Foot fetishism; Jones, Angela; Women)

EUROPE

Impressed by the quality of the *Reservoir Dogs* script, Jersey Films offered Tarantino a $900,000 advance for his second feature. With his future secure, Tarantino decided to move to Amsterdam in March 1992 in order to concentrate his thoughts on writing the screenplay for an anthology film he and Roger Avary had originally devised as *Black Mask* in 1989. *Pulp Fiction*, as the film was ultimately titled, came together over the following ten months - much of which Tarantino spent touring European film festivals promoting *Reservoir Dogs*.

Fare maiden: Angela Jones as Esmarelda Villalobos in *Pulp Fiction*.

The time Tarantino, and later Roger Avary, spent writing *Pulp Fiction* in Amsterdam had a profound influence on the script. Vincent Vega enters the film having just spent three years in Amsterdam (running a club for Marsellus, according to Tarantino's non-scripted history for the character). The conversation he has with Jules comparing the 'little differences' between Europe and the US has become some of *Pulp Fiction*'s most famous dialogue. Tarantino's surroundings also influenced the nationalities of the characters in the script: the barman at Sally Leroy's is called 'English Dave' (although his name is Paul and he is clearly American), Lance's friend Trudi is Irish and Fabienne, Butch's girlfriend, is French.

French and Italian cinema remain two of Tarantino's great passions - the work of Jean-Luc Godard (qv) clearly informs *Pulp Fiction*. Italian Spaghetti Westerns and exploitation horror films are similarly influential. The Dario Argento shocker *Opera* is one of Tarantino's favourite Italian films; its influence is felt during such pivotal scenes as the massacre in the diner during the opening scene of *Natural Born Killers* and the torture of the cop in *Reservoir Dogs*. The debt owed by *From Dusk Till Dawn* to Italian horror films was more formally acknowledged in the screenplay, which opens with 'I earnestly wish an end would come to this bloody race I am forced to run' - a quotation from the Countess in Jess Franco's *La Comtesse Noire*.

(See also: Horror; *Killing Zoe*)

EZEKIEL 25:17

'There's a passage I got memorized', claims *Pulp Fiction*'s Jules, 'Ezekiel 25:17. "The path of the righteous man is beset on all sides by the inequities of the selfish and the tyranny of evil men. Blessed is he who, in the name of charity and good will, shepherds the weak through the valley of darkness, for he is truly his brother's keeper and the finder of lost children. And I will strike down upon thee with great vengeance and furious anger those who attempt to poison and destroy my brothers. And you will know my name is the Lord when I lay my vengeance upon you."' Chapter 25, verse 17 of *The Book of the Prophet Ezekiel* actually reads, of the Philistines, simply this: 'And I will execute great vengeance upon them with furious rebukes; and they shall know that I am the LORD, when I shall lay my vengeance upon them.' Jules's speech actually originated in an early draft of *From Dusk Till Dawn* and was modelled after that given by Sonny Chiba throughout the TV series *Kage No Gundo* (aka *Shadow Warriors*); Chiba's character recites a similarly involved cant - 'The only people who hear this speech die' - immediately before executing one of his enemies. Chiba's Streetfighter film persona is itself exhaustively chronicled by *True Romance*'s Clarence; Chiba himself visited the *Pulp Fiction* set. (Some have claimed, however, that Jules's mode of speech owes more to that of preacher Harry Powell, Robert Mitchum's fanatical pastor in 1955's *Night of the Hunter*. Note also that, throughout 1989's *Batman*, Jack Nicholson's Joker adopts a similarly quasi-Biblical pre-murder phraseology: 'Did you ever dance with the Devil on a moonlit night? . . . I always ask that of all my friends. I just like the sound of it.')

(See also: Jules Winnfield; Morality; Redemption)

f

FABIENNE

The character of Fabienne was originated by Roger Avary in his script *Pandemonium Reigns*. Originally an American woman called Christine, Avary was upset to see Tarantino change the character's name and nationality when he integrated the story into *Pulp Fiction*. Tarantino asserts that the scene Butch and Fabienne share in the motel bathroom is the only one in the entire film that preserves Avary's original dialogue verbatim.

In the film, Butch's French 'sugar pop' appears to be in a child-like world of her own, a million miles away from the murder and deception of her boyfriend's recent activities. Upon Butch's return from his fight, she asks if they can 'make spoons' and pontificates the pleasures of having a pot belly before she even gets round to asking him, 'Are you the winner?'

Her devotion to Butch is absolute - she cannot bear to listen to his fights on the radio, is terrified at the thought of his returning to their apartment and bursts into tears at the sight of his resulting broken nose. Her insecurity demands reassurance from Butch that he wants to be with her forever. The couple's sexual relationship enjoys similar reciprocation - oral

sex is a shared indulgence, even after the physical rigours of Butch's fight.

There is little more to say about Fabienne - all that 'oral pleasure' has given her an appetite for blueberry pie for breakfast, she likes being called 'tulip', doesn't like being called 'retard', and regards Bora Bora as an ideal location to spend her boyfriend's ill-gotten gains. In short, Fabienne projects a naive innocence, possesses an assured sexuality and maintains a carefully cultivated ignorance. Her personality is entrancing enough to transform the ruthless, amoral Butch into a sweet-natured child who tempers his worst excesses. At the close of *The Gold Watch*, it is difficult to imagine his new life with Fabienne ever again descending to the ruthless brutality of recent events.

(See also: De Medeiros, Maria; Dialogue; Foot fetishism; Quarterpounders; Women)

FICTIONAL FILMS AND TELEVISION

The pop culture of Tarantino's fictional world is but one step removed from our own; endlessly bizarre yet horribly credible. Tarantino's dream films include, in *True Romance*, the Lee Donowitz-produced Vietnam epic, *Comin'*

Home in a Body Bag: 'after *Apocalypse Now*', believes Clarence, 'the best Vietnam movie ever', and 'the first movie with balls to win a lot of Oscars since *The Deer Hunter*'. (Donowitz was consciously reconfigured by director Tony Scott as a caricature of action producer Joel Silver - who does not, of course, share Donowitz's less savoury habits). The Mickey and Mallory Knox movie, *Thrill Killers* - 'a Wagnerian love story', according to its writer/director Neil Pope - starred the previously unknown Jessie Alexander Warwick and Buffy St McQueen as the husband-and-wife mass murderers; ending with Mallory blowing her own head off for Mickey, its poster showed the gun-toting pair 'in a romantic pose, *à la Gone With the Wind*' (this sequence was removed from *Natural Born Killers* by director Oliver Stone). Also in *NBK*, we meet bodybuilding film stars The Brothers Hun, who headline, amongst others, *Conquering Huns of Neptune*; an especial influence upon Mickey and Mallory, apparently (see Avary, Roger). Segments of Wayne Gale's weekly TV show, *American Maniacs*, underscore much of *Natural Born Killers* (note, however, that sitcom *I Love Mallory* was neither a Tarantino invention, nor a 'real' fiction, taking place as a fantasy inside Mallory's head). In *Pulp Fiction*, Mia relates the tale of her involvement with a pilot for a formulaic TV series in the *Charlie's Angels* mould. Entitled *Fox Force Five*, it concerned a team of five female secret agents: Mia played knife expert Raven McCoy alongside actress Sommerset O'Neal, ex- of yet another fictional series, *Baton Rouge*. And, in *The Man From Hollywood*, Tarantino's *Four Rooms* segment, we learn that Chester Rush's hit movie, *The Wacky Detective*, has made a staggering $72.1m on domestic takings alone. Early drafts of the script also made mention of the follow-up, *The Dog Catcher*, and featured an additional character unseen in the film: Connie Bakalinkoff, 'a rough and dangerous action movie star'. With a resume comprising such undoubted meisterworks as *Three Kicks to the Head*, *Powder Keg*, *Mr Nitro*, and *Three Kicks to the Head II*, it would be tempting to surmise that the character was devised as a satire on the *Die Hard* persona oft-attached to the segment's uncredited co-star, Bruce Willis (qv).

(See also: Films; Television)

FILMS

The mention of films, film stars and film styles, both in dialogue and setting description, proliferate Tarantino's scripts and screenplays. The extent and variety of these references render any attempt to read meaningful patterns into their deployment difficult. They do, however, highlight the writer's reliance on movie culture as his principal reference framework. The degree of this reliance is best illustrated by listing the descriptive short-cuts and characterising name-drops labelled by film references:

True Romance

In the bar, Clarence eulogises *Jailhouse Rock*.

As a birthday treat, Clarence goes to the cinema to watch a triple bill of Sonny Chiba martial arts movies - *The Streetfighter*, *Return of the Streetfighter* and *Sister Streetfighter*.

In the diner after the movies, Alabama tells Clarence that her favourite movie star is Burt Reynolds, and that Mickey Rourke is also a turn-on.

'That's a pretty original moniker there', Clarence tells Alabama. 'Sounds like a Pam Grier [qv] movie.'

'Did you know they came out with dolls for all the actors in *The Black Hole*?' Clarence asks Alabama, in the Heroes For Sale comic shop. 'I always found it funny that somewhere there's a kid playin' with a little figure of Ernest Borgnine.'

When Alabama tells Clarence about her life as a call girl, she describes the better paid hookers as living like Nancy Allen in *Dressed to Kill*.

The newlywed Clarence and Alabama are watching *The Incredible One-Armed Boxer vs. the Master of the Flying Guillotine* on television when Clarence asks, 'Did you ever see *The Chinese Professionals?*' (In Scott's film, they watch *A Better Tomorrow Part 2* at home)

When Clarence visits Drexl, *The Mack* is playing on the television screen behind them.

Drexl likens Clarence to the Charles Bronson character Mr Majestyk.

'Next time you bogart your way into a nigger's crib . . . make sure you do it on white boy day', Drexl warns Clarence.

Dicks hangs a poster for the William Conrad film *My Blood Runs Cold* in his bathroom. Fearful of telephone tapping while talking to Lee Donowitz, Clarence describes his suitcase of cocaine as *Doctor Zhivago*.

Clarence alludes to the car chase in *Bullit* before he takes off in his Mustang.

Police detective Nicholson tells his commanding officer, Captain Bufford Krinkle, that he doesn't care if he enlists the ghost of Steve McQueen as long as he and Dimes take the credit for busting Lee Donowitz.

In Lee's hotel room, bodyguard Boris asks Clarence what compelled him to bring a gun. Clarence replies, 'The same thing that compelled you, Beastmaster, to bring rapid-fire weaponry to a business meeting.'

Clarence later describes the bodyguards as '*Soldier of Fortune* poster boys'.

In a speech largely cut from the film screenplay, Clarence complains to Lee about the supposed poor quality of most Oscar-winning films: *Sophie's Choice, Ordinary People, Kramer vs Kramer, Gandhi*. All that stuff is safe, geriatric, coffee-table dog shit . . . Like that Merchant-Ivory clap-trap. All those assholes make are unwatchable movies from unreadable books.'

Later in the same conversation, Clarence includes Lee Donowitz's *Comin' Home in a Body Bag* amongst his own favourite films. '*Mad Max*, that's a movie. *The Good the Bad and the Ugly*, that's a movie. *Rio Bravo*, that's a movie. *Rumble Fish*, that's a movie. And, *Comin' Home in a Body Bag*, that's a movie. It was the first movie with balls to win a lot of Oscars since *The Deer Hunter*.'

When Clarence retires to the bathroom, his concerns about his performance in front of Lee are allayed by Elvis, who tells him, 'All anybody saw was Clint Eastwood drinkin' coffee.'

After Clarence's death, the widowed Alabama remembers his words, 'She's a sixteen-calibre kitten! . . . Alabama Whitman is Pam Grier!'

Natural Born Killers

'I'm a detective', Scagnetti tells Squeri. 'You want an errand boy, call Jerry Lewis'. Scott,

Wayne's cameraman, wears a t-shirt with *She Devils On Wheels* on the front.

A conversation between Wayne, Scott and Roger is described as being played at a rapid *His Girl Friday* pace. Wayne tells the others that '. . . this is Truffaut setting the record straight on Hitchcock . . .'.

Roger jokingly alludes to Raymond Burr witnessing the destruction of Tokyo in the first *Godzilla* film.

One of Wayne's interviewees likens Mickey and Mallory to 'that crazy mother in the first *Dirty Harry* movie'.

The bodybuilding Hun brothers are similarly impressed, rating the Knoxes over Arnold Schwarzenegger in *Pumping Iron*.

The poster for *Thrill Killers*, a film based on Mickey and Mallory's exploits, has the two of

Ricky Nelson and John Wayne in *Rio Bravo* - 'that's a movie'.

them in a romantic pose in the manner of *Gone With the Wind*.

Grace tells Mickey that Tim studied Jeet Kune Do because it was Bruce Lee's fighting style.

Scott is incredulous at Roger's belief that *Indiana Jones and the Temple of Doom* is Steven Spielberg's finest film.

'We're after a *cinema-verite*, anything can happen, truth twenty-four times a second kinda feel.' Wayne tells Scott.

'Did you ever see *El Dorado?*' Mickey asks Scagnetti, referring to Howard Hawks's 1967 follow-up to *Rio Bravo*.

Mallory suggests that she and Mickey go down with all guns blazing, as in the climax to *Butch Cassidy and the Sundance Kid*. (The script later decribes the two of them firing just like Butch and Sundance.)

Just before Mickey shoots Wayne, he does an impression of John Wayne from *Rio Bravo*: 'Let's make a little music, Colarada.'

Reservoir Dogs

Mr Blue refers to well-endowed porn star John Holmes during his lecture on the supposed meaning of *Like a Virgin*. 'Then one day she meets a John Holmes motherfucker, and it's like, whoa baby. This mother fucker's like Charles Bronson in *The Great Escape*. He's diggin' tunnels.'

Joe describes his new wife's accent as being like that of *L'il Abner*.

'You're a big Lee Marvin fan aren't you?' Mr Blonde asks Mr White. 'Me too.'

Holdaway tells Freddy that when working undercover he must be a great actor, like Marlon Brando.

Freddy's fabricated story contains an interruption while he's trying to watch *The Lost Boys*.

While giving Mr Orange some advice on crowd control, Mr White tells him what to do 'If you get a customer or an employee who thinks he's Charles Bronson . . .'

Pulp Fiction

Pumpkin and Honey Bunny's dialogue is described as being spoken in a rapid *His Girl Friday* fashion.

Jules and Vincent's colleague, Antwan Rockamora, is nicknamed Tony Rocky Horror.

'Cut. Print. Let's go eat.' Mia tells Vincent.

The script describes the walls of Jack Rabbit Slim's as being plastered with posters for 1950s AIP movies *Rock All Night*, *High School Confidential*, *Attack of the Crab Monster* and *Machine-Gun Kelly*. One of the waitresses is a double of Marilyn Monroe - her skirt is duly seen to billow under an air vent.

Vincent orders a steak named after film director Douglas Sirk and Mia asks for a milkshake named after Dean Martin and Jerry Lewis.

As Vincent eats his steak, he scans the restaurant the script describes as 'Hellsapoppinish'. He soon spots a Mamie Van Doren waitress and notes the absence of 'Jayne Mansfield'.

When Vincent drives the comatose Mia to Lance's house, the script describes his 'having one hand firmly on the wheel, the other shifting like Robocop'.

Lance is watching *The Three Stooges* just prior to their arrival.

When Vincent is shown how to resuscitate Mia, the script describes it thus: 'Lance demonstrates a stabbing motion, which looks like the The Shape killing its victims in *Halloween*.'

In the motel, Butch wakes up to the television playing a scene from *The Losers*.

When Winston Wolf discusses details of *The Bonnie Situation* with Marsellus, his notes reveal that Vincent resembles Dean Martin.

Jules is furious at having to wipe up Marvin's brain tissue from inside the Chevy Nova: 'Every time my fingers touch brain, I'm *Superfly TNT*', he tells Vincent. 'I'm *The Guns of Navarone*.'

Winston compares the argumentative Vince to Western character Lash Larue.

As Jules and Winston part company, Winston grabs Jules's wrist and 'pantomimes like he's in a *Dead Zone* trance.'

Jules, unimpressed with Vincent's theory about animals' personalities compensating for their supposedly dirty habits, tells him that any swine winning his respect would have to be 'the Cary Grant of pigs'.

Four Rooms: Penthouse:
The Man From Hollywood
Director Ted Post is namechecked on Chester's list of famous Teds.

As part of a protracted discussion about bellboys, Chester Rush makes extensive reference to The Who film *Quadrophenia* and the Jerry Lewis movie *The Bellboy*.

From Dusk Till Dawn
The script opens with a quotation from Jess Franco's *La Comtesse Noire*.

Seth and Richard's car is a 1975 Plymouth. The script specifies it is just like the one driven by

Charley Varrick in the Don Siegel film of the same name. (The car ultimately featured in the film is a Cougar.)

'I'll turn this fuckin' store into *The Wild Bunch* if I even think you're fuckin' with me.' warns Richard Gecko. The script also mentions Peckinpah's Western when events at The Titty Twister culminate in a Mexican stand-off (qv).

Scott wears a t-shirt displaying the name of the heavy metal garage band he plays guitar for - Precinct 13. This is possibly inspired by the James Cameron movie *Assault on Precinct 13*, seen by many as a new take on Howard Hawks's *Rio Bravo* and which bears a number of similarities to *From Dusk Till Dawn* itself.

The script quotes *The Jazz Singer* in describing the Geckos' destination: 'If the Titty Twister looked like the asshole of the world from the outside, in the immortal words of Al Jolson, "You ain't seen nothin' yet."'

Photographs of cult film star wrestler Santo are stuck to the Titty Twister's walls.

Big Emilio walks steadily through the bar, 'like Godzilla walks through Tokyo'.

The script describes how 'The biker has turned into Captain Sex Machine, Vampire Hunter.' This is possibly an allusion to the Hammer horror film *Captain Kronos Vampire Hunter*.

Sex Machine refers to Hammer's version of *Dracula*, when he advocates creating a crucifix by putting two sticks together: 'Peter Cushing does that all the time.'

(See also: *Crimson Tide*; Horror)

FINGERS
When it comes to grievous bodily harm, fingers actually figure more prominently in Tarantino's work than ears (qv).

During the opening scene in *Natural Born Killers*, Mickey begins his attack on one of the ogling hillbillies by causing him a little separation anxiety. The script describes the action: 'Mickey whips a large buck knife out from its sheath and, in a flash, slices off Sonny's finger.' The scene is preserved in Oliver Stone's film, the bloody digit falling onto Sonny's boot. He shakes it off in a panic.

Although ears take centre stage in *Reservoir Dogs*, Mr White's crowd control advice to the inexperienced Mr Orange includes the following handy tip about uncooperative store managers: 'If you wanna know something he won't tell you, cut off one of his fingers, the little one, then tell him his thumb's next. After that he'll tell you if he wears ladies' underwear.'

The threat of finger-severing hovers over Zed in *Pulp Fiction* when Butch returns to the pawnshop's back room to save Marsellus. Having already speared Maynard with the Samurai sword, he then turns the weapon onto Zed. As Zed's hand reaches towards his gun, Butch waves the sword before him, daring him to risk the loss of his fingers. As luck would have it, Zed is rescued by the appearance of a recovered Marsellus. Who promptly blasts him with a pump-action shotgun.

The ultimate in finger severance is the highlight of *Four Rooms: Penthouse: The Man From Hollywood*. In a reconstruction of a bet Chester saw staged in the *Alfred Hitchcock Presents* (qv) episode *Man from the South*, Norman wagers he can light his Zippo ten times in a row. If he succeeds, he wins Chester's Chevy Chevelle. If he fails, he has his little finger severed by Ted. A bucket of ice is prepared for the finger, in case Norman has to be rushed to hospital for micro surgery. The film ends with Norman failing to light his Zippo even once, and his pinkie duly being chopped. The ice bucket is filled and the penthouse suite promptly vacated.

The precedence of a finger-chopping bet in an episode of *Alfred Hitchcock Presents* (qv) allows Tarantino to defer a potential moral tangle of *Reservoir Dogs* proportions. That the director is once more presenting another gory scene where a hapless character has a body-part sliced off (and this time in the name of comedy) is no longer his responsibility - Roald Dahl wrote the story. Tarantino sidesteps the moral question in the same way Ted sidesteps his conscience in taking Chester's money. Remarkably, Tarantino admits to never having seen the actual episode of *Alfred Hitchcock Presents*, only having seen a 1985 colour remake starring John Huston.

The theme was revisited yet again in *From Dusk Till Dawn* - angry at the unhealthy interest shown in Kate, Seth grabs hold of Chet Pussy's finger and 'bends it backwards till the bone snaps in two'. Unluckily for Seth, Chet later turns out to be the type to bear a grudge.

Tarantino's fixation with finger mutilation finds its closest reflection in the unsavoury practises of the Japanese mafia. The punishment for disloyalty has long been 'yubizume' - the severing of a finger. Such is the proliferation of yubizume, that a surgical procedure transplanting a toe onto the afflicted finger stump is now available.

(See also: Honda Civic; Violence)

FLOWERS ON THE WALL

Pulp Fiction's Butch is such a fan of this 1966 Statler Brothers hit that he is able to sing along with the lyrics when he hears it driving back from his trip to collect The Gold Watch. In the 1995 film *Die Hard With a Vengeance*, cop John McClane (to whom Butch bears a striking resemblance) is similarly familiar with the chorus of this jaunty country tune.

Originally formed in 1955, The Statler Brothers took their name from an American tissue manufacturer in 1960 (prior to this they had been known as The Kingsmen). While they continue to be hugely successful country artists and live performers in the USA, *Flowers on the Wall* remains their only significant crossover into the mainstream charts, reaching number 4 in the US and number 38 in the UK. The single originally appeared on the album *Flowers on the Wall*, released in 1966.

The song was selected for *Pulp Fiction* after it was presented as a possible contender by music supervisor Karyn Rachtman. 'I could see Bruce singing that song, and Bruce loved it', claimed a similarly enthused Tarantino, 'so it was just a total marriage made in heaven'.

Fortuitously, the lyrics 'It's good to see you, I must go, I know a look a fright', occur just at the point when Butch witnesses arch-nemesis Marsellus crossing the road directly in front of him.

FOOD
(See: Quarterpounders)

FOOT FETISHISM
'I've given a million ladies a million foot massages and they all meant somethin',' claims *Pulp Fiction*'s Vincent. 'There's a sensuous thing goin' on . . .'. This dialogue on the etiquette of foot massage serves merely as circumstantial evidence in an effort to prove Tarantino's foot fetishism (note also that, according to writer Jami Bernard, he wrote a foot massage scene into *Past Midnight* [qv] which was altered prior to shooting at the insistence of the director). Consider this, however: all the lead female characters in Tarantino's directorial canon are seen on-screen

sans footwear. In *Pulp Fiction*, a close-up of Mia's upturned sole signifies her readiness to leave for Jack Rabbit Slim's; later, she removes her shoes to do the twist. (Even her portrait is rendered barefoot.) Jody eschews slippers at night, and Esmarelda - oddly enough - drives unshod. Fabienne, too, is seen naked from the ankle down, and, in the *Man From Hollywood* section of *Four Rooms*, Angela, likewise, goes soleless. *From Dusk Till Dawn*'s script goes further, specifying that one of the Geckos' hostages in Benny's World of Liquor be 'a pretty blonde girl in cutoffs and bare feet'. Later, while the Geckos and the Fullers make for the border, Richard, played by Tarantino himself, ogles Kate's plates (the screenplay specified a slow zoom to Kate's bare feet, then an extreme-close-up of Kate's toes, which wiggle).

Most incriminating of all, however, is the scene in which Mexican love-goddess Santanico Pandemonium 'scans the table, zeroing in on our boy Richard [Tarantino again]. She stands over him. While moving her body to the music, she lifts up the whiskey bottle from the table, and pours the whiskey down her leg. She lifts up her foot, with the whiskey dripping from her toes, and sticks it in Richard's face . . . Richie, mesmerized, sucks the whiskey off her toes.' Incredible but true . . .

(See also: Women)

FOUR ROOMS: PENTHOUSE: THE MAN FROM HOLLYWOOD
(See appendix)

FROM DUSK TILL DAWN
(See appendix)

g

GODARD, JEAN-LUC (1930 -)

Unlike Tarantino's other preferred directors -
Brian De Palma, Howard Hawks - it is possible
to see much that is directly Godard-influenced
in Tarantino's *oeuvre* (particularly *Pulp Fiction*).
Tarantino in *The Guardian*, 4 February 1995:
'It's so easy to say Godard taught me invention. He did, but you know, it sounds so small
compared to what he taught me but more
than anything, he inspired me and made me
want to make movies like him.'

Jean-Luc Godard rose to prominence in the
early Fifties, initially as a writer and film theo-
rist (via magazine *Cahiers du Cinema*), later as
a fully-fledged director; his first feature, *A
Bout de Souffle* (aka *Breathless*), was released in
March 1960. Godard's work - and that of the
nouvelle vague, the era's so-called French New
Wave - followed largely in the tradition of
writer Andre Bazin, *Cahiers du Cinema*'s key
contributor. Bazin believed that mainstream
narrative cinema had evolved an undesirable
aesthetic; that it manipulated reality where it
should passively record it. Godard politicised
these ideas; over time, he came to believe that
filmic devices which sought to reflect 'real life'
within a bogus fictional framework were
inherently bourgeois, and sought to expose

both they and 'hidden' narrative codes in general. Thus his early films - particularly *A Bout
de Souffle*, *Bande a Part* (1964) and *Pierrot le
Fou* (1965) - parodied and inherently criti-
cised Hollywood conventions: the first two
of the gangster thriller, the latter of the
'love-on-the-run' sub-genre (see *Badlands*,
qv). Godard sought to 'denaturalise' these narratives by mixing genre trademarks: thus the
dance sequence in *Bande a Part* - which
inspired Mia and Vincent's twist contest turn
in *Pulp Fiction* - suddenly apes the language
of the American musical within the structure
of the thriller. 'His films constantly refer
outside themselves to other films, other tradi-
tions, using this method of extra-textual
reference and quotation to bring together
apparently incompatible ideas and forms to
contradict and conflict with one another',
wrote Pam Cook of Godard in *The Cinema
Book* (1985): the quote might be equally apt
of Tarantino himself.

In addition, Godard and his ilk were given to
flourishes which would remind an audience
that they were watching a constructed fiction:
mimicking such, Jim McBride's 1983
American remake of *A Bout de Souffle*,
Breathless, runs obviously back-projected

often chooses to underline these breaks with monolithic subtitles (in *Pulp*, he uses an extra title to signal both Winston Wolf's arrival and the subsequent descent of the film into black farce). Mia's 'magic square' in *Pulp* is another example; *FilmMaker*, however, suggested this might be seen as a nod to comedy director Frank Tashlin (*The Girl Can't Help It*, *Will Success Spoil Rock Hunter?*, etc). (In either context, the square achieves the effect of distancing the audience's actuality from the constructed artificiality of the film. Note also the similarly disruptive effect of Jules's line, 'Let's get into character.') Tarantino makes another pointed nod to Godard in *Reservoir Dogs*: the jewellery store - the site of the film's key inciting events which are convention-defyingly unseen on screen - is named Karina's, after Godard's *Bande a Part* actress, Anna Karina (see also the name given to Tarantino and Bender's production company, A Band Apart).

Perhaps prophetically, Pauline Kael, discussing both *Bande a Part* and Godard in general, wrote in 1965: '. . . until recently people were rather shamefaced or terribly arch about relating their reactions in terms of movies . . . Godard brought this way of reacting out into the open of new movies . . . By now - so accelerated has cultural history become - we have those students at college who when asked what they're interested in say, 'I go to a lot of movies.' And some of them are so proud of how compulsively they see everything in terms of movies and how many times they've seen certain movies that there is nothing left for them to relate movies to. They have been soaked up by the screen.' Several *Four Rooms* magazine features made great play of announcing the film's four authors as 'the American New Wave': Quentin Tarantino, Godard *fils* and heir apparent? Or Hollywood's revenge; a human sponge, mindlessly regurgitating pop culture past? You never can tell . . .

(See also: Europe; *You Never Can Tell*)

Tete-a-tete: Jean-Luc Godard with Anna Karina during rehearsals for *Bande a Part*.

process shots behind Richard Gere as he drives through an evidently ersatz California (this device is pointedly reprised in *Pulp Fiction*'s Butch/Esmarelda scenes). Likewise, Tarantino usually breaks linear film narrative - *True Romance* being a key exception, but Tarantino's original script, unlike the film, constantly flashes back and forward, to and fro - and

GIRL, YOU'LL BE A WOMAN SOON

Mia returns home the triumphant winner of the Jack Rabbit Slim's twist contest. While Vincent goes to the toilet, she carefully lines up Urge Overkill's *Girl, You'll Be A Woman Soon*. Pressing 'play', she gyrates around the room, singing along with the lyrics. While Vincent wrestles with his conscience in the bathroom mirror, one of *Pulp Fiction*'s greatest dramas unfolds next door.

Girl, You'll Be A Woman Soon was a US top twenty hit for singer/songwriter Neil Diamond in May 1967. For the *Pulp Fiction* soundtrack Tarantino turned to a more recent version of the song by Urge Overkill, who had originally recorded it as a sincere tribute to Diamond. 'At the pre-production stage of *Pulp* I had about six different songs for the Mia dance number sequence and I was moving back and forth, changing my mind all the time,' explained the director. 'I played Urge Overkill's mini-LP [*Stull*] and the first track on there was a remake of *Girl, You'll Be A Woman Soon*. Some people I know said, "Oh they just adore Neil Diamond, they just love Neil Diamond." Well, I love Neil Diamond too. I've always loved Neil Diamond's version of that song but their version is even better. Beyond a shadow of a doubt this was the song Mia had to dance to by herself. It was one of those things where I was in love with four or five songs, then I found my true love.'

GRIER, PAM (1949 -)

Early Seventies black cheesecake superchick. In the *True Romance* script, Clarence riffs on his suggestion that the name Alabama Whitman 'sounds like a Pam Grier movie' ('She's a sixteen-calibre kitten, equally equipped for killin' and lovin'!'). Grier debuted in exploitation pics such as Russ Meyer's *Beyond the Valley of the Dolls* and *The Big Bird Cage*: come 1973, she got her first lead as an avenging Angel in *Coffy*. She played to type in films like *Black Mama, White Mama, Foxy Brown, Sheba Baby*

and *Friday Foster* before her star waned; although last seen in a bit-part in *Bill and Ted's Bogus Journey* (1991) and on TV's *The Fresh Prince of Bel-Air*. Tarantino, the Hudlin brothers and Tim Burton are all reported to be currently developing projects for her. (Allegedly, Grier was considered for a role in *Pulp Fiction*.) In *Reservoir Dogs*, *Get Christie Love* is recalled as 'a Pam Grier TV show without Pam Grier'; networked on ABC, this ground-breaking series starred Teresa Graves as black undercover LAPD operative Christine 'Christie' Love. Partnered by Lieutenant Joe Caruso (Andy Romano), Christie would never shoot to kill - 'just enough to stop 'em' - and was much given to the exclamation, 'You're under arrest, sugar!' After a successful pilot, the series ran for 22 x 50-minute episodes between 11 September 1974 and 18 July 1975. (It's been suggested that *Pulp Fiction*'s Bonnie, qv - a night nurse - was modelled after Grier's character in *Coffy*.)

(See also: Blaxploitation)

GYPSYS TRAMPS AND THIEVES

The first draft of *Reservoir Dogs* features a reference to this song, a top ten hit for Cher on both sides of the Atlantic in 1971. The track is mentioned during the lengthy Pancake House sequence, during the discussion about K-Billy's Super Sounds of the Seventies weekend.

Following Nice Guy Eddie's confession that he has only just realised who shot who in the lyrics of *The Night The Lights Went Out In Georgia*, Mr Pink causes much hilarity by adding, 'You know the part in *Gypsys Tramps and Thieves*, when she says "Poppa woulda shot his if he knew what he'd done?". I could never figure out what he did.'

In the finished screenplay, this dialogue is replaced with a more succinct response to Nice Guy Eddie's discovery - Mr White simply says, 'Who gives a damn?'

h

HARRELSON, WOODY (1961 -)
Mickey Knox, *Natural Born Killers*

At 21, Woodrow T Harrelson saw his father imprisoned for the killing of a federal judge. Having also been allegedly connected to the Kennedy assassination, Charles Voyde Harrels on continues to serve two life sentences.

Back on the chain gang - Woody Harrelson in *Natural Born Killers*.

Harrelson Jr majored in Theatre Arts and English at Indiana's Hanover College, and

thereafter pursued a stage career in New York. After a small early film role in the comedy *Wildcats*, he was cast as barman Woody Boyd in TV series *Cheers* - a role which garnered him a 1989 Emmy award. In interviews, Harrelson pithily described playing mass-murderer Mickey Knox - a part earmarked for, among others, Michael Madsen (qv) - as 'a journey into the heart of darkness . . . It took time to get into Mickey's skin, but once I was in it, it really felt like my rage was a hair-trigger thing, like the [Jungian] demon coming out . . .'. Harrelson surrounded himself with serial killer memorabilia while preparing to play Mickey, and, according to *Time Out*, 'as part of his *NBK* working regime . . . "conserved his semen" during sex'. Other credits include: *Casualties of War* [with Ving Rhames, qv] (1989), *White Men Can't Jump* (1992), *Indecent Proposal* (1993), *The Money Train* (1995).

(See also: Mickey Knox)

HEIST MOVIES

In 1903, American cinematic pioneer Edwin S Porter directed a twelve-minute long, thirteen-shot film, *The Great Train Robbery*.

Arguably the first classic narrative film, Porter's short certainly, nonetheless, scored a remarkable double first: not only was it the first Western, but also the first in a long line of heist movies, of which Tarantino's *Reservoir Dogs* can be identified as the foremost latterday example.

Crime and punishment, of course, have been a staple of the cinema ever since: the gangster movie - typified, perhaps, by Howard Hughes's *Scarface* - dominated Hollywood's golden age, but depicting the heist as such remained taboo. The Hays Code expressly forbade criminal methods to be 'explicitly presented or detailed': the Code remained sacrosanct until the immediate post-war era, when a handful of *noir*-influenced 'B' thrillers began to test the waters, focussing on the build-up to, and the execution of, large-scale robberies. In Joseph H Lewis's seminal love-on-the-run flick, *Gun Crazy* (1949), for example, the viewer is party to the conversation between robbers John Dall and Peggy Cummins as they drive slowly to the bank that they're about to hold up, all shot in one single unbroken take from the back seat, and Richard Fleischer's LA-bound *Armored Car Robbery* (1950), despite concentrating largely on police methodology, contains enough of the titular heist's set-up to be of interest.

Street With No Name (William Keighley, 1948) takes as its protagonist Mark Stevens' FBI man, infiltrating a gang led by crime boss Richard Widmark, in one of his early tough-guy roles. Stevens' FBI agent is so successful

Gang of four: the hooligan, the lieutenant, the Big Man and the seasoned hand divide the loot in *The Asphalt Jungle*.

Heist movies: *The Taking
of Pelham 123.*

movie: its characters included the Big Man (Emmerich, or Joe Cabot), his lieutenant (Cobby, or Nice Guy Eddie), a 'hooligan' (Dix Handley, or Mr Blonde) and a ruthless old pro (Doc Riedenschneider, or Mr White). The low-lifes which inhabited the seedy urban dystopia were unflinchingly realised, yet sympathetically portrayed; a combination which led Louis B Mayer famously to condemn his own studio's feature as 'full of nasty, ugly people doing nasty things. I wouldn't walk across the room to see a thing like that.' (The film contains yet more elements later influential upon *Reservoir Dogs* - a friendship is struck up between a young, green gang member and an old hand; one of the gang is shot in the stomach during the course of the robbery; the gang disintegrates in mutual mistrust and recrimination; the stolen jewels are kept in a briefcase.) So successful was *The Asphalt Jungle* that it has been remade three times: as a 1958 Western, *The Badlanders*, in 1963 as *Cairo*, and in 1972 as *Cool Breeze*. It spawned a wave of imitators throughout the Fifties and Sixties, of varying merit: 'caper' movies such as 1955's *Five Against the House* and 1960's *Seven Thieves* rarely rose above the level of the 'B' feature, usually substituting fabulous casinos for mundane banks, but 1955's cool French *Rififi* and Stanley Kubrick's 1956 *The Killing* further developed the sub-genre's cold and paranoid edge; both are oft cited as a *Dogs* influence.

in penetrating the gang that he becomes Widmark's most trusted lieutenant. Widmark's eventual suspicions trigger the violent and ironic climax, which anticipates many of *Reservoir Dogs'* plot points. The same plot was reworked in a Japanese setting for Sam Fuller's 1955 *House of Bamboo*, with Robert Ryan as the ex-GI Tokyo crime boss and Robert Stack as the Military Police undercover man. Both movies dwell on the aftermath of unsuccessful heists, and the clouds of distrust which quickly form around suspected moles.

However, the first major studio picture explicitly to contravene the code, and the first 'true' heist movie, was MGM's *The Asphalt Jungle*, released in 1950. Directed and co-scripted by John Huston and starring Sterling Hayden, Louis Calhern, Sam Jaffe, James Whitmore and Marc Lawrence, *The Asphalt Jungle* concerned an ex-con assembling a gang to pull a jewel robbery, and the thieves' subsequent in-fighting, dissolution, and downfall. Told from the gang members' viewpoint, using their jargon-laden slang, and more concerned with character than plot, it forged the template for the heist

Aka *Du Rififi Chez les Hommes*, *Rififi* - a slang term meaning 'trouble' - was directed by Jules Dassin, and detailed the robbery of a jewellery store; the heist itself was presented as a silent, thirty-minute long sequence. As was fast becoming convention, the film concluded with a shoot-out between not only the gang members themselves, but a set of rival mobsters as well, (semi-sequels *Du Rififi Chez les Femmes*, *Rififi a Tokyo*, and *Du Rififi a Panama*, followed). *The Killing*, likewise, featured a gang attempting to rob the robbers and a subsequent bloody shoot-out. More significantly, it utilised a flashback-laden narrative structure whereby each gang member was granted separate scenes showing their individual function in the successful execution of a racetrack heist (Sterling Hayden, Ted de Corsia, Joe Sawyer, Elisha Cook Jnr, and Timothy Carey portrayed the gang). (Note also that a constituent element of 1946's *The Killers*, remade in 1964, was the story of a gangland murder related to a payroll heist; much was related in flashback, as per *film noir* convention.)

There are many other gangland characters considered quintessential background to

Jean-Hugues Anglade as Eric and Gary Kemp as Oliver in Roger Avary's directorial debut, *Killing Zoe*.

Monte Hellman directing
Two Lane Blacktop.

In Joseph Sargent's 1974 *The Taking of Pelham 123*, four ruthless gunmen code-named Mr Blue (Robert Shaw), Mr Green (Martin Balsam), Mr Grey (Hector Elizondo), and Mr Brown (Earl Hindman) hijack New York subway car Pelham One Twenty-Three, demanding a million-dollar ransom in exchange for their hostages; one of the gang is eventually shot by an undercover cop, and one - Brown - is executed by another, Blue. Several Hong Kong action thrillers, particularly 1987's *City on Fire* (qv) would likewise strongly inform *Reservoir Dogs*.

Post-*Dogs*, the heist movie has undergone something of a renaissance, with both Roger Avary's *Killing Zoe* (qv) and Bryan Singer's tortuous, flashback-laden *The Usual Suspects* holding up diverse strands of the tradition. 'Making the greatest western is a pretty tall order', notes Tarantino. 'But if you set out to make the greatest heist movie, you'll probably get in the top 15 if you make a good one . . .'

HELLMAN, MONTE (1931 -)
Executive producer, *Reservoir Dogs*

A one-time film editor whose directorial debut, 1959's *The Beast from Haunted Cave*, was produced by Roger Corman (and who later co-directed, with Francis Ford Coppola, Corman's 1962 *The Terror*), Hellman's place in Tarantino lore is affirmed by his nearly having directed *Reservoir Dogs*. Much admired by Tarantino for 'his naturalistic style and pace, his invisibly punchy editing rhythms, and the journeys his characters inevitably set sail on', and, more importantly, for 1966's *Ride in the Whirlwind* - 'one of the most authentic and brilliant westerns ever made' - Hellman's resolutely independent career encompasses both cult road movie *Two Lane Blacktop* and straight-to-video horror *Silent Night, Deadly Night III - Better Watch Out!* He also helped launch the career of Jack Nicholson, who featured in four Hellman movies in the space of a year. ('Jack's a

Dogs. In Larry Cohen's 1982 *Q - The Winged Serpent*, a member of a gang of jewel thieves (Jimmy Quinn, played by Michael Moriarty), discovers the egg of the eponymous monster. Coincidentally, in a later scene, one cop suggests to another, upon finding a decapitated corpse, that the head might have simply 'floated away like a balloon' - whereupon the film cuts to a shot of a pink balloon. (Note the shot in *Dogs* where an orange balloon can be seen, according to some indicating the identity of the informant.)

very similar personality to Quentin's', claims Hellman. 'They both just had absolute authority and assurance in their own stardom.')

In autumn 1990, Hellman's attention was drawn to the recently-completed *Reservoir Dogs* screenplay by a friend who knew Lawrence Bender's (qv) room-mate. After reading Tarantino's hand-written script, he typed it out on computer, and called Bender, intending to direct the film himself. He later met with Tarantino on Hollywood Boulevard but, according to Hellman, 'The day I met him he sold *True Romance* and so he said, "This is all I need to hold out for directing *Reservoir Dogs*. Much as I admire you, I'm going to direct this movie myself."'

Undeterred, Hellman consented to act as executive producer on the project, cold-calling industry acquaintances and arranging meetings. It was Hellman who handed the script to Richard N Gladstein of eventual producers Live Entertainment (qv), and attempted to allay any doubts that Gladstein may have had concerning the abilities of the untested Tarantino. He also suggested Tarantino attended the Sundance Institute's workshop, nominated *Dogs*'s director of photography, Andrzej Sekula (qv) - and put forward Michael Madsen (qv) for a role in the film, having previously cast him in 1988's *Iguana*. Hellman advised on trims to the film's rough cut.

In return, Tarantino and Bender have, apparently, volunteered to work in an executive capacity on future Hellman projects, including the mooted prison drama *Red Rain*. In 1995, Hellman said, modestly, of his former protege, 'I think that he's been more helpful to me than I was to him . . . His backing and his stamp of approval mean a lot.' Wrote Tarantino, in *Sight and Sound*: 'Movie theatres would be much happier places with a new Monte Hellman movie playing in them.'

HONDA CIVIC

Mr Orange and Marvin bleed all over Chevy Novas, Vincent has his Chevy Malibu vandalised and Norman loses his finger for a Chevy Chevelle. At the other end of the scale from these relatively exotic machines is the humble Honda Civic. In *Pulp Fiction*, Butch takes Fabienne's Honda Civic to make the risky journey back to his apartment to pick up his watch. It's the last trip the little white car makes. In *Four Rooms: Penthouse: The Man From Hollywood*, Norman declares, 'I drive a motherfuckin' Honda my sister sold me. You hear what I'm sayin'? A little white motherfuckin' Honda Civic.' His avarice for Chester's car is such that it drives him towards a fatal risk. 'That's a 1964 nigger-red, rag-top Chevy Chevelle,' he tells Ted. 'And I love that car more'n I love hips, lips, and fingertips.'

While an impoverished video store clerk, the young Tarantino would drive to work in a silver Honda Civic. The traffic violation tickets the small vehicle attracted on its abandonment once landed its owner in prison for non-payment.

HOPPER, DENNIS (1936 -)
Clifford Worley, *True Romance*

Having begun his career as a juvenile supporting actor in the Fifties (*Rebel Without a Cause*, etc), and having managed a directorial CV in tandem from 1969 on, independently-minded Hollywood veteran Hopper had been one of those mooted by financiers Live Entertainment for a role in *Reservoir Dogs*: in January 1991, Harvey Keitel (qv) sent Hopper the screenplay, seeing him as a possible Mr Pink. 'I loved it and I wanted to do it', recalled Hopper, in conversation with Tarantino for *Grand Street* magazine, 'but I had to do something else.' Prior to being cast by Tony Scott (qv) in *True Romance*, Hopper had - albeit unknowingly - been stalked by Tarantino and Roger Avary (qv) regarding the film: in the late Eighties, the struggling pair had driven past Hopper's house several times, trying to drum up the courage to give Hopper their script for him to direct (they bottled out). A genuine admirer and supporter of Tarantino's - 'he's the Mark Twain of the Nineties' - Hopper was particularly impressed by the quality of his *True Romance* speech concerning the ethnicity of the Sicilians, telling the young writer-director, 'It was great to act your words, man.' Other acting credits include: *Giant* (1956), *The Trip* (1967), *Cool Hand Luke* (1967), *Apocalypse Now* (1979), *Rumble Fish* [with Chris Penn, qv] (1983), *Blue Velvet* (1986), *The Pick-Up Artist* [with Robert Downey Jr and Harvey Keitel, both qv] (1987), *Chattahoochee* [with Gary Oldman, qv] (1989), *The Heart of Justice* [TVM, with Eric Stoltz, qv] (1992), *Speed* (1994). Films as director include: *Easy Rider* (1969), *The Last Movie* (1971), *Kid Blue* (1972), *Out of the Blue* (1980), *Colors* [with Randy Brooks, qv] (1988), *Catchfire* (1989), *The Hot Spot* (1990), *Chasers* (1994).

(See also: Clifford Worley; Ears)

HORROR

His enthusiasm never fully demonstrated on screen until *From Dusk Till Dawn*, Tarantino's love of the horror genre was sparked by 1948's comedy-horror *Abbott and Costello Meet Frankenstein* (aka *Abbott and Costello Meet the Ghosts*), starring the eponymous comedians as themselves with support from Lon Chaney Jr, Glenn Strange, and Bela Lugosi (who was later impersonated in *Ed Wood*, Tarantino's preferred film of 1994). The Abbott and Costello/Universal monsters sequence he admires particularly for their unevenness and lack of compromise: 'The Abbott and Costello stuff was funny, but when they were out of the room and the monsters come on, they'd kill people!' *From Dusk Till Dawn* had, at one stage, been mooted as part of one of the *Tales From the Crypt* anthology series (and later, was due to head-

line Robert Englund, eternally *A Nightmare On Elm Street*'s Freddy). The narrative structure of the eventual screenplay - wherein a crime thriller turns halfway into a down-the-line horror movie - might be said to owe something to the structure of Alfred Hitchcock's *Psycho* (*Psycho* is also fleetingly referred to in the *Pulp Fiction* scene where Marsellus turns and sees Butch driving, which apes a shot of Janet Leigh's Marion Crane fleeing town in the former). Tarantino, however, told *Fangoria*: 'The first half is closer to [The] *Silence of the Lambs* . . . while the second half turns into this big, wild carnival of horrors like [The] *Evil Dead II* . . . in that there's humour and one damn thing after another coming at you.' There are photographs of cult Mexican wrestler Santo - star of such mock-horror classics as *Santo Versus the Vampire Women* - on the Titty Twister's walls. The 'stomach mouth vamp bitch' bites the head off one of the bar's customers in homage to John Carpenter's 1982 Howard Hawks remake *The Thing* (some of *The Thing*'s paranoid atmosphere might be said to replicated in *Dusk*'s closing scenes). *Dusk* also makes mention of Hammer horror star Peter Cushing, and possibly also references Hammer's 1972 *Captain Kronos Vampire Hunter*. The film's screenplay opens with a quotation from European exploitation guru Jess Franco's 1973 *La Comtesse Noire*, aka *The Bare-breasted Countess / Female Vampire*.

Other genre favourites of Tarantino's include the work of splatter directors Mario Bava, Dario Argento, Alberto De Martino and Lucio Fulci: 'the sense of over-the-topness in them is really cool', he told fanzine *Giallo Pages*.

(See also: Awards; Europe; Savini, Tom; Unfilmed projects)

HOTELS

Hotel culture has been an occasional, but nonetheless significant, motif in Tarantino's

cooler-than-cool Winston Wolf is to be found, tuxedo-clad, shooting craps in a plush hotel suite at around nine o'clock in the morning.

Four Rooms's Mon Signor, however, is but the latest in a very long line of fictional grand hotels to provide the core setting for a filmic *portmanteau*. The original, 1932's *Grand Hotel*, featured a guest list comprising Joan Crawford, John Barrymore, Lionel Barrymore, Wallace Beery and Greta Garbo (as a woesome ballerina; it's the source of her immortal line 'I want to be alone'). Beyond its only true remake (1945's *Weekend at the Waldorf*), a multiplicity of pictures of the era used a similar setting in a similar style: *International House* (1933), *Hotel Berlin* (1945), *Separate Tables* (1958), and, more recently, *Hotel* (1967), *Plaza Suite* (1971), and *California Suite* (1978) have all benefited from a *Grand Hotel* format. 1989's *Mystery Train*, directed by Jim Jarmusch (and featuring, in a small role, Steve Buscemi, qv), was set in a down-at-heel Memphis hotel and concerned three separate sets of temporary residents whose stories - ostensibly connected by the figure of Elvis Presley (qv) - were gradually seen to become fully interlinked.

Porter Ted's various gurnings, meanwhile, owe something not only to Jerry Lewis as *The Bellboy* (see Martin and Lewis, qv) but to one of the earliest examples of the type: the Marx Brothers's first feature, 1929's *The Cocoanuts*, in which Groucho, attempting to manage a Florida hotel, has to cope with an array of assorted human detritus (usually Chico and Harpo). Other prominent bellhops - sardonic, comedic, or otherwise - can be seen in 1991's *Barton Fink* (as portrayed by Steve Buscemi), that same year's *Blame It on the Bellboy* (as portrayed by Bronson Pinchot, qv), and in *Killing Zoe* (qv). (*The Man From Hollywood*'s script also makes mention of the character Bellboy from 1979's *Quadrophenia*.)

work prior to *Four Rooms*. In the climax to *True Romance*, the environs of the Beverly Ambassador, wherein Clarence makes his (metaphorical) last stand, permit a bloody coming-together of all the film's major plot strands. In *Pulp Fiction*, Butch and Fabienne make use of a seedy motel room, and the

i

I GOTCHA

While Nice Guy Eddie discusses the botched robbery with Dov on the phone, a bound policeman is being savagely beaten by Mr Blonde, Mr White and Mr Pink at the warehouse rendezvous. K-Billy plays the pounding *I Gotcha* by Joe Tex as the hapless cop is mercilessly attacked.

Although he originally made an impact as a songwriter in the early Sixties, Joe Tex (born Joseph Accrington Jnr) made his big breakthrough in January 1965, scoring a top ten hit in the US with the groundbreaking sound of *Hold On To What You've Got*. A number of successful singles followed, most notably *Skinny Legs And All* and *Men Are Gettin' Scarce*, before his popularity seemed to dwindle. His career was reinvigorated by *I Gotcha*, a major US hit in March 1972, but Tex decided to turn his back on the resulting recognition, devoting himself instead to the Muslim religion. After spending some time lecturing on spiritual faith under the name Yusuf Hazziez, he resumed his career, experimenting with dance and country music. He enjoyed his last big hit in 1977 with the cheeky *Ain't Gonna Bump No More (With No Big Fat Woman)*. Following this, however, Islam once more took precedence over his

musical career and there were no further comebacks. He died of a heart attack in 1982.

Aside from the *Reservoir Dogs* soundtrack, *I Gotcha* can be found on the 1972 Joe Tex album of the same name.

INFERNO

Captain Koons tells the young Butch that when two men are in a 'pit of hell' together, they each owe the other something. This principle is subsequently followed to the letter by the adult Butch, when he finds himself sharing a very real pit of hell with his mortal enemy Marsellus Wallace. Through chance alone (Zed's 'Eeny meeny minie moe'), it is Butch who escapes. After hesitating briefly, Butch ventures back into the hellhole under the Mason-Dixon pawn shop to rescue Marsellus. His departure on a chopper clearly labelled 'Grace' can be taken to signal his spiritual awakening.

Hell as an eschatological concept still holds a surprisingly active place in popular culture - almost independent from any decline in organized Christian worship (a phenomenon far less noticeable in the USA than in Europe).

A hit movie such as *Ghost*, for example, coolly sends dead unrepentant sinners straight to Damnation. Leading comics such as Image's *Spawn* and DC's *Hellblazer* draw indirectly from the Church Father's vision of hell as originally adumbrated by St Thomas Aquinas and expressed most completely in the *Inferno* section of Dante's *Divine Comedy*. Dante's *Inferno* itself has been adapted in comic-book form on several occasions, notably in 1980's *X-Men Annual*, when the members of this superhero team plus occult magus Doctor Strange take a perilous journey through the circles of Dante's Hell.

Dante's Hell is strictly for the Unbaptised and the Damned. There is no escape from it - except for Dante and his companion Virgil, who are present only to record its terrors. In many ways the 'pit of hell' in which Butch achieves Grace through his rescue of Marsellus Wallace more closely resembles the spiritual trials of Mount Purgatory, the setting for part two of the *Divine Comedy*. The pains of Purgatory are embraced willingly by the dead souls as their only path to redemption.

(See also: Deliverance, Redemption)

IT'S PAT
(US, 1994, dir. Adam Bernstein)
Tarantino performed a minor, uncredited rewrite on this vehicle for Julia Sweeney's indeterminately-gendered *Saturday Night Live* character; Sweeney had appeared as *Pulp Fiction*'s Raquel. The film bombed, and loiters in video hell.

j

JACK RABBIT SLIM'S

'It's like a wax museum with a pulse' - Vincent
Vega, *Pulp Fiction*.

'This is Jack Rabbit Slim's', Mia tells Vincent.
'An Elvis man should love it.' An Elvis man
should also find the Fifties theme diner from
Pulp Fiction strangely familiar - Tarantino
requested it should resemble a club seen in
the Elvis Presley/Nancy Sinatra film *Speedway*
(1968). Another influence on the impressive
design was the Howard Hawks racing car
drama *Red Line 7000* (1965). The electric toy
cars and two of the most prominent movie
posters on the wall continue the theme:
Motorcycle Gang (1957) concerned the
authorities' efforts to restrict a bunch of wild
bikers, while *The Young Racers* (1963) was
about an ex-racing driver's attempts to write
an expose on the sport.

Tarantino's script, however, highlighted a more
contemporary reference: 'In the past six years,
1950s diners have sprung up all over LA, giving Thai restaurants a run for their money.
They're all basically the same. Decor out of an
'Archie' comic book, golden oldies constantly
emanating from a bubbly Wurlitzer, saucy
waitresses in bobby socks, menus with items

like the Fats Domino Cheeseburger, or the
Wolfman Jack Omelette, and over-prices that
pay for all this bullshit.'

The $150,000 set itself was the ultimate
responsibility of David Wasco and Sandy
Reynolds-Wasco, production designer and set
decorator respectively. The huge diner was
constructed in a warehouse in Culver City and
became the largest component in a mini-com-
plex of *Pulp Fiction* sets which also included
Brett's apartment, Butch's motel room and the
back of the Mason-Dixon pawnshop.

The jiving bunny logo for the restaurant was
realised by two of Tarantino's former Video
Archives colleagues - Russell Vossler and
Gerald Martinez. Their names are immortalised
in lights outside the theatre where Butch's
'Battle of the Titans' fight takes place. Vossler
also designed the logo seen on the side of the
cab Butch makes his escape in, paying tribute
to his friend with a caricature and the title 'Big
Jerry Cab Co'.

Although only ever visited in *Pulp Fiction*,
Jack Rabbit Slim's is first referred to in
Reservoir Dogs. The background radio chatter
on K-Billy's radio station (which Tarantino

co-wrote with Roger Avary) includes a commercial for the diner which can be just be heard after Mr Orange shoots Mr Blonde. In *Pulp*, while Butch is taking the long route back to his apartment to recover his watch, a similar commercial is playing in a house he passes. The latest Jack Rabbit Slim's reference occurs in Tarantino's segment of *Four Rooms*. While Chester Rush holds court in the penthouse suite, a gap in the curtains behinds him offers us a glimpse of a familiar neon rabbit. Ted could do a lot a lot worse than pop in on his way home to experience a comparatively sane night out.

Jack Rabbit Slim's itself is a physical embodiment of the pop culture melting pot inside Tarantino's head. All the essential ingredients are there - the influence of Roger Corman is acknowledged with posters for such films as *Machine-Gun Kelly* (1958) adorning the walls; the music is supplied by rock 'n' roll legends Ricky Nelson and Chuck Berry; Fifties' films constantly play on a huge screen and Marilyn Monroe serves the customers' drinks. Indeed, as Gavin Smith pointed out in *Film Comment*, Jack Rabbit Slim's is surely the only diner in Los Angeles 'that inverts the archetypal waitress-to-superstar legend'.

This Ed Sullivan-hosted melee certainly struck a chord somewhere - one restaurant chain apparently applied to Miramax for a Jack Rabbit Slim's licence. On this occasion at least, good taste prevailed.

(See also: Amos 'n' Andy; Buscemi, Steve; Martin and Lewis; Miller, Dick; Sirk, Douglas)

JACKSON, SAMUEL L (1949 -)
Big Don, *True Romance*
Jules Winnfield, *Pulp Fiction*

Born in Chattanooga, Tennessee, Samuel Leroy Jackson studied drama at Georgia's Morehouse College in the late Sixties, and was suspended for his involvement in a Black Power sit-in. He furthered his career in rep at Yale and Seattle, sometimes playing August Wilson roles; after working on a number of Shakespeare Festival productions in New York - 'Othello. A cat who went all over the world kickin' ass, raping women and he falls in love with a teenager and gets punked out totally' - he transferred to film and TV, playing largely gangsters and brutes in series such as *Spenser For Hire*. Remembering the meagre pickings of his typecast days, he told the *LA Times*: 'It's easy to just go in and play the result. "You have a criminal who's got a gun, he's gonna rob somebody, and that's what we want you to do, Sam." But you have to sit at home and say to yourself, "OK, this guy's gonna rob somebody, but why? Is he an addict? Is he a veteran who couldn't get a job? Is his rent due? Is his kid sick? . . . You have to have had a life before they saw you on screen, and a life that's going to go on when you leave the screen."' After appearing in several Spike Lee joints, Jackson was auditioned by Tarantino and producer Lawrence Bender in New York for the part of Holdaway, Freddy's contact in *Reservoir Dogs*; he was passed over in favour of Randy Brooks (qv). Jackson was later cast as dealer Big Don Watts in Tony Scott's *True Romance*; his one scene consisted largely of a three-way dialogue between Drexl, Floyd and Don on the etiquette of cunnilingus - 'I eat everything. I eat the pussy. I eat the butt. I eat every motherfuckin' thang' - but much of this explicit scene was cut. However, Jackson was to be afforded the opportunity to do his homework on *Pulp Fiction*'s Jules Winnfield, a part written with him in mind (he was, nevertheless, required to audition for the role, narrowly winning out over Laurence Fishburne and Paul Tatagliarone). The backhistory Jackson created for Jules was thorough, as related in several interviews: 'He did go to church and Sunday school . . . he and Marsellus grew up in the same neighbourhood together. They were in the same gang. He had been doing this stuff for Marsellus all his life 'cause Marsellus never got his hands dirty. In his absence, Marsellus

AUSGEZEICHNET MIT DER GOLDENEN PALME

QUENTIN TARANTIN

Pulp Fictio

EIN FILM IM VERLEIH DER SCOTIA DEUTSCHLAND/IM VERTRIEB DER BUEN

John Travolta and Samuel L Jackson in *Pulp Fiction*.

has hired [Vincent]. Then Jules comes back from prison and has to sort of keep [Vincent] in line because he's got this drug problem.' And, after that fateful breakfast in the diner: 'He starts travelling around the world, getting into these adventures and meeting people. Now, that doesn't necessarily mean that he stops killing people. But when he's out trying to find the true meaning of why he was saved, he can still fall back into the same things that he was in before. But not necessarily with the same kind of purpose . . .'. Nominated for an Oscar as best supporting actor for Jules, Jackson went on to star alongside Bruce Willis (qv) in *Die Hard With a Vengeance* (qv) wherein the two *Pulp* alumni shared an on-screen in-joke. (Incidentally, Jackson shares with Tarantino a love for Hong Kong movies and blaxploitation comics.) Other credits include: *Sea of Love* (1989), *Do The Right Thing* (1989), *Goodfellas* (1990), *Mo' Better Blues* (1990), *Jungle Fever* (1991), *Amos and Andrew* (1992), *Jurassic Park* (1993), *National Lampoon's Loaded Weapon 1* [with Bruce Willis in uncredited cameo] (1993), *Menace II Society* (1993), *Fresh* [producer Lawrence Bender] (1994), *Trees Lounge* [director Steve Buscemi, qv] (1996).

(See also: Awards; Jules Winnfield; Race)

JACOB FULLER

From Dusk Till Dawn begins with the 44-year old ex-minister still reeling from the agonised death of his wife in a car accident. Jacob's resulting loss of faith seems permanent. 'I'm just not connected any more', he tells his disbelieving daughter, Kate. 'I'm not going through a lapse. What I've experienced is closer to awakening.'

Forgoing his new motor home for a night at the Dew Drop Inn proves a mistake - it is there that he, his daughter and his adopted son Scott are kidnapped by the Gecko brothers. The safety of his children remains his priority - he offers to go with the Geckos and act as their hostage alone. In Kate's case, his growing unease about Richard is justified: 'If he touches her, I'll kill him', he warns Seth. 'I don't give a fuck how many guns you have, nothing will stop me from killing him.'

After staring into the depths of hell at The Titty Twister, Jacob regains his faith and becomes the humans' most valuable weapon against the vampires. 'If we're gonna get out of this we're gonna need each other', he tells Seth, extending their uneasy co-operation beyond its previous bounds of mutual threat. His restored faith empowers him to bless the water inside the balloon bombs and etch crosses into the remaining bullets. Even after he's been bitten by the vampirised Sex

Machine, his children's safety still comes first. He is able to stave off his transformation long enough to warn them that 'I won't be Jacob any more. I'll be a lap dog of Satan.'

At least Jacob meets his end with his last vestige of humanity imbued with a refound faith. It may prove much-needed fortification for the trials still to come.

(See: Keitel, Harvey)

JIMMIE DIMMICK

(See: Alter egos; Jules Winnfield; Names; Yuppie scum)

JOE CABOT

An elderly hoodlum, *Reservoir Dogs*'s Joe Cabot is old-fashioned enough to contact Larry by telegram and refer to the forthcoming diamond robbery as 'a caper'. His strength of character similarly belongs to a different age - he treats the gang to breakfast at Uncle Bob's Pancake House prior to the robbery, insists that Mr Pink leaves a tip and reveals, in an overheard telephone conversation, how he has the decency to allow a friend in need more time to repay an outstanding debt.

Joe is a crime boss of some distinction - his son, Eddie, claims his father has a wide ranging operation and we discover that Mr Pink can't swap his code-name for Purple because 'some guy on some other job is Mr Purple'. Joe enjoys a paternal relationship with his most trusted partners in crime - Larry has earned the title 'junior' and the stillness of Vic's tongue throughout his jail sentence (he was arrested working for Joe) is rewarded with regular packages and a cover job on his release.

Perhaps the most intriguing insight into Joe's character was cut from the finished print of

Reservoir Dogs. In the 'Mr White' segment, Joe tells Larry that he has recently married someone called Tammy. 'She used to be a regular on *Hee-Haw.* You know that country show with all those fuckin' hicks.' Joe has genuinely fallen in love, even allowing himself to be persuaded into reading Sylvia Plath's *The Bell Jar* so he can discuss the book with his new wife afterwards. 'Look', he explains, 'I know everybody thinks I'm a chump, but they're wrong and I'm right. I know how she feels about me, and how she makes me feel when I'm with her. And that's good enough for me.'

According to Freddy, Joe resembles The Thing from *The Fantastic Four* and is 'a cool guy, a funny guy'. Joe also shares the racist tendencies exhibited by his son, and the same finely tuned instinct. At the climax of *Reservoir Dogs,* Eddie has a hunch that Mr Orange is the rat in their midst. Joe is convinced - and dies trying to prove it.

(See also: Heist movies; Tierney, Lawrence)

JONES, ANGELA
Esmarelda Villalobos, *Pulp Fiction*
Angela Jones was recruited into the *Pulp Fiction* fold after being seen by Tarantino in a festival short, *Curdled,* in which she played a character who, rather like Winston Wolf, cleans up murder scenes. So impressed was Tarantino with *Curdled* that he agreed to take an executive producer's credit on a full-length remake, also starring Jones; Tinderbox Productions's feature version, co-written by Reb Braddock and John Mass - director and producer respectively - was premiered at Nottingham's Shots in The Dark film festival in June 1996. She also made a brief appearance in Tarantino's 1995 *ER* episode, *Motherhood* (qv).

JONES, TOMMY LEE (1946 -)
Dwight McCluskey, *Natural Born Killers*
Tommy Lee Jones studied English at Harvard University, appeared on the off-Broadway stage, and made his film debut as a Harvard student in 1970's *Love Story.* He won an Emmy award for his portrayal of convicted murderer Gary Gilmore in 1981 TV movie *The Executioner's Song,* and a best supporting actor Oscar for *The Fugitive.* Jones had appeared in two earlier Oliver Stone movies - *JFK* and *Heaven and Earth* - prior to being cast in *NBK* as doomed prison warden McCluskey: a shot of McCluskey's head impaled on a pole was cut from the film. He made his directorial debut with the 1994 TV movie *The Good Old Boys.* Other credits include: *Jackson County Jail* (1975), *Rolling Thunder* (1977), *The Eyes of Laura Mars* (1978), *The Client* (1994), *Batman Forever* (1995).

JULES WINNFIELD
'Look, you wanna play blind man, go walk with a shepherd. But me, my eyes are wide fuckin' open' - Jules, *Pulp Fiction.*

Like his wallet, Jules Winnfield is one Bad Motherfucker. He lives in Inglewood, which Lance sneeringly infers is a black neighbourhood, and has been reciting Ezekiel 25:17 (qv) as a preamble to murder 'for years'; it seems reasonable to assume, therefore, that his entanglement with Marsellus is long-lived (he's certainly familiar with The Wolf). Jimmie Dimmick is his 'buddy' in Toluca Lake; it may be that Jimmie is an ex-Wallace employee, pre-Bonnie up to his neck in 'gangsta' shit' (given the director's preoccupation with film cross-referencing, it's worth invoking Francois Truffaut's *Jules et Jim* here). Jules will give a foot massage to any woman, including his mother (after all, 'foot massages don't mean shit'). From the outset, however, Jules is obviously undergoing some kind of realignment of his ideas and principles: he's critical of Marsellus's defenestrative treatment of 'Tony Rocky Horror'; his girlfriend is a vegetarian, and, in turn, he won't touch pork, because 'pigs are filthy animals' (nevertheless, he can still appreciate a good burger). All in all, he's more than ready to allow the possibility of a miracle into his life; when it happens, he announces his resignation on the spot. He still has to be cleansed, however, and learn the true significance of those words in the Bible, but afterwards he's going to 'walk the earth . . . like Caine in *Kung Fu*'.

(See also: Blaxploitation; Jackson, Samuel L; Morality; Race; Redemption)

JUNGLE BOOGIE

Pulp Fiction shares its opening credits with *Jungle Boogie*, a US top ten hit from February 1974. Jules is clearly a big fan of the group that recorded it - 'That's Kool and the Gang', he reassures Jimmie during *The Bonnie Situation*.

Robert 'Kool' Bell had been playing jazz-influenced soul/funk with his 'Gang' under a number of different names until the group settled on its best-known title in 1969. Kool and the Gang's highly successful chart career

kicked off with *Funky Stuff* in 1973 and continued with *Jungle Boogie* the following year. The pioneering funksters went on to have seventeen further top forty hits in the US, and contributed *Open Sesame* to the *Saturday Night Fever* soundtrack album in 1977. In the UK, their chart career began in 1979, and encompassed a similarly impressive eighteen top forty hits in a mere seven years. In 1984, Bell sang on the Band Aid record *Do They Know It's Christmas?* and changed his name to Khalis Bayyan in 1988 wen he gave himself to Islam. *Jungle Boogie* originally appeared on the 1974 album *Light of Worlds*.

Tarantino, clearly aware that the group's sound firmly dated them to the pre-discotheque funk boom, was unrepentant about including the track in *Pulp Fiction*. 'Growing up in the Seventies gives you an appreciation for music that came out in the Seventies that no-one else on the planet has an appreciation for unless you grew up listening to it. I really don't come from the attitude of "It's so cheesy I like it". . . *Jungle Boogie* is not a novelty record, that's an intense black rhythm and blues instrumental. That's a cool song.'

k

KATE FULLER

Jacob Fuller's 19-year-old daughter begins *From Dusk Till Dawn* as an inquisitive teenager, and emerges from the ordeal at *The Titty Twister* a resourceful adult.

The script describes Kate as 'a young beauty, who possesses what can only be described as an apple pie sensuality'. Confused at her father's waning faith and restricted by his authoritative air, her family's kidnap by the Geckos brings some much-needed excitement into Kate's life. When the motley crew arrive at the Mexican border, she is smart enough to drop her pants round her ankles and sit on the toilet, successfully embarrassing the inspecting guards into leaving them alone. Her arrival at The Titty Twister whets the appetite of its lecherous bouncer. 'What's this?' Chet observes. 'A new flavour approaching. Apple Pie Pussy.' Perhaps inspired by the sexual assertiveness of Santanico Pandemonium, Kate soon proves that apple pie is off the menu - she uses her crucifix to inventively defend herself from the vampirised Chet, and later turns into a one-woman vampire-killing army. Once the creatures have been dispatched, she directs her venom against the police and saves Seth, her new ally, from recapture.

'I gotta hand it to ya Pops', Seth tells Jacob. 'You raised a fuckin' woman.'

(See also: Lewis, Juliette)

KEITEL, HARVEY (1941 -)
Mr White/co-producer, *Reservoir Dogs*
Winston Wolf, *Pulp Fiction*
Jacob Fuller, *From Dusk Till Dawn*

A graduate of Method guru Lee Strasberg's Actors' Studio, ex-US Marine Keitel - rightly acclaimed for his ongoing commitment to both aspirant filmmakers and 'dangerous' roles - stood for some time in the shadow of his prominent Studio stablemate, Robert De Niro, with whom he'd co-starred in Martin Scorsese's 1973 feature, *Mean Streets*. Keitel's fulsome endorsement of Tarantino came as his star was once again in the ascendant in the wake of his portrayal of Judas Iscariot in Scorsese's 1988 *The Last Temptation of Christ* and his Oscar nomination for 1991's *Bugsy*.

Brooklyn-born, and of Polish descent, Keitel, having recently returned from serving in Beirut, was scraping by as an odd-jobbing actor in 1965 when he was cast in *Who's That Knocking On My Door?*, a New York University student production directed by college boy Martin Scorsese; the film was uncompleted until 1969. Scorsese would cast Keitel in the former's feature debut proper, *Mean Streets*: it was only after this that Keitel, who'd been auditioning - unsuccessfully - for several years, was finally admitted to the Actors' Studio. In 1980, Keitel was cast as Willard, the lead in Coppola's *Apocalypse Now*; dismissed after two weeks on location, he was replaced by Martin Sheen.

Producer Lawrence Bender was responsible for Keitel's recruitment into the *Reservoir Dogs* fold: he'd shown the script to one of his acting coaches, Lily Parker, telling her that Keitel was their preferred choice for White. Coincidentally, Parker knew Keitel through the Actors' Studio, and duly sent him the screenplay. 'I was stirred by its content', said Keitel later. 'It is a brilliantly written piece . . . I felt it was important to make. I phoned Quentin and Lawrence and said I wanted to make the film and we began a dialogue on how I would help them raise the money to put the film into production.' Settling for the role of White after due consideration of both Pink and Blonde, Keitel initiated and attended the film's casting sessions (he paid Tarantino and Bender's air fares to the New York auditions), and was duly rewarded with a co-producer's credit.

Keitel's role as Winston Wolf in *Pulp* was a virtual retread of his portrayal of 'The Cleaner' in 1993's Nikita remake, *Point of No Return* (aka *The Assassin*); he was responsible for introducing his *Pulp* co-star, Bruce Willis (qv), to Tarantino. In the summer of 1995, Keitel was cast as minister Jacob Fuller in the Tarantino-scripted horror, *From Dusk Till Dawn*. 'When he got out to the set', recalled executive producer Lawrence Bender in *Fangoria*, 'and was yelling and screaming while working with all these monsters, we teased him and said, "Hey, Harvey, this is what all your work has led to."' Other credits include: *Alice Doesn't Live Here Any More*

(1974), *Taxi Driver* (1976), *The Duellists* (1977), *Bad Timing* (1980), *The Pick-Up Artist* [with Robert Downey Jr and Dennis Hopper, both qv] (1987), *Two Evil Eyes* [with Tom Savini, qv] (1990), *Thelma and Louise* [with Michael Madsen, qv] (1991), *Bad Lieutenant* (1992), *The Piano* (1993), *Somebody To Love*

Harvey Keitel as *Reservoir Dogs'* Mr White.

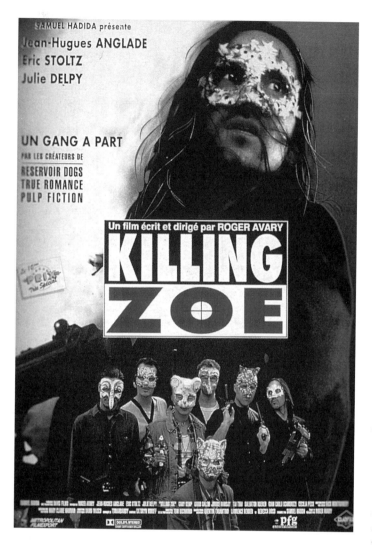

French poster for the release of *Killing Zoe*. The design and copylines stress the film's link to *Reservoir Dogs* and other Tarantino movies.

scout. According to Avary, 'Lawrence [Bender, qv, producing] called me up and said, "Oh my God, we've found this great bank, and you've gotta come down and check it out. We have no use for it in *Dogs*, but it's a great location." So I went down, and he said, "If you have any scripts that take place in a bank, we could kick together a hundred or two hundred thousand dollars and make a movie here." So I drew a map of the bank and went home and wrote the script in about a week, week and a half . . .'

In the film, American safecracker Zed (Eric Stoltz, qv) arrives in Paris to help out with a Bastille Day bank robbery planned by his childhood friend, Eric (Jean-Hugues Anglade), now a heroin-addicted sociopath. After a long night's hallucinogenic revelry, the gang arrive at the bank, and Zed discovers that one of the hostages is a part-time prostitute, Zoe (Julie Delpy) whom he'd slept with earlier. The film's title is loaded: 'zoe' means 'life' in Latin. 'I wanted to write an extreme example of what my generation is about - people who are living for the moment', claims Avary. Tarantino and Bender were recruited to act as Executive Producers on the film, alongside Becka Boss; reports vary on the extent of their actual involvement and remuneration. (It's probable that their names were invoked merely to ensure that responsibility for the film's final cut would stay in Avary's hands. Nevertheless, Tarantino's name would figure prominently on *Killing Zoe*'s poster, which was realised using distinctively *Dogs*-style typography.) Eric Stoltz was cast, according to Avary, 'because I wanted someone who could play me and looked a little like me'. (Apparently, it was Tarantino, by chance sighting Stoltz in the street, who first told the actor of the role.)

[with Eddie Bunker, Steve Buscemi, and Quentin Tarantino, director Alexandre Rockwell, all qv] (1994), *Get Shorty* [with John Travolta, qv] (1995).

(See also: Jacob Fuller; White; Winston Wolf)

KILLING ZOE
(US, 1994, dir. Roger Avary)

Sometimes cheekily labelled 'Reservoir Frogs', Tarantino collaborator Avary's directorial debut, concerning a bungled Parisian bank heist, owed its conception to *Dogs*'s location

Killing Zoe was shot in Paris and downtown Los Angeles in the spring of 1993; the bank itself was a stone's throw from the Los Angeles Mission. The locations were largely shot *in situ*, although the walls of the bank's lower levels were painted red: 'Being inside of the bank is like being inside of Eric's brain', explains Avary. 'The further you descend, the more confusing the labyrinth of walls becomes. It parallels Eric's descent into madness.' The actors playing the gang members were told to read books on Viking legends. Avary: 'Viking berserkers used to light their beards on fire, attack villages and scare the hell out of people. That is how I wanted these men to approach life. I wanted to inject a little myth into the story.' Richard Turner, who played the loudmouth American tourist ruthlessly despatched by Eric, had previously appeared as a sheriff in *Dogs*.

Perhaps inevitably, bearing in mind the background common to the two, Tarantino and Avary's respective directorial and writing styles share many motifs. Beyond the obvious *Dogs* comparisons - seven men pull a bank heist, for example - *Killing Zoe* demonstrates a number of similarities in theme, content and style to portions of Tarantino's overall work. There's a shared Europhilia; the name, 'Zed' (qv); a passenger inveigled into conversation with a taxi driver, *pace Pulp Fiction*'s Butch/Esmarelda scene; the phrase, 'supercool', *pace Dogs*'s Freddie Newendyke psyching himself up; Zed sees himself as a professional, 'on business', after Mr Pink; scenes in hotel suites (one with a comic-relief bellboy), *pace True Romance, Pulp* and *Four Rooms*; Zoe is a reluctant call-girl ('I'm not a prostitute'), after *True Romance*'s Alabama ('I'm not a whore'); heavy-duty drug-taking, including heroin injection ('doing heroin here is safer than Amsterdam'); the tripping Zed's seeing animated musical notes emanating from the Dixie band's instruments might be acknowledged as a self-conscious swipe at a distancing Realism, *pace* Mia's 'magic square' in *Pulp Fiction*; betrayal between erstwhile friends; and, *mais oui*, the obligatory Mexican stand-off at the finale.

There are also, of course, a plethora of banal pop culture/film references and allusions,

including 1922's *Nosferatu: Eine Symphonie des Grauens* (showing on the TV set in Zed's hotel room, and intercut with shots of Zed and Zoe having sex); Marvel Comics's *Captain America*; Viking movies (a poster for *La Reine des Vikings*, and Gary Kemp's Oliver later claims to have got 'some videos of Viking stuff made in Norway, which is excellent'); Eric furious because 'your leetle sheet monkey pissed on my Billie 'Olliday al-burms'; children's author Dr Seuss; psychedelic Sixties TV series *The Prisoner* (Oliver: 'What I was telling you is, in the final conflict between Six and Number Two to find out who is Number One, Number Six realises that he is Number One . . . It's like, we're all prisoners of ourselves, y'know? But the best episode is *A, B & C*, where he takes three drugs and he realises three different alternate universes and . . . [snorts coke] This is really good gear, isn't it?'); and a discussion of the merits of Dixieland music. There are moments of blank, po-faced surrealism akin to David Lynch (the dead cat in the hallway, Eric's revelatory experience towards the climax), and Zoe's shooting Eric in the foot appears to be a nod in the direction of a similar sequence in *Straw Dogs* (also possibly invoked in *True Romance*). *Sight and Sound* commented on the piece's overall similarity to *Dog Day Afternoon*, and Eric's eventual slo-mo execution owes a great deal to Al Pacino's bullet-ridden death in 1983's *Scarface*.

(See also: Avary, Roger; De Palma, Brian; Heist movies; Mexican stand-offs; Peckinpah, Sam)

KISS ME DEADLY
(US, 1955, dir. Robert Aldrich)

Adaptation of a Mickey Spillane Mike Hammer novel, and a major influence upon *Pulp Fiction*. Not only does *Pulp* replicate *Kiss Me Deadly*'s 'mysterious suitcase', albeit unintentionally - 'I came up with the suitcase and said let's not say what's in the suitcase. I then realised it was *Kiss Me Deadly*. The cart wasn't before the horse' - but the character of Butch shows some of his roots herein. Tarantino: 'I wanted Butch to be a complete fucking ass-hole. I wanted him to be basically like Ralph Meeker as Mike Hammer in Aldrich's *Kiss Me Deadly*. I wanted him to be a bully and a jerk . . .".

(See also: Briefcase; Pulp)

KNOXVILLE, TENNESSEE

The place of Quentin Jerome Tarantino's birth, on 27 March 1963. Quentin (named after Quint Asper from the television Western *Gunsmoke*, and a character in Faulkner's *The Sound and the Fury*) was born to Connie and Tony Tarantino, although the teenage Connie had already left her actor husband by the time of the birth. Connie remarried in 1965, and Quentin's birth certificate was adapted to show her new surname Zastoupil. He

reclaimed Tarantino in 1979, apparently tired of being teased about his surname's resem-blance to 'disaster pill' at school. He was also mindful that 'Tarantino' might hold him in better stead throughout his intended career as an actor.

Tarantino has harked back to his birthplace on several occasions throughout his scripts. *Natural Born Killers'* Mickey and Mallory Knox possibly derive their surnames from Knoxville. A more obvious reference wasn't made until *Pulp Fiction* - before Captain Koons gives the young Butch Coolidge his late father's gold watch, he tells the boy it was bought during the First World War from a general store in Knoxville. Later during the same story, the escaping Butch tells his unseen telephone con-tact 'It should take us a couple of days to get into Knoxville.'

LEONARD, ELMORE (1925 -)

US thriller writer and occasional screenwriter: his novel *The Switch* was unsuccessfully shoplifted from a K-Mart in Torrance by the fifteen-year old Tarantino, who, tearful, was duly arrested and escorted home in handcuffs. Leonard's work would later affect the genesis of *True Romance* - 'When I wrote *True Romance*, I was really into Elmore Leonard. In fact, I was trying to write an Elmore Leonard novel as a movie, though I'm not saying it's as good'. Tarantino's script also made reference to the 1974 Charles Bronson actioner *Mr Majestyk* (also written by Leonard), and *Natural Born Killers*'s Mickey was partly

Elmore Leonard, pictured during production of *Get Shorty* in 1995.

named in tribute to *The Switch*'s protagonist. And, regarding *Pulp Fiction*, Tarantino elaborated on Leonard's influence upon his writing. '[*Pulp*] has a lot to do with real-life crime', he told *Time Out*. 'I'm taking genre characters and applying them to real-life circumstances. I guess the master of that is Elmore Leonard.' In 1995, Miramax, at Tarantino's request, optioned four Leonard novels - *Killshot*, *Bandits*, *Freaky Deaky* and *Rum Punch* - to be developed by Tarantino and Bender, with Bruce Willis attached to the first two. Also in 1995, MGM, in association with Danny De Vito's Jersey Films (co-producers of *Pulp Fiction*) shot Leonard's *Get Shorty*, starring John Travolta as 'loan shark turned movie producer' Chilli Palmer. Tarantino had to talk Travolta into accepting the role after the latter had, apparently, turned it down twice: 'He said, "This is the one script that you should do . . .'''

(See also: Pulp)

LET'S STAY TOGETHER

Pulp Fiction's Marsellus Wallace holds court at Sally LeRoy's. Butch Coolidge listens impassively as he receives instructions from 'The Big Man' about throwing a fight. As Marsellus

offers him the bribe money, Al Green's *Let's Stay Together* plays over the background.

Let's Stay Together was a top ten hit on both sides of the Atlantic in January 1972, and hails from what many regard as the most fertile period of Al Green's long and varied career. It followed such classics as *I'm Tired of Being Alone* (1971) and preceded *Here I Am (Come and Take Me)* (1973) and *L.O.V.E.* (1975). A series of personal tragedies drew Green closer to God (he became a priest in 1976) and his work resultingly took on a Gospel flavour towards the late Seventies. His best-known songs are acknowledged soul classics, but with the exception of 1988's *Put a Little Love in Your Heart* (a cover of the Jackie DeShannon song, performed as a duet with Annie Lennox) his work has failed to find a wide audience for some time.

'That's almost like a hypnotic score', claims Tarantino, describing his use of *Let's Stay Together* in *Pulp Fiction*. 'The majority of the song plays as you're staring at this long take of Bruce Willis listening to somebody off screen. You hear that Al Green song in a way you've never listened to it before.'

LEWIS, JULIETTE (1973 -)
Mallory Knox, *Natural Born Killers*
Kate Fuller, *From Dusk Till Dawn*

California-born Lewis, the daughter of actor Geoffrey (*Every Which Way But Loose*, etc), made her first film appearance at age seven with a bit part in *Any Which Way You Can*. She played her first lead at 12 years in a TV mini-series, *Homefires*; later television work included TV movie *Too Young To Die?*, which concerned a 14 year-old raped by her stepfather. Oscar-nominated in 1991 as best supporting actress for her role in Martin Scorsese's *Cape Fear*, she went on to play one half of a couple of young-and-in-love serial killers on the road in mid-America in 1993's *Kalifornia* (alongside *True Romance*'s Brad

Pitt); she would partially reprise the role as Mallory in *NBK*. It's said that she had to meet with director Oliver Stone (qv) five times before she finally agreed to play Mallory, insisting upon one major script addition, the *I Love Mallory* sitcom sequence: she told *Premiere*, 'I actually asked Oliver - told Oliver - "You've got to show that something happened to this girl"' . . . Callousness and cruelty come from pain, not because you don't give a shit.' She also instigated a shift of emphasis in the scene where Mallory seduces the petrol-pump attendant. (Lewis is rumoured to have gone to see *NBK* with Tarantino incognito; they walked out after twenty minutes, allegedly.) Cast as the cross-bow-wielding Fuller daughter, Kate, in *From Dusk Till Dawn* because, according to executive producer Lawrence Bender (qv) in *Fangoria*, 'we felt she was really part of this world and thought she would be a good daughter for Harvey [Keitel]', Lewis's role was part-rewritten by Tarantino prior to principal photography to better demonstrate the actress's strengths. Other credits include: *My Stepmother Is an Alien* (1988), *Husbands and Wives* (1992), *What's Eating Gilbert Grape?* (1993), *Romeo Is Bleeding* [with Gary Oldman, qv] (1994), *Strange Days* [with Tom Sizemore, qv] (1995).

(See also: Kate Fuller; Mallory Knox)

LIGHTERS

Anyone who's anyone in Tarantino's *oeuvre* owns a sophisticated cigarette lighter or, more specifically, a Zippo. The flip-top devices serve several functions - Cliff favours his Zippo over Coccotti's matches; Virgil and Mia both pass time by fiddling with the hinged lid; Vincent uses his Zippo to heat Lance's heroin before shooting up and Norman bets Chester he can light his Zippo ten times in a row, *à la Alfred Hitchcock Presents* (qv). Scagnetti in *Natural Born Killers* is unusual in simply using his to light cigarettes.

Juliette Lewis and Woody Harrelson in *NBK*.

Zippos prove problematic for a number of characters - Mr White struggles with his lighter in the *Reservoir Dogs* warehouse, and Norman's faith in his lighter proves tragically misjudged at the climax of *Four Rooms*. In the pre-credit sequence of *From Dusk Till Dawn*, Seth Gecko finds an altogether more destructive use for a Zippo - he uses his to light the paper towel fire bombs that torch Benny's World of Liquor.

LONESOME TOWN
Ricky Nelson's US top ten hit from November 1958 is heard after a briefly-glimpsed performance by an impersonator during the Vincent Vega & Marsellus Wallace's Wife segment of *Pulp Fiction*.

Eric 'Ricky' Nelson began his recording career in 1957, and he went on to become one of America's premier teen idols of the late Fifties/early Sixties. His popularity extended further than the musical world - in 1959 he starred alongside John Wayne and Dean Martin in *Rio Bravo*, later to become Quentin Tarantino's favourite film. Growing up with his audiences, Ricky became Rick in 1961, and went over to performing country music in 1966. Widely acknowledged as an accomplished songwriter as well as singer by this point, he continued playing live after his record sales finally diminished in the early Seventies. He was killed when a plane taking him to a concert in Dallas crashed on 31 December 1985.

The laid back, melancholy tones of *Lonesome Town* signpost a more relaxed pace for the Jack Rabbit Slim's sequence in *Pulp Fiction*, and prove a perfect appetiser for Vincent and Mia's 'awkward silence'.

'The movie doesn't move like a bullet', stresses Tarantino, 'I don't want it to move like a bullet. I want it to move like a bullet when it's supposed to, and then at other times I want it to kinda hang out for a while . . . the music is very important in that regard - it really helps me create that rhythm.'

LOVEBIRDS IN BONDAGE
(US, 1983, dir. Scott McGill & Quentin Tarantino [uncompleted])
Tarantino's first foray into amateur film-making was as star, co-writer and co-director of this black comedy about a car accident victim and her lover. Tarantino collaborated with Scott McGill, an aspiring film-maker he had first met while a customer at the Video Outtakes rental store in 1983. Soon, the two began filming their co-written script *Lovebirds in Bondage*; McGill operated the camera and shared the direction with Tarantino.

The destruction of what little footage was shot, and McGill's subsequent suicide in 1987, mean that very little is known about the project. The plot concerns a girl who suffers brain damage after an accident in a car. Her erratic behaviour sees her admitted to an institution - unfortunately, her lovesick boyfriend is so devoted he decides to get himself admitted as well so he can be with her.

Casting never progressed beyond Tarantino taking the role of the boyfriend, and the project was soon abandoned. McGill later claimed the footage had been destroyed by his mother, but many, including Tarantino, now believe that he destroyed the film himself. The friendship McGill shared with Tarantino, and especially Roger Avary, nevertheless continued, and he went on to act as co-cinematographer on Tarantino's next 'film', *My Best Friend's Birthday*.

m

MADSEN, MICHAEL (1958 -)
Mr Blonde ('Toothpick' Vic Vega),
Reservoir Dogs

A one-time motor mechanic, and brother to actress Virginia (*Slam Dance*, etc), Michael Madsen broke into acting after giving an impromptu audition at Chicago's Steppenwolf Theatre to actors John Malkovich and Gary Sinise. He made his film debut in 1983's *War Games*. Somewhat portentously, in John Dahl's 1988 thriller *Kill Me Again*, his character tied an unfortunate individual to a chair and slit their throat. He was apparently handed early draft scripts of both *True Romance* and *Natural Born Killers* to read by Stephen Sachs, an associate of Lawrence Bender; nothing came of this (he'd later be earmarked as *True Romance*'s Vincenzo Coccotti, a part eventually played by Christopher Walken). Madsen was cast in *Dogs* at the instigation of executive producer Monte Hellman; he'd appeared in Hellman's 1988 *Iguana* (note, however, that some sources claim that Harvey Keitel, his earlier *Thelma and Louise* compadre, put Madsen's name forward as a potential Mr Blonde). An unrepentant improviser, Madsen ad-libbed Blonde's line - 'Hey, what's goin' on? Did ya hear that?' - into Nash's severed ear. Post-*Dogs*, he was once more offered a role - thought to be that of Mickey Knox - in *Natural Born Killers* by director Oliver Stone; Madsen had appeared in Stone's earlier *The Doors*. Having taken a leading part in the children's adventure *Free Willy* in a bid to avoid being typecast as a smirking psycho *pace* Blonde, he turned down a semi-reprisal of his *Dogs* role as *Pulp Fiction*'s Vincent in favour of 1994's *Wyatt Earp*. Other credits include: *Sea of Love* (1989), *Trouble Bound* [with Patricia Arquette, qv] (1992), *The Getaway* (1994), *Species* (1995), *Mulholland Falls* [with Chris Penn, editor Sally Menke, both qv] (1995).

(See also: Baltz, Kirk; Blonde; Ears; *Stuck In The Middle With You*)

MALLORY KNOX

'That's a bitch outta hell, son', claims Otis upon seeing natural born killer Mallory Knox, and he isn't far wrong. Mickey's wife is a wildcat perfectly tuned in to his philosophy of mass destruction. Her savage tendencies are rarely tempered: she calls 911 in remorse after chainsawing B-movie stars The Hun Brothers, and later apologises to Wayne Gayle for swearing on television ('Oh

I'm sorry - Can I say fuckin'? I can't, can I?'). Elsewhere, however, Mallory is the perfect partner - we learn from McClusky that she drowned her father in a fish tank and helped Mickey torch her mother in her bed - just because they wouldn't bless the couple's forthcoming marriage. They then blew up Mallory's house, taking half the block with it.

We discover little about Mallory's feelings on her forthcoming secondment to the Nystrom Asylum for the Criminally Insane - a year of solitary confinement has improved her singing voice but ingrained something of a nihilistic outlook. 'Let's do a Butch Cassidy and the Sundance Kid', she recommends to her husband when things get tricky during their escape. Mickey has more faith and the couple bust out to pursue their nightmarish romance along the road.

Oliver Stone's film gave Mallory the maiden name Wilson, and added a lengthy examination of the sexual abuse that engendered her all-consuming hate. Tarantino left police detective Scagnetti to sum up Mallory's motivation. 'When they gave you a polygraph', he tells her, '"I love Mickey" was the only thing you said that registered as the truth.'

(See also: *Badlands*; Lewis, Juliette; Mickey Knox; Stone, Oliver; Women)

MAN FROM RIO, THE

(See: *Alfred Hitchcock Presents: Man From the South*)

MARSELLUS WALLACE

(See: Butch Coolidge; Inferno; Men; Names; Race; Rhames, Ving)

MARTIN AND LEWIS

Comedy partners Dean Martin and Jerry Lewis, like Amos 'n' Andy (qv), would be commemo-rated in *Pulp Fiction* as a Jack Rabbit Slim's milkshake (vanilla-flavoured, presumably, as opposed to Amos 'n' Andy's chocolate); a pair of impersonators can also be glimpsed doing their *schtick* beside the bar. Martin and Lewis became famous as occasional co-hosts of NBC TV's whiter-than-white *Colgate Comedy Hour*, appearing 28 times in the five years to November 1955. The pair split shortly after, each enjoying solo success. In Tarantino's *NBK* script, Scagnetti blows out Captain Squeri with the retort, 'I'm a detective. You want an errand boy, call Jerry Lewis' - a reference to Lewis's title role in 1960's *The Bellboy*, itself extensively discussed by Chester Rush in the script to *Four Rooms*: 'Didja ever see *The Bellboy*? . . . You should, it's one of Jerry's better movies. He never says a word through the entire film . . .'

(See also: Hotels)

MEN

'Let's not start sucking each other's dicks quite yet' - Winston Wolf, *Pulp Fiction*.

The sophistication of Tarantino's male characters forms a stark contrast to the perfunctory attention paid to the few leading ladies in his scripts. Tarantino seems more comfortable establishing complex relationships between male characters than he does between males and females. After all, as Mr White tells Joe, 'You push that woman/man thing too long and it gets to ya after a while.'

Inexorable bonds form between certain men - often fiercely loyal relationships that one or the other partner will risk death for. In *Reservoir Dogs*, Mr White and Mr Orange share a discreet understanding which often sees the older White acting like a father figure to the younger Orange. Mr White gives Mr Orange some informal advice on crowd control prior to the robbery, and drives his dying colleague back to the warehouse afterwards. Once there, he threatens to kill Mr Pink when they argue

over the risk of taking Orange to hospital, and later risks his life defending 'a good kid' against Joe Cabot. His loyalty stems from a paternal instinct towards Orange and a feeling of responsibility for the wound he sustained in the getaway. Mr Orange rewards his friend's loyalty with the painful truth in the closing moments of the film.

The relationship between Nice Guy Eddie, Joe Cabot and Vic Vega was put to the test following Vic's arrest in 'a company warehouse full of hot items'. Vega served a four year jail sentence, refusing throughout to rat on Joe. On Vega's release, his first meeting with Eddie is taken up with a play fight in Joe's office which Eddie seems to interpret as a sexual assault.

Man to man to man: Tarantino, Buscemi and Keitel rehearse *Reservoir Dogs*'s early confrontation between Mr Pink and Mr White.

'Don't try to fuck me, Vic', he tells his old friend. 'I like you a lot buddy, but I don't dig you that way.' The bond between Eddie and Vic is nevertheless strong enough to make Nice Guy unhesitatingly assume that Mr Orange is lying when he claims Blonde was planning to escape with the jewels.

The relationships between *Pulp Fiction*'s males are as revealing. Following Butch's escape from the pawnshop, he turns around and risks his life to save Marsellus, the man who earlier that day had tried to murder him. Butch's motivation is never made explicit; attempting to win back Marsellus's respect by murdering his assailants seems illogical - Butch could make his getaway to Knoxville before Marsellus ever gained his freedom, assuming he ever did. More likely, Butch recalls the testimony imparted to him by Captain Koons, his late father's comrade-in-arms: 'We were in that Hanoi pit of hell together five years . . . when two men are in a situation like me and your Dad were . . . you take on certain responsibilities of the other.' Thus Butch continues a Coolidge tradition of laying his ass on the line to free Marsellus, who is undergoing the insertion of something altogether less comfortable than a gold watch.

Jules's outraged reaction to Vincent's asking whether he'd ever given a man a foot massage leaves us in no doubt that *Pulp Fiction*'s characters share a similarly intolerant stance towards homosexuality as those in *Reservoir Dogs*.

Elsewhere, Jules and Jimmie (or should that be *Jules et Jim*?) prove themselves as loyal to each other as their namesakes in Truffaut's 1961 film. Although Jimmie clearly doesn't have a sign out the front of his house that says 'dead nigger storage' he reluctantly lets Jules use his garage for just that purpose. It is revealing that it is not being landed with Jules and Vincent's bloody predicament that upsets Jimmie as much as his wife's likely reaction to it on her return from work - 'no marriage counselling,

no trial separation, I'm gonna get fucking divorced . . . there's nothing that you're gonna say that's gonna make me forget that I love my wife.' By this stage of play, it is unsurprising that an absent woman threatens a bigger wedge between Jules and Jimmie than the possibility of wrongful arrest as an accessory to murder.

The code of honour between straight male friends isn't just exceeded by the dumping of dead bodies in their garages. A man will go a long way for a Malibu - in *Pulp Fiction* Lance regards the recent vandalism of Vincent's Malibu as a crime punishable by death, '. . . no trial, no jury - straight to execution'. The selling of the heroin he's weighing while he says all this clearly presents no quandary at all. In the first draft of *Four Rooms*, Pete is prepared to risk his little finger to win a Malibu in a bizarre bet. 'I drive a Honda Civic', he says. 'I love Chester's car more than I've ever loved a woman.' The finished screenplay had Norman risk his finger for Chester's Chevy Chevelle, but the principle remained the same.

From Dusk Till Dawn (initially drafted around the same time as *Reservoir Dogs* but only completed some years later) revisits the idea of male bonding. In much the same way that Mr White is blind to the finger of guilt pointing to his friend Mr Orange, Seth Gecko overlooks his brother Richard's pychosis time and again. In self-denial over his brother's most recent rape and murder victim, Seth hugs Richard, whispering, '[When] we get into Mexico . . . none of this shit's gonna matter.' After Richard falls victim to Santanico Pandemonium, Seth holds his dead brother's hand and apologises to him. 'Richie, I'm sorry I fucked things up. You'd really like it in El Ray [sic]. We'd find peace there. I love you little brother, I'll miss ya bad.' 'I'm glad you feel that way, Seth,' the corpse suddenly replies. 'I love you, too.'

In Tarantino's world, the most sophisticated and realistic relationships are those between heterosexual men who share unspoken bonds and discreet loyalties. While there are clearly defined parameters to these relationships ('You don't fuck with another man's vehicle . . . It's against the rules' - Vincent) even the most disloyal and selfish behaviour will be tolerated if that relationship is in danger of being infringed by a woman or a homosexual. Whether motivated by a lack of personal experience or a fear of constricting his genre neverland, Tarantino largely steers clear of seriously tackling either in his work.

(See also: Alter egos; Butch Coolidge; *Deliverance*; Jules Winnfield; Seth Gecko; Trust and betrayal; Women)

MENKE, SALLY
Editor, *Reservoir Dogs*
Editor, *Pulp Fiction*
Editor, *Four Rooms: Penthouse: The Man From Hollywood*

Oscar-nominated for *Pulp Fiction* - the rough cut of which was trimmed from some 200 minutes - Menke graduated from New York University's film school, becoming Tarantino's editor of choice via such diverse pictures as the 1984 comedy *Cold Feet* and 1990's *Teenage Mutant Ninja Turtles*. Other credits include: *The Search For Signs of Intelligent Life in the Universe* (1991), *Heaven and Earth* [co-edited; with Tommy Lee Jones, director Oliver Stone, both qv] (1993), *Mulholland Falls* [with Michael Madsen and Chris Penn, both qv] (1995).

(See also: Dialogue)

MEXICAN STAND-OFFS
The Mexican stand-off first appears in *True Romance*, where all the story's various elements converge in Lee Donowitz's hotel room and fight for possession of Blue Lou Boyle's cocaine. The police, led by Nicholson and Dimes, confront Boris and Monty, Lee's bodyguards, and the mafia hitmen, led by Dario and Lenny. 'This is a Mexican stand-off if ever there was one', the script says. 'Gangsters on

Pulp Fiction's Mexican stand-off - a stand-off in a sitting position.

The Mexican stand-off from *The Good, The Bad and the Ugly* is about to be set in motion . . .

police detective, as if to underline the point. In Oliver Stone's film, the confrontation is transferred to a corridor outside, Scagnetti being otherwise indisposed inside Mallory's cell during Mickey's escape. With Mickey and Mallory united, they leave the prison using Wayne Gale and Deputy Sheriff Duncan as human shields. As they prepare to leave, the scene, preserved in Stone's film, is described in the script as 'a silent stand-off'.

The legendary *Reservoir Dogs* stand-off, initiated by the incredible 'Stop pointing that fucking gun at my dad!', is resolved thus: Joe shoots Mr Orange, Mr White shoots Joe, Eddie shoots Mr White and Mr White finally shoots Eddie. Only Mr White and Mr Orange survive the confrontation. Such was the debate surrounding this sequence that 'Who Shot Nice Guy Eddie?' t-shirts became a familiar sight at the time of the film's release.

one end with shotguns. Bodyguards with machine-guns on the other. And cops with handguns in the middle.'

In Tarantino's script, the stand-off becomes a pitched battle during which the following principal fatalities occur: Nicholson shoots Lee; Nicholson is then shot by Boris and Marvin; Clarence is shot by Dimes and Dario; Frankie is shot; Elliot is shot; Monty is shot by Marvin and some cops; Dario is shot by some cops; Dimes shoots Boris, and finally Alabama shoots Marvin, Dimes and Wurlitzer.

In Tony Scott's film, the shoot-out in Donowitz's room at the Beverly Ambassador is altered in several significant ways. After the pitched battle, Dimes shoots Boris as revenge for the murder of Nicholson, and is then murdered himself. The most significant difference, however, is that although Clarence is still shot by Dimes, he doesn't die. Alabama is able to drag him away from the hotel unnoticed amidst the chaos.

Natural Born Killers features two significant stand-offs - the first between Mickey and Scagnetti when the serial killer makes his escape attempt from inside a cell. 'Looks like we got a Mexican stand-off', he tells the

The climax of *Pulp Fiction* sees a stand-off (or rather sit-off) between Jules, Pumpkin and Honey Bunny in the Hawthorne Grill. 'Normally both your asses would be dead as fuckin' fried chicken,' Jules tells them, 'but you happened to pull this shit while I'm in a transitional period and I don't wanna kill you.' They are later joined by Vincent, who seems more than happy to oblige. Jules's spiritual rebirth leaves Pumpkin $1500 richer, and Honey Bunny heading for the nearest toilet. Jules is trying real hard to shepherd the weak Pumpkin, and for the only time in any of Tarantino's scripts such an encounter is bloodless. Jules replaces the safety catch on his gun and earns the right to walk away from violence.

The less austere stand-off that brings *Four Rooms* to its giddy conclusion is modelled on the Roald Dahl/*Alfred Hitchcock Presents* story *Man From the South*. For a fee of $1000, Ted the bellhop poises a meat cleaver over Norman's little finger. If Norman can light his Zippo ten times in a row, he wins Chester Rush's Chevy Chevelle. If he fails at any point, he forfeits his pinkie. He fails on the first attempt, and the resolution of the stand-off brings another Tarantino movie to a close.

The climax of *From Dusk Till Dawn* is similarly anticipated by a tense confrontation. When the beleaguered humans edge away from the Titty Twister's back room and into the bar, the vampire creatures cautiously retreat from their home-made holy weapons. 'What we have here is a Mexican stand-off, *à la The Wild Bunch*', describes the script. 'A moment of peace before the battle. The vamps just watch the humans. The humans just watch the vamps.'

Tarantino is well aware of his reputation for liberally sprinkling his scripts with the same dramatic device. 'Well, when you're doing a gangster film, the Mexican stand-off is like the modern equivalent of a Western showdown,' he told *Q* magazine's Andy Gill. 'If I were doing a bedroom comedy, I probably wouldn't end it with a Mexican stand-off. Though who knows, maybe I will . . .'

It isn't difficult to trace the inspiration for this prediliection. *Il Buono, il Bruto, il Cattivo* (better known as *The Good, The Bad and the Ugly*) is Tarantino's second favourite Western, next to *Rio Bravo* (1959). The Mexican stand-off was probably never used to better effect than in this, Sergio Leone's 1967 conclusion to the Clint Eastwood so-called 'Dollars' trilogy. The second instalment, *For A Few Dollars More* (1965), had already seen Gian Maria Volonte dispatched in similarly stand-offish style by the supercool Clint Eastwood. Such confrontations achieved unprecedented heights of dramatic tension in the Western, earning a notoriety shared only by the famous gunfight in *High Noon* (1952). It took *Reservoir Dogs* to wrest the device away into a different genre, and a new level of public recognition. This recognition, and possibly an acknowledgement of its catalyst, didn't go unnoticed at New Line Cinema. In June 1994 *Variety* reported that the organisation had paid $400,000 for the rights

to an unpublished action novel called *The Stand-off*. It was written by one Chuck Hogan, a 26-year old assistant video store manager from Boston.

(See also: Fingers; Lighters; *Killing Zoe*; Redemption; Trust and betrayal; X-rated)

MIA WALLACE

'My favourite character I've ever written' - Quentin Tarantino.

The Big Man's young wife in *Pulp Fiction* is a devious minx from the outset - when Vincent arrives at her house to take her out, he finds a message telling him to go ahead and pour himself a drink while she gets dressed. A fully dressed Mia uses this opportunity to check out her stoned escort on her surveillance cameras and indulge herself with some cocaine before she finally appears. Vincent has every right to be apprehensive about his date - Mia is an actress rumoured to accept foot massages from her husband's employees. The rumour that such employees are then thrown out of fourth storey windows, thus developing 'speech impediments', makes him understandably curious about her.

He has nothing to worry about. While Mia is undeniably attractive and sensual, she finds it hard to follow up her sophisticated entrance. She takes Vincent to Jack Rabbit Slim's, an incredibly tacky Fifties theme restaurant where milkshakes cost $5.00 and waiters dress like Buddy Holly. She soon confesses to being unable to roll a cigarette, enters them both into a twist contest with unabashed vigour and later fails to distinguish between heroin and cocaine with disastrous consequences.

Tarantino's original screenplay played more on Mia's predatory instincts during her initial meeting with Vincent. In a sequence that never made it into the finished film she interrogates Vincent, recording his responses on her camcorder. In order to find out what sort of person he is before they leave, she asks him about some popular culture preferences. Does he prefer *The Brady Bunch* or *The Partridge Family*? *Bewitched* or *[I Dream of] Jeannie*? On *Rich Man, Poor Man* did he prefer Peter Strauss or Nick Nolte? If he were Archie, who would he fuck first: Betty or Veronica? She finishes by asking him if he has ever fantasised about being beaten up by a girl. 'Sure,' Vincent replies. 'Emma Peel on *The Avengers*. That tough girl who usta hang out with Encyclopedia Brown. And Arlene Motika . . . Girl from sixth grade, you don't know her.'

Mia's limited acting career has included a co-starring role in the pilot episode of a television series called *Fox Force Five*. As a member of a gang of female supersleuths, Mia's jet black hair made her ideal for the role of Raven McCoy - the deadliest woman in the world with a knife. Her character was a circus performer whose grandfather, an old vaudevillian, had taught her numerous corny jokes, one of which she would repeat in each episode. If Vincent is struck by the similarities with Willie Garvin and Modesty Blaise, the heroes of the Peter O'Donnell book he reads on the toilet, then he keeps quiet about them.

Aside from all this, we learn that Mia has a portrait of herself (in bare feet, of course)

Dick Miller (right) as Monster Joe in *Pulp Fiction*. You haven't forgotten this part of the movie - it was cut prior to release. Harvey Keitel plays Winston Wolf.

hanging on the wall, is fond of visiting Amsterdam to 'chill out' about once a year, dislikes uncomfortable silences (who doesn't?) and eschews digital technology when it comes to her music collection - Dusty Springfield is played on vinyl while Urge Overkill appear on a reel-to-reel tape machine. It is fitting that Mia knows all the words to *Girl, You'll Be A Woman Soon* - she is clearly a little girl striving not to be 'a square' with a cocaine-fuelled self-confidence not entirely matched by her experience or sophistication.

And what about that foot massage? Just a rumour. Apparently.

(See also: Drugs; Foot fetishism; *My Best Friend's Birthday*; Quarterpounders; Thurman, Uma; Vincent Vega)

MICKEY KNOX

Natural Born Killers's Mickey Knox is an enigma that McClusky nevertheless labels with consummate ease: 'Mickey and Mallory Knox are without a doubt the most twisted, depraved group of fucks it's ever been my displeasure to lay eyes on.'

A seemingly motiveless killing spree which leaves 49 people dead begins at Mallory's house and ends in the court room when Mickey murders one of the witnesses during his trial. Even after sentencing, he and his wife go on to kill a criminal psychologist and several guards in three jails. It seems they are unstoppable, and it is only the threat of imminent transfer to the Nystrom Asylum for the Criminally Insane (nicknamed 'Lobotomy Bay') that prompts Mickey into a degree of cautious co-operation with Wayne Gayle. While undoubtedly psychotic, at no point does Mickey appear to suffer from the schizophrenia that blighted some of his most admired predecessors. In fact, Wayne Gayle describes him as 'charismatic', Dr Emil Reinghold as 'exciting' and one of his fans as 'romantic'. Mickey has a more philosophical view of himself: 'I used to be you', he tells Wayne, 'then I evolved'. His bloated ego demands that one person is always left alive at the scene of every crime to tell the story of their Bonnie and Clyde-style rampage, and he retains a curious control over his surroundings, playing hard to get with Wayne even when bound in chains.

Exactly what Mickey has evolved into isn't made clear, and we never quite share the author's obvious fascination with the most dangerous man in the world. Ultimately, we are told it is enough to know that Mickey is a natural born killer, and that prison was small price to pay for his crimes. 'Was an instant of purity worth a lifetime lie?' he asks Wayne. 'Yeah, it was.'

(See also: *Badlands*; Harrelson, Woody; Mallory Knox; Yuppie scum)

MILLER, DICK (1928 -)
Monster Joe, *Pulp Fiction*

Heavy-lidded actor in US exploitation pictures from the Fifties on; particularly associated with *schlock* legend Roger Corman, Miller's brief appearance as *Pulp Fiction*'s Monster Joe - 'I'll tell ya what, if you ever need it, I'll dispose of a body part for free' - would be cut prior to release. Posters for two of Miller's AIP features - *Sorority Girl* (UK title: *The Bad One*) and *Rock All Night*, both 1957 - are displayed on the walls of Jack Rabbit Slim's. Other credits include: *It Conquered the World* (1956), *Not of this Earth* (1957), *A Bucket of Blood* (1959), *The Little Shop of Horrors* (1960), *The Terror* [co-director Monte Hellman, qv] (1962), *After Hours* [with Rosanna Arquette and Bronson Pinchot, both qv] (1985).

MISIRLOU

Tarantino, a self-confessed surf-guitar enthusiast, had clear motives in selecting the main theme for *Pulp Fiction*: 'To me, opening credits are very important, because that's the only mood time most movies give themselves. Having *Misirlou* as your opening credits is just so intense . . . it's so loud and blaring - it throws down a gauntlet that the movie just has to live up to. It says "We're big!"'.

Misirlou was the work of the legendary Dick Dale and his Del-Tones. Richard Monsour adopted the name Dick Dale at the suggestion of a Los Angeles country DJ, and spent the late Fifties struggling to make an impact in showbusiness. A number of indifferent singles and a small role in the Marilyn Monroe film *Let's Make Love* (1960) led to nothing. In August 1961, however, Dale made his mark on the world by recording the guitar instrumental *Let's Go Trippin'*. A musical sub-genre was born, the newly-crowned 'King of Surf Guitar' pioneering the thundering instrumental style which became so closely associated with California's favourite water sport. Released in May 1962, *Misirlou* was Dale's third instrumental single and saw the emergence of his distinctive high-octane rattle.

Despite appearances in the film *Muscle Beach Party* (1964) and on *The Ed Sullivan Show*, Dale's loyal fan base extended little further than Southern California and his popularity waned when surfing and hot-rod music gave way to The Beatles' Merseybeat in the mid-Sixties. In 1966, serious illness forced Dale to retire to Hawaii. He has since juggled a successful career in real estate with several showbusiness comebacks - the first in Las Vegas during the early Seventies. The most important catalyst in resurrecting his popularity came in 1994 with the release of *Pulp Fiction*; the renewed interest in his work has led to new recordings and his first gigs outside the US. Perhaps the most notable of these was a powerful performance of *Misirlou* on Jools Holland's New Year's Eve programme in 1995.

'The style of music I developed was the feeling I got when I was out there eating it on the waves,' Dale recently told enthusiast Robert J Dalley. 'It was that good rambling feeling I got when I was locked in a tube with the white water caving in over my head. I was trying to project the power of the ocean to the people.'

Enthused by the recent resurgence in his popularity, Dale released a well-received album, *Calling Up Spirits*, in 1996 and is optimistic about the future. 'It just needs the explosion like when I started it back in 1961. If I really come back, you'll see that explosion again!'

MORALITY

There has been no shortage of detractors willing to rage against the supposed im- or amorality of Tarantino's works. For some, such as Finlan O'Toole, writing in the otherwise liberal *Guardian* newspaper on 3 February 1995: 'What Tarantino has done with movie violence is precisely what the makers of cheap pornography have done with movie sex . . . He has dispensed with sequential plot . . . has disavowed all moral or social intent, and gone straight for the sadism.' O'Toole concludes: 'His films should be studied as Exhibit A in the museum of post-modern moral vacuity.' Under the headline 'Sickening amorality masquerading as culture', the *Daily Mail*'s Mary Kenny slavered on 22 October 1994: '*Pulp Fiction* [is] a symbol and a metaphor for so much of the value-free and value-less culture of our time, representing a nihilism which nearly always ends up with boring, mindless cruelty . . . [It is] a negation of civilized values - which is, of course, a definition of decadence.' According to Kenny (who, bizarrely, suggests that 'cynical drug dealer' Lance is 'visibly modelled on Rembrandt's most famous picture of Jesus'), 'art, including the cinema, [has] a teaching role, an inspirational role which . . . should seek to make men and women better'; her point of view is shared by the *Evening Standard*'s Peter McKay who, five

days later, attempted to contextualize Tarantino as part of ongoing narrative cinema history by comparing his films to those of John Ford. Writes McKay: '[Ford] took the trouble to put senseless violence and killing into some kind of moral context. He made sure that good triumphed over evil in the end . . . Neither Tarantino nor [Oliver] Stone bothers with this convention . . . they shoot violence as a random, conscienceless, casual and sometimes rather witty expression of human tedium or contemporary anger. There are no goodies who'll win in the end and no baddies who'll get their just deserts . . . Surely most of us think that any artist should strive to give meaning to human life, to encourage decency and self sacrifice.'

The auteur has done little to shield himself from such accusations: when, of *Reservoir Dogs*'s 'ear' scene, he remarks in the *Village Voice*, 'I'm a little surprised by how many people were horrified by what happened to the cop. I mean, I don't like cops. I don't give a shit about cops', he seems thoroughly deserving of such criticism. When questioned directly about the moral framework of his movies, Tarantino himself ducks the issue, often stating that his characters dictate their individual fates, that they (or divine inspiration, perhaps) decide the resolution of their, not his, narrative: interviewed by Graham Fuller, he claimed that constantly, throughout the scripting process, 'the characters will do something that just blows me away. With regard to the torture scene in *Reservoir Dogs* . . . I didn't sit down and say, 'OK, I'm gonna write this really bitchin' torture scene.' When Mr Blonde reached into his boot and pulled out a straight razor, I didn't know he had a straight razor in his boot. I was surprised.' Yet the purpose of this scene - in narrative terms - is to incite Mr Orange to reveal himself to the audience as undercover cop Freddy Newendyke: indeed, the remainder of the film springboards almost entirely from this most significant of moments. Orange's clear (moral) choice not to permit Marvin to be murdered, and to therefore execute the plainly evil Blonde, leads ultimately to Orange's own death, and that of the remaining Dogs bar Pink, whose amoral self-proclaimed 'professionalism' exempts him from the choices made by the rest of the gang. Pink's conspicuous survival appears to suggest that in a twisted world, to make any moral choices - good or bad, regardless - is futile, self-delusory and ultimately doomed.

Pulp Fiction, however, appears to contradict this; invert it, even. Two major moral decisions are fought out on screen: Butch's decision to return and save his enemy Marsellus (dramatically necessary to underline this segment's 'pit of hell' motif: see Inferno, qv), and Jules's revelatory experience in Brett's apartment, wherein he chooses to renounce violence and thereby save the day. The latter, significantly, is scripted to make his dilemma clear: immediately before opening the suitcase for Pumpkin, Jules fantasises coldly executing first Honey Bunny, then Pumpkin - but Honey Bunny, firing wildly as she falls, shoots a bystander dead. (This scene, we understand, was shot, but later cut, from the completed film: perhaps Tarantino's audience was considered unable to accept such a stark underlining of the futility of gunplay. Notably, the crisis is resolved by the threat of bullet-laden reprisal.) Earlier, Honey Bunny and Pumpkin, through their dialogue, have made a significant point: 'He looks like the hero type to me!' says Honey Bunny, gun trained at the diner's manager. 'Execute him!' snarls Pumpkin. In Tarantino's world, heroes - and villains likewise - get hurt. Heroes and villains receive no reward. Only, like Pink, by opting out from good versus bad relativism, shall you survive. Probably.

Pulp Fiction's conclusion makes a virtue of the fudge at the heart of its discourse. 'Maybe it means you're the evil man', says Jules to Pumpkin, 'and I'm the righteous man. And Mr .9mm here, he's the shepherd . . . Or it could mean you're the righteous man and I'm the shepherd, and it's the world that's evil and selfish. Now I'd like that. But that shit ain't the truth. The truth is you're the weak. And I'm the tyranny of evil men. But I'm tryin'. . .'. It's a genuine anticlimax anathema to the tradition of classic narrative, *High Noon* cinema popularised by Hollywood's true pulpmongers. (Lest there be any doubt that the comparison is relevant, Tarantino has frequently described Jules and Vincent's story strand in such terms. It 'starts with Jules and Vincent going to kill some guys. That's like the opening five minutes of any Joel Silver movie [*Lethal Weapon*, *Predator*, *Die Hard* etc] - a bunch of guys show up and pow, pow, pow kill somebody and then the credits start and then you see Arnold Schwarzenegger'.)

Equally anticlimactic, albeit in a different manner, is the conclusion of *Reservoir Dogs*: the (faceless) forces of law and order may prevail, but it is White who metes out retribution and (inverted) justice as his final act, an apparent denial of 'normal' film morality (in *True Romance*'s script, Clarence dies, a victim of his self-imposed transformation from a 'real' person to a film character, a hero or villain). Through rejecting a 'correct' moral choice as a concluding message, Tarantino effectively circumvents clear interpretation; nothing is to be learned from his cinema, other than that cinema is an unsuitable medium to learn from (note also that some of his characters appear to endorse the line on causality adopted by Tarantino's detractors: see Causality and imitation, qv).

In Tarantino's endless invocation of cinema past, we see the constantly-tendered promise of clear resolution, one upon which he will always renege. Unlike, say, the pulp fictions of John Ford, *Pulp Fiction*'s only profundity lies in its rejection of capital-m Meaningfulness, in its rejection of the conventionally Moral. Would a conclusion wherein Honey Bunny and Pumpkin lie dead (at the cost of an innocent's life), to quote Kenny, 'make men and women feel better'? Would Orange's living to tell the tale, receiving backslaps from his LAPD compadres as White and Pink are led away, to invoke McKay, 'give meaning to human life'?

Maybe they would. Maybe Tarantino's a weak writer; maybe his shots are shots in the dark. But maybe the very greyness at the heart of his films's discourse, their avoidance of too-easy moralizing - their very amorality, if you must - is in itself a profoundly moral choice. Maybe, like Jules, he's tryin' real hard to be a shepherd.

(See also: Redemption; Violence)

MUSIC

The importance of film score to Tarantino is best illustrated by the unrivalled precedence he grants music in the creative process. Whereas directors such as Stanley Kubrick have created some of the most memorable marriages of pictures and sound by deciding on score once shooting is completed, Tarantino has created some of his most successful sequences by deciding on the right tracks before shooting, or even scripting, has begun.

Pulp Fiction's opening theme, *Misirlou* (qv) by Dick Dale and his Del-Tones, was pinpointed in an early shuffle through Tarantino's record collection. 'I'm always trying to find the right opening credit or closing credit sequence music early on, when I'm thinking about the story. Once I find it, that really triggers me in to what the personality, the rhythm, of this piece should be.' Obtaining permission to use another song, Dusty Springfield's *Son of a Preacher Man* (qv), became crucial - it decided whether or not the scene it accompanied was included in the film.

In *Reservoir Dogs*, the soundtrack entirely comprised source music - specifically Seventies tracks heard on K-Billy's Super Sounds of the

Seventies weekend. Once the dramatic premise of a nostalgia radio station familiar to all the key characters was established in the pre-credits sequence, Tarantino was free to draw upon a variety of different songs and manipulate their value as ironic counterpoints to on-screen action. This most famously occurs when the smooth easy listening of Stealer's Wheel's *Stuck In The Middle With You* (qv) seduces us into a sadistic slice of switchblade torture.

'I went out of my way to get bubblegum songs', Tarantino remembers. 'I didn't have Led Zeppelin or Marvin Gaye - I wanted the 1910 Fruitgum Company, that kind of thing.' One particular track that Tarantino cites in illustrating this approach is Edison Lighthouse's number 1 hit from 1970, *Love Grows (Where My Rosemary Goes)*. Although never actually used, its appearance is scripted in both *Reservoir Dogs* and *Natural Born Killers*.

The premise of the radio station also allowed Tarantino to manipulate the volume of background music without appearing overly contrived. This is perhaps most obvious when the heavyweight funk of Joe Tex's *I Gotcha* (qv) accompanies the brutal beating of the bound policeman. The seamless fusion of the same song played at different volumes between two scenes (one in Eddie's car, the other immediately afterwards in the warehouse) illustrates the effectiveness of the device. In contrast, *True Romance* employs Tony Scott's more traditional approach - the background music in Drexl's house simply mounts in volume mid-scene prior to his murder. Although effective, the credibility of the sequence is ultimately compromised.

Tarantino imposes a strict examination of previous use on all songs considered for his films. 'You are such a poseur and such a lame-o for using a song that another movie has "christened" . . . When *Dirty Dancing* used *Be My Baby* it's like, 'Excuse me, that is the opening theme to *Mean Streets*.' Whenever

I hear *Be My Baby* I see Harvey Keitel leaning back on his pillow.'

Pulp Fiction's more diverse soundtrack was unafraid to suggest a humorous tone (the use of *Comanche*, qv, by The Revels in the pawnshop rape scene bordered on comic) but worked in better harmony with the action. Tarantino also felt less obligated to provide an on-screen premise for the appearence of certain songs. While the music played at Mia's house and Jack Rabbit Slim's is initiated by characters in the film, many other songs are employed purely as score. This approach was taken to its next logical step when some much-needed glue was applied to *Four Rooms* with a specially composed score performed by Combustible Edison. The group's innovative jazz went some way towards papering over the cracks between the four directors' contrasting styles.

The successful soundtrack albums of *Reservoir Dogs* and *Pulp Fiction* apparently stand comparison to the tapes Tarantino is fond of compiling for his friends. Both feature favourite tracks from the director's record collection, and while the soundtracks feature snatches of movie dialogue ('we're trying to give it a personality, like a mini-offshoot of the movie') the tapes intermingle music with sound effects, radio jingles and comedy sketches. For Tarantino, compiling home-made music compilations is comparable to his other great love. 'Making tapes is very similar to directing movies - you're taking a bunch of artists who are all doing their own thing and by mixing them, putting them together and choosing how they appear you're creating something that says an aesthetic of yourself.'

When interviewed about his favourite music in July 1994, Tarantino told *Melody Maker* that his favourite albums were Bob Dylan's *Blood On The Tracks* ('It's his masterpiece'), followed by Freda Payne's *Band Of Gold* and Elvis Presley's *The Sun Sessions*. Aside from soundtrack composers, his other favourite artists

were folk singers Suzanne Vega and Phil Ochs. Vega was namechecked in the screenplay of *Pulp Fiction* (Vincent tells an incredulous Mia that his cousin is also called Suzanne) but the sequence never made it into the finished film.

MY BEST FRIEND'S BIRTHDAY
(US, 1985-87, dir. Quentin Tarantino [uncompleted])

This seminal project was, by Tarantino's own admission, the closest he ever came to film school training.

Tarantino met Craig Hamann at The James Best Theater Center in early 1981, and the two soon became friends. In late 1984, when they were both working at the Video Archives store, Hamann devised a semi-autobiographical story called *My Best Friend's Birthday*. Following an initial draft script, Tarantino joined his friend and the two collaborated on what ultimately became an expanded screenplay designed to highlight their talents as actors. Tarantino decided to shoot *My Best Friend's Birthday* as a 16mm black and white film containing a mere thirty scenes.

My Best Friend's Birthday was intended to be a screwball comedy of errors set in and around Tarantino's neighbourhood of Torrance. Mickey Burnett (Craig Hamann) loses his job and his girlfriend the day before his dreaded thirtieth birthday. His best friend, extrovert rockabilly Clarence Pool (Quentin Tarantino) decides to cheer him up by throwing a party for him at a local bar. Mickey is unimpressed, so Clarence tries another tack by hiring a prostitute, Misty Knight (Crystal Shaw), for his friend. Clarence gives the hooker the keys to Mickey's house, and Mickey arrives to find her waiting. Misty's inexperience proves problematic. The arrival of her pimp (Al Harrell) proves even more difficult - while he and Mickey fight, Misty leaves with Clarence. The two fall in love and get down to some kinky sex. Later, Mickey goes to Clarence's house, bumping into his ex-girlfriend (Linda Kaye), who mistakenly believes he has been seeing the prostitute. Mickey and Clarence end up fighting over the disastrous outcome of the evening, and Mickey winds up face-down in his own birthday cake. The reappearance of the pimp means that Mickey once more loses out on Misty's affections and he becomes utterly dejected. The two friends eventually make up, and return to the bar where the whole debacle began. Before Clarence goes in for a drink he hands Mickey a joint and tells him to relax with it before he joins him inside for a beer. Mickey perches on a nearby vehicle and lights up. Unfortunately, just as he begins to enjoy his smoke, the vehicle's headlights switch on - revealing it to be a police car. Mickey's under arrest. 'Nothing much happens in Torrance', reads the script. 'But occasionally you can have a bad night there.'

Shooting began in 1985 using a variety of rented or borrowed equipment. Incredibly, the tortuous filming schedule spanned three years, progress often being halted by a lack of funds, unsuitable locations, unreliable actors and archaic cameras. The final budget lay somewhere between $5000 and $8000, most of which was footed by the crew, who mainly comprised members of the Video Archives crowd and their friends. One influential newcomer was Rand Vossler, who acted as co-cinematographer (with former Video Outtakes staffer Scott McGill) and overall producer. Rand, the brother of Tarantino's friend Russell, left the project to join McGill in more 'legitimate' film-making for producer/director Don Coscarelli (*Phantasm, Survival Quest*). McGill committed suicide in 1987. Vossler went on to co-produce Oliver Stone's *Natural Born Killers*.

Hamann and Tarantino soldiered on through 1986 and beyond, but early excitement over the quality of their footage turned to bitter disappointment when the final two reels of film were ruined in a laboratory processing accident. Tarantino initially entertained the idea of remounting the film, but Hamann had little enthusiasm left for the project. While acknowledging the value of the experience he gained from directing *My Best Friend's Birthday*, Tarantino now claims to be embarrassed by the results of his work. Aside from the appearance of a brief clip on the BBC's *Omnibus* documentary *Quentin Tarantino: Hollywood's Boy Wonder*, the remaining footage has never been publicly exhibited.

Although *My Best Friend's Birthday* was forgotten, its influence continued to be felt in Tarantino's work for some time. Cast member Rich Turner later appeared as the moustachioed sheriff in the *Reservoir Dogs* public toilet scene and was heard as a sportscaster on Esmarelda's radio in *Pulp Fiction*. Another of the four sheriffs in the *Reservoir Dogs* public toilet scene was played by Stevo Poliy, who appeared in *MBFB* as a DJ. Craig Hamann's voice can be heard as a cop in *Reservoir Dogs*, while Mickey's ex-girlfriend, Linda Kaye, is the 'shocked woman' dragged from her car by Mr Pink. She makes a similarly fleeting appearance in *Pulp Fiction*, shot by Marsellus after Butch's car crash.

More importantly, Tarantino recycled many of the film's dramatic devices for future scripts. The character name Clarence and the idea of hiring a hooker as a birthday present found their way into *True Romance* - as did the comics references (Misty Knight is a character from the Marvel Universe, *True Romance*'s Clarence works in a comics store). Clarence's opening speech about Elvis in *True Romance* also originated in *MBFB*. Mickey lent his name to the serial killer in *Natural Born Killers*, and K-Billy's radio station, seen extensively in *MBFB*, reappears in *Reservoir Dogs*. Finally, the pre-credit sequence, during which Clarence snorts some itching powder believing it to be cocaine, has similarities to Mia's accidental overdose in *Pulp Fiction*.

n

NAMES

'Who cares what your name is?' Mr White tells Mr Pink. 'Who cares if you're Mr Pink, Mr Purple, Mr Pussy, Mr Piss . . .'. Although this statement on the unimportance of names never made it from the *Reservoir Dogs* script into the finished film, the sentiment was echoed by Butch in *Pulp Fiction*. 'I'm an American', he tells Esmarelda,'our names don't mean shit'.

This irreverence may well be a veiled expression of the author's own feelings towards naming his characters - the same names are often attached to totally unrelated protagonists throughout his scripts. There are cases where the reuse of certain names is clearly deliberate - Vic Vega (*Reservoir Dogs*) and Vincent Vega (*Pulp Fiction*) were originally intended to be brothers, the Bonnie mentioned in *True Romance*, *Reservoir Dogs* and *Pulp Fiction* is possibly the same nurse, and the Alabama seen in *True Romance* and mentioned in *Reservoir Dogs* could well be the same 'good little thief'. Elsewhere, however, the unrelated use of certain names are harder to explain. It is feasible that in at least some of these cases, Tarantino simply attaches particular names to particular character types . . .

Alabama Clarence's wife in *True Romance* and Larry's ex-partner in *Reservoir Dogs*.

Bonnie This character is mentioned in the film of *True Romance* , discussed at greater length in the original script of *Reservoir Dogs*, and briefly glimpsed in *Pulp Fiction*.

Clarence The rockabilly in *My Best Friend's Birthday*, and the Elvis-worshipping wide boy of *True Romance*.

Dimick/Dimick Dimick is Larry's surname in the original script of *Reservoir Dogs*, and Dimmick is Jimmie's surname in *Pulp Fiction*.

Earl A redneck knifed by Mickey at the beginning of *Natural Born Killers*, and the Texas ranger shot by Richard at the beginning of *From Dusk Till Dawn*.

Floyd One of Drexl's hapless colleagues and Dick's stoned flatmate in *True Romance*, and the boxer Butch kills in *Pulp Fiction*.

Jacobs/Jacob The former a suspected pseudonym for *Reservoir Dogs*'s Larry Dimick; the latter the Christian name of the disaffected preacher in *From Dusk Till Dawn* (both parts were taken by Harvey Keitel).

Jodie/Jody Jodie is a police computer operator in the original script of *Reservoir Dogs*, and Jody is Lance's body-pierced wife in *Pulp Fiction*.

Joe Nice Guy Eddie's father in *Reservoir Dogs*, and Raquel's father in sequences ultimately cut from *Pulp Fiction*.

Koons Vic Vega's parole officer in the first draft of *Reservoir Dogs*, and the army captain who visits the young Butch in *Pulp Fiction*.

Marcellus/Marcellus Prior to his recent arrest, Marcellus moved Larry's stolen 'ice' in *Reservoir Dogs*. Marsellus is 'The Big Man' in *Pulp Fiction*.

Marvin A television interviewee in *Natural Born Killers*, one of Coccotti's 'wise guys' in the original script of *True Romance*, and the tortured police officer in *Reservoir Dogs*.

McClusky/McCluskey The Chairman of the California Prison Board in *Natural Born Killers*, and the computer operator at Freddy's police headquarters in the original script of *Reservoir Dogs*.

Mickey Mickey Burnett is the hapless character celebrating *My Best Friend's Birthday*, and Mickey Knox is one of the *Natural Born Killers*.

Nash A patrolman murdered by Mickey and Mallory in *Natural Born Killers*, and the cop tortured by Mr Blonde in *Reservoir Dogs*.

Newendyke One of the rioting prisoners in *Natural Born Killers*, and Freddy's surname in *Reservoir Dogs*.

Norman A television interviewee and Arnold Schwarzenegger fan in *Natural Born Killers*, and the loser of Chester's gruesome bet in *Four Rooms: The Man from Hollywood*.

Otis A K-Billy DJ in *My Best Friend's Birthday*, and a redneck pummelled by Mickey and Mallory at the beginning of *Natural Born Killers*.

Pete Chester's fingerless chum in the first draft of *Four Rooms: Penthouse: The Man from Hollywood* (then entitled *Thrill of the Bet*) and a clerk at Benny's World of Liquor in *From Dusk Till Dawn*.

Pool The surname of Clarence in *My Best Friend's Birthday*, and one of the rioting prisoners in *Natural Born Killers*.

Scagnetti A police detective in *Natural Born Killers*, and Vic Vega's 'motherfucker' of a parole officer in *Reservoir Dogs*.

Spivey The surname of drug-pushing pimp Drexl in *True Romance*, one of the rioting prisoners in *Natural Born Killers*, and the surname of Larry's former contact Marcellus in *Reservoir Dogs*.

Vega Vic Vega is the psychotic Mr Blonde in *Reservoir Dogs*, and Vincent Vega is the drug-addicted hitman in *Pulp Fiction*. The first draft of *Pulp Fiction* had Vic Vega in the lead role, but when Michael Madsen declined to reprise his performance the character name was changed. The two men are now intended to be seen as brothers. Inspiration for the surname possibly comes from Tarantino's record collection - folk singer Suzanne Vega is one of the director's favourite musicians.

Vic Although unnamed on screen, 'Tooth-pick' Vic is a member of the squad Coccotti takes to visit Cliff in *True Romance*. 'Tooth-pick' is also Vic Vega's nickname in *Reservoir Dogs*.

Wurlitzer The head IA officer overseeing Elliot's trap in *True Romance*, and the LA County Jail superintendent in *Natural Born Killers*.

Elsewhere, Tarantino borrows the names of friends and colleagues for the characters in his scripts . . .

Big Don Blue Lou Boyle's murdered drug courier in *True Romance* is named after 'Big' Don Watts, the brother of one of Tarantino's mother's friends. Tarantino credits him with originating Cliff's speech about the ancestry of Sicilians.

Dave *Pulp Fiction*'s barman, 'English Dave' (in actual fact an American called Paul) was possibly named after 'Dave the British guy' who once shared a house with Tarantino and Stevo Poliy.

Dov Joe Cabot's unseen accomplice in *Reservoir Dogs* was named after Dov Schwarz, a sound technician friend of Rand Vossler's who once donated a car battery to keep the cameras rolling on *My Best Friend's Birthday*. It is likelier, however, that the inspiration came from one Dov S-S Simens, the self-professed 'greatest film instructor in the history of the universe.' A set of informative audio tapes produced by Simens had a profound motivational effect on Tarantino prior to the production of *Reservoir Dogs*.

Grace The court witness knifed by Mickey in *Natural Born Killers*, and the name of Zed's chopper in *Pulp Fiction*. Grace is the name of Quentin Tarantino's long-time girlfriend.

Heide Vogel In *From Dusk Till Dawn*, it is reported that Heide Vogel, a sixth grade teacher, has been run over by the Gecko

Scagnettis. Is the detective in *Natural Born Killers* (left, played by Tom Sizemore), any relation to the unseen parole officer from *Reservoir Dogs*?

brothers during a high speed pursuit through Wichita. This is presumably after she co-produced *Four Rooms*.

Lance Clarence's boss in *True Romance*, and Vincent's heroin dealer in *Pulp Fiction*. Both characters were named after Lance Lawson, Tarantino's boss at Video Archives (qv); a 'Lawson' also appears in *Crimson Tide* (qv).

Martinez A rioting prisoner in *Natural Born Killers* and Vossler's unseen opponent in a boxing match advertised in *Pulp Fiction*. The characters were named after Tarantino's Video Archives colleague Gerald Martinez. Tarantino's old friend was also the inspiration for the 'Big Jerry Cab Co' logo seen on the side of Esmarelda's taxi. Martinez served as Chief Graphic Designer on *Pulp Fiction*.

'Nice Guy' Eddie Joe Cabot's son in *Reservoir Dogs* was named after 'Nice Guy' Eddie Karpinsky, an occasional employee at the Video Outtakes store where Tarantino rented his tapes in 1983.

Roger The soundman in *Natural Born Killers* was possibly named after Roger Avary, who worked as a crew-member on *My Best Friend's Birthday* and collaborated on *True Romance*, *Natural Born Killers*, *Reservoir Dogs* and *Pulp Fiction*.

Scott The cameraman in *Natural Born Killers*, and Jacob Fuller's adopted son in *From Dusk Till Dawn*. The characters were possibly named after one of two Scotts in Tarantino's life - the late Scott McGill, who collaborated on *Lovebirds in Bondage*, or director Scott Spiegel, who introduced him to future producer Lawrence Bender.

Stevo Bishop's unfortunate colleague at the 7-Eleven store that Mickey and Mallory raid in *Natural Born Killers*. Stevo Poliy was Tarantino's flatmate and friend while they both worked at Video Archives. He appeared in *My Best Friend's Birthday* and *Reservoir Dogs*.

Unruly Julie Wayne Gayle's mute assistant in *Natural Born Killers* is named after 'Unruly' Julie McClean, someone who joined the staff at Video Archives after Tarantino left. Julie McClean can be spotted as 'Left Redhead' at a party in *Four Rooms*.

Vossler Russell Vossler is a Harvard law student interviewed by Wayne Gayle in *Natural Born Killers*; another Russell Vossler is the communications op in *Crimson Tide* (qv). Vossler is the surname of one of the contenders in the boxing match that preceded Butch's fight in *Pulp Fiction*, and the room where Marsellus is raped in the Mason-Dixon pawnshop is referred to as 'Russell's old room'. Russell Vossler was one of Tarantino's colleagues at Video Archives, and was credited as Character Artist on *Pulp Fiction*. His brother, Rand, produced *My Best Friend's Birthday* and *Natural Born Killers*.

Zastoupil Dr Zastoupil is Laura's GP in *Past Midnight* (qv); Zastoupil is Tarantino's mother's surname (see Knoxville, Tennessee).

NATURAL BORN KIILLERS
(See appendix)

NICE GUY EDDIE
The yuppie of the *Reservoir Dogs* pack belongs to the generation that regards the Seventies as nostalgia and is never seen anywhere without a mobile phone. 'Nice Guy' Eddie Cabot's manner is as loud and brash as his taste in shell suits, his personality hallmarked by traits of ruthlessness, racism and anti-semitism.

'You know, all things considered, this was pretty successful', Eddie tells Mr White, estimating the value of the stolen diamonds as over $2 million in a sequence cut from the film. Unfortunately, the 'all things considered' include the death of two members of the gang, the fatal wounding of Mr Orange and

the massacre of the cops and customers foolish enough to get in the robbers' way. Eddie dismisses these complicating factors as callously as he shoots the tortured Marvin Nash on his return to the warehouse. He is unmoved by Mr Orange's protestations about Mr Blonde's behaviour towards the policeman. 'Who cares what he was gonna do to this fuckin' pig?'

Eddie is a key middle man in his father Joe's organisation. Liaising with his daddy and the unseen Dov, he arrives at the warehouse to assess the post-robbery situation, later leaving Mr Orange and Marvin in the care of Mr Blonde. Nice Guy has a lot of friends in low places - he has worked with Larry (Mr White) before and is able to convince Bonnie to nurse the dying Mr Orange until a doctor can be found. Eddie's devotion to his father is rivalled

only by his loyalty to Vic Vega (Mr Blonde). Their friendship is strong enough to withstand Eddie's taunts about Vic's supposed homosexual rape and a resulting play fight. Eddie sets Vic up with a covering job as a dock worker in Long Beach (perhaps with Freddy's dubious character reference, 'Long Beach Mike'?) and initiates his involvement in the robbery. Eddie's faith in Vega is so unshakeable that Mr Orange's accusations about Mr Blonde's plans immediately plant seeds of suspicion. These seeds of suspicion, and Eddie's loyalty to his father, lead to his undoing. (In 1996, Britpop *arrivistes* Sleeper released *Nice Guy Eddie*, the second single from thir album, *The It Girl*, presumably in tribute).

(See also: Names; Penn, Chris; Race; Suits; Trust and betrayal; Yuppie scum)

Mickey and Mallory Knox, the *Natural Born Killers*.

O

OLDMAN, GARY (1958 -)
Drexl Spivey, *True Romance*

London-born actor, the son of a welder; his second marriage was to Uma Thurman (qv). After graduating with a BA in Theatre Arts from the Rose Buford College of Speech and Drama in 1979, Oldman learned his craft on stage at the Greenwich Young Peoples' Theatre. In 1983, he appeared in the largely improvised Mike Leigh Film on Four, *Meantime*, alongside Tim Roth (qv; he would later resume his on-screen relationship with Roth in 1990's arthouse two-hander, *Rosencrantz and Guildenstern Are Dead*). Oldman's first major film appearance was as the hapless, hopeless, helpless Sid Vicious in Alex Cox's 1986 biopic, *Sid and Nancy*; his next lead role - as gay play-wright Joe Orton in Stephen Frears's 1987 *Prick Up Your Ears* - resurrected yet another doomed pop culture icon. He leaped at the chance to play repulsive white Rasta Drexl in *True Romance* - 'I've always wanted to play a pimp because I liked Harvey Keitel [qv] so much in *Taxi Driver*', he told *Premiere* - and spent a mere five days on set. 'I loved the whole cocktail of it, and playing a part like Drexl, I thought I could exercise my tool, lubricate my tool. Drexl is very high energy. It's a firework display - just light the fuse and

I'm a rocket.' Drexl's voice was partly based on that of a security guard whom Oldman had encountered on the set of *Romeo Is Bleeding* (a film in which he featured alongside Juliette Lewis [qv]). With much of his first scene cut (see Jackson, Samuel L), Oldman received mixed reviews for *True Romance* - *Sight and Sound* called his casting 'audacious and ridiculous'. He also claims that, in the light of the number of scripts by Quentin wannabes foisted upon him ever since, 'Tarantino has done such a disservice to young writers'. Other credits include: *We Think the World of You* (1988), *Criminal Law* (1988), *Chattahoochee* [with Dennis Hopper, qv] (1989), *JFK* [director Oliver Stone, qv] (1991), *Bram Stoker's Dracula* (1992), *Leon* (1995), *Murder in the First* [with Christian Slater, qv] (1995).

OPEN ROAD, THE

Video Archives clerk Roger Avary (qv) wrote *The Open Road*, a script that would prove ultimately crucial to Tarantino's career, in 1985. It concerned a comic store worker writing a road movie about a pair or rampaging serial killers. Throughout the course of the story, however, the would-be writer finds his life developing along alarmingly similar lines.

Reservoir Dogs: Mr Orange bleeds to death. Mr White considers his options.

In 1987, an impressed Tarantino offered to develop the script when Avary lost interest in the project. With the help of fellow Video Archives colleague Craig Hamann, Tarantino set to work on the story. Soon, its burgeoning length proved such a problem that he split the story in two, taking the fictional serial killers, Mickey and Mallory, into an independent story of their own. Initially concentrating on the other half of the story, Tarantino blended elements of *My Best Friend's Birthday* into the remaining storyline and *True Romance* was born. Although the new script bore little relation to *The Open Road*, *True Romance* contained much of Avary's work in amongst Clarence and Alabama's tale of love on the run. Avary would belatedly return to the project to supplement the film version's screenplay some six years later.

ORANGE (FREDDY NEWENDYKE)

Reservoir Dogs's Freddy Newendyke, alias Mr Orange, is an idealistic young cop who takes an enormous risk in infiltrating Joe Cabot's squad of jewel thieves. He is given the job of guarding the doorway of Karina's during the robbery, ensuring that no-one leaves or enters. The deception is so carefully cultivated that the only clue we receive about his real role within the gang occurs when he rats on Mr Pink for not tipping the waitress. Elsewhere, we discover little about Freddy - we learn he has a notorious sense of humour, numbers DIY and comic collecting amongst his hobbies (the unimpeachable *Silver Surfer* is a natural favourite), wears a wedding ring and hangs a silver crucifix on the wall of his apartment. A strong code of personal morality makes him patently unsuited to the task in hand. While an excellent liar, Freddy is unable to disguise his self-loathing after defending himself against the female driver who shoots him. When he kills her in a momentary lapse of reason he reveals the same signs of mortification he feels at the death of Mr Brown.

Freddy's LAPD backup is fully established in Tarantino's original script. The cop is seen relaxing in his apartment, flipping through a series of mug shots until he finds one of Mr White - real name Lawrence Dimick. Freddy discovers more at the police station - and at a meeting with fellow officer Jodie McCluskey, who fills him in on Larry's violent criminal history. In the film, Freddy's police contact is restricted to clandestine meetings with officer Holdaway, and involves a series of intensive acting lessons which help fabricate Freddy's assumed identity as a drugs dealer. While Freddy succeeds in becoming as 'naturalistic as hell', it is his incredible tenacity that makes him ultimately convincing. Even after being fatally wounded, he is able to feign unconsciousness while Mr Blonde is torturing Marvin and later shoots the psychotic killer as he prepares to 'pull a burn'. Even though he is bleeding to death, Freddy exaggerates his plight in the back of the stolen car Mr White is driving. He elicits considerable sympathy from Mr White - and uses the opportunity to confirm the criminal's first name.

Mr White is one of Freddy's earliest criminal contacts, and a father/son relationship soon develops between the two men. Mr White takes the younger man under his wing, specially advising him on crowd control, and risks his life defending him against Joe and Nice Guy Eddie. Such is the strength of Mr Orange's loyalty that, once the triangular shoot-out is over, he feels he must reciprocate Mr White's trust. He gives him the only thing he has left - the truth: 'I'm a cop, Larry. I'm so sorry, I'm a cop.' These prove to be his last words.

(See also: Morality; Names; Roth, Tim; Trust and betrayal)

p

PAST MIDNIGHT
(US, 1991, dir. Jan Eliasberg)

In late 1990, *True Romance*'s tortuous development path took one step closer to production. Hoping to direct the film, Bill Lustig (previously responsible for *Relentless* and *Maniac Cop*) brought the script, and its author, to the attention of production company Cinetel.

Intending to commence shooting in 1991, the company first hired Tarantino to undertake an extensive rewrite on Frank Norwood's script for a forthcoming thriller, *Past Midnight*. With the encouragement of CineTel staffer Catalaine Knell, Tarantino overhauled the script - much to the alleged dismay of Norwood, director Jan Eliasberg and star Rutger Hauer.

Past Midnight concerns a social worker, Laura Matthews (Natasha Richardson) and her growing confusion over client Ben Jordan (Rutger Hauer). In 1975 Jordan is arrested for the murder of his heavily pregnant wife - an event largely captured on silent 8mm film by the murderer. Fifteen years later he is released, and sent to Matthews who helps him find employment. To the alarm of her friends and colleagues, Matthews pores over the serial killer's footage and becomes convinced that

Jordan, who is never actually seen in any of the murder films, was wrongly imprisoned. She falls in love with Jordan, and becomes pregnant with his child. Her sexual relationship hampers an investigation already complicated by prejudice, self doubt, and the violent intervention of an unseen assailant.

Despite compelling performances from Hauer and Richardson, *Past Midnight* is an unremarkable mystery that draws upon *Peeping Tom* (1960) and *Jagged Edge* (1985) for much of its suspense. Although Tarantino's input was extensive, the reported reluctance of Rutger Hauer and director Jan Eliasberg to implement elements of his dialogue mean that few characteristic touches are still in evidence. Some interesting snippets nevertheless remain: 'Maybe Jordan just isn't a natural born killer', argues policeman Lee Samuels, suggesting that murder didn't come easy to the suspect. Elsewhere, Jordan compares his IQ to that of Ted Bundy (in *Natural Born Killers*, Mickey Knox compares his television ratings to those garnered by the serial killer). In rewriting the script, Tarantino took the liberty of naming Laura Matthews's GP after his mother - it is Dr Zastoupil who breaks the unwelcome news that her patient is pregnant.

Genius at work: a grizzled
Sam Peckinpah framing
*Pat Garrett and Billy the
Kid* (1973).

Never theatrically released, *Past Midnight* first
appeared on cable television in the US, and
went straight to video in the UK. Tarantino
was granted an on-screen credit as 'associate
producer' alongside his friend Catalaine Knell.

(See also: Foot fetishism; Knoxville, Tennessee)

PECKINPAH, SAM (1925-1984)

Principally notorious for two visceral medita-
tions on violence, 1969's *The Wild Bunch* and
1971's *Straw Dogs*, writer/director Sam
Peckinpah's bloody legacy can be seen in
several Tarantino moments.

Peckinpah's career was forged scripting Fifties
television Western serials; he soon graduated
to the cinema, working occasionally for director Don Siegel. In 1961, he wrote the first
draft screenplay for Brando's *One-Eyed Jacks* -
yet another Tarantino enthusiasm - embarking
thereafter upon a fully-fledged directorial
career with that year's *The Deadly Companions*
and his masterpiece, 1962's *Ride The High
Country* (aka *Guns in the Afternoon*).

As a child, Tarantino was taken by his mother
to see *The Wild Bunch* as half of a double-bill
with John Boorman's *Deliverance* (qv; a film,
incidentally, Peckinpah was once slated to
direct). It's been noted elsewhere that the
gang members's slo-mo stroll to camera
under the *Reservoir Dogs* titles would appear
to be a nod in the direction of the similar
strut adopted by the remaining four members
of Pike Bishop's Bunch as they prepare to take
on certain death at the hands of General
Mapache's 250 soldiers in the climax to
Peckinpah's film (note that the latter scene is
immediately preceded by Bishop's snarled
'Let's go!'). The Bunch and the Dogs share a
similar composition - a seasoned perpetrator
who finds his moral sense to be flawed, and is
prepared to die in order to justify himself
(Bishop/White); a younger, idealistic outsider
whose betrayal of the gang's contract with
Mapache/Joe Cabot fuels both films' bloody
finales (Angel/Orange); cannon fodder for
the original heist (note that both the man
Bishop 'puts down' and Brown have been
temporarily blinded by blood in their respective flights from the scene); a 'psycho' who
goes trigger-happy in the bank (Crazy
Lee/Blonde); and shallow, reprehensible 'professionals', concerned mostly for their cut of
the spoils (The Gorches/Pink). More substantially, key themes of trust, betrayal and
redemption which power many Peckinpah
narratives are reprised, especially, in both
Dogs and *Pulp Fiction*: the *Wild Bunch* line, 'I
go with you, Jefe. When you side with a man
you stick with him' closely resembles the sentiments which underscore Captain Koons's 'pit
of hell' speech in *Pulp*. And critic Paul Seydor
- quoted in David Weddle's Peckinpah biography, *If They Move . . . Kill 'Em!* - comments
that the active question underlining (particularly) *Ride The High Country* is, 'What does it
profit a man to gain the world if he loses his
soul?' - which pertinently rationalises the
gory, self-determined apotheoses of both
Bishop and White (and perhaps, also, explains
Pumpkin's willingness to back down in the

Pulp climax after seeing the supernatural contents of Marsellus's 666-coded briefcase).

The memorable and extraordinarily violent farmhouse siege which concludes *Straw Dogs* sees David Sumner (Dustin Hoffmann) and wife Amy (Susan George) fend off a posse of blood-baying rural Cornish vigilantes by a variety of means: boiling liquid is thrown into a face, someone is shot in the foot, and Amy is forced to coldly execute the last of the aggressors with a shotgun. These core elements are all present in *True Romance*'s Virgil/Alabama scene, with some adjustment: for boiling oil, read ignited hairspray, and a corkscrew, rather than a bullet, penetrates the foot. The shotgun-blows-off-toes motif is also reprised in Roger Avary's *Killing Zoe* (qv). *Straw Dogs*'s central theme - that even the most apparently civilised of men can be pushed to commit the most terrible violence - might be echoed in the 'liberation' of the odious Wayne Gale towards the end of *NBK*.

Tarantino and Peckinpah's names are often linked: both - justified or not - have become synonyms for film violence. Tarantino plays down Peckinpah's alleged influence, but much contained in 1972's *The Getaway* would appear to countermand his denials. Released from an *NBK*-style prison at the behest of a corrupt businessman, Beynon, Doc McCoy (Steve McQueen) takes charge of a bank heist Beynon has planned. McCoy and his wife, Carol (Ali McGraw), are assigned two back-up men, Rudy Butler (Al Lettieri) and Frank Jackson: the latter unnecessarily kills a bank guard at the heist and is in turn executed by Butler, who plans to take the money for himself. The McCoys escape Butler with the $500,000 proceeds; Butler shadows them as they flee for the Mexican border . . .

The Getaway, then, is a heist movie which mutates into a 'love-on-the-run' melodrama akin to *Badlands* (qv): *True Romance*, perhaps, via *Reservoir Dogs*. Comparisons to the latter

are legion: the gang assemble at a restaurant to plan the robbery of a 'walk-in' bank: 'You don't have to be Dillinger for that, man,' remarks Butler. 'Dillinger got killed,' McCoy reminds him (see Tierney, Lawrence). At the First Bank of Beacon City, 'psycho' Jackson starts the shooting *à la* Blonde; afterwards, McCoy changes, sporting thereafter a black suit, white shirt, black tie - and he carries the loot in a battered leather holdall. Even more strangely, the wounded Butler pursues the McCoys with the enforced assistance of husband and wife hostages Harold and Fran Clinton: en route, the flighty Fran's allegiance switches to her captor. Harold is tied to a chair and, like Marvin the Cop, is tortured - he is forced to endure the sight of Fran and Butler making love before his gaze (later, he kills himself). And, like the Worleys in *True Romance*, the lovers plan to flee to Mexico (as do both *From Dusk Till Dawn*'s Gecko brothers and Pike Bishop's *Bunch*); again, like the Worleys, the McCoys finally confront their various nemeses during a three-way shoot-out inside an hotel.

Trust, honour, redemption, guns, and blood: in Tarantino's men, especially, we see descendants of Peckinpah's tormented protagonists. 'That's the trouble with this goddamned world,' remarks a truck driver at the climax of *The Getaway*. 'There ain't no morals . . .'

(See also: *City on Fire*)

PENN, CHRIS (1958 -)
Nice Guy Eddie, *Reservoir Dogs*
Nicky Dimes, *True Romance*

The son of writer-director Leo, and younger brother to Sean. (Sean was formerly married to Madonna; as Nice Guy Eddie, Chris joins in a perhaps rather less than proper discussion of his erstwhile sister-in-law's sexual persona in *Reservoir Dogs*). Penn has been acting since the age of 12; he studied his craft at LA's Loft Studio. He made his first major film appearance in 1983's *Rumble Fish*, alongside Dennis Hopper (qv); in 1985, he appeared in *At Close Range* playing the younger brother to brother Sean's character (the film also featured Christopher Walken, qv). Once cast in *Dogs*, it was Penn who nominated his friend Eddie Bunker (qv) as a potential Blue. Director Tony Scott had originally intended that Steve Buscemi (qv) should play either Dimes or Elliot in *True Romance*; Penn was quickly recruited as doomed Detective Dimes when Buscemi passed on the roles. Scott's original intention that Dimes should be killed by Alabama was altered at the insistence of the Motion Picture Association of America's censors; Dimes would have to be shot by one of the Italians (see X-rated). Offered a role in *Natural Born Killers* by director Oliver Stone (qv), Penn refused. Other credits include: *Footloose* (1984), *Pale Rider* (1985), *Mobsters* [with Christian Slater, qv] (1991), *Short Cuts* (1993), *To Wong Foo, Thanks For Everything, Julie Newmar* (1995), *Mulholland Falls* [with Michael Madsen, editor Sally Menke, both qv] (1995), *Funeral* [with Christopher Walken, qv] (1996).

PINCHOT, BRONSON (1959 -)
Elliot Blitzer, *True Romance*

Once a regular in US TV series *Perfect Strangers*, Bronson Alcott Pinchot has latterly been seen as recurring villain Kyle Griffin, aka *The Prankster*, in *Lois and Clark*, aka *The New Adventures of Superman*. Regarding the role of hapless, hopeless Hollywood PA Elliott - a part Steve Buscemi (qv) had been considered for - Pinchot told writer Jami Bernard in her book, *Quentin Tarantino: The Man and his Movies*: 'You were supposed to cheer when [Elliott] died . . . [Director] Tony Scott said to me that devilishly, mischievously, surreptitiously and quietly I had construed a character who is sympathetic...' (Scott's original intention had been to have Elliott's head blown off his shoulders and fly across the hotel suite). Other credits include: *Risky Business* (1983),

Beverly Hills Cop (1984), *After Hours* [with Rosanna Arquette and Dick Miller, both qv] (1985), *Blame It On the Bellboy* [see Hotels, qv] (1992).

(See also: Yuppie scum)

PINK

In *Reservoir Dogs*, Nice Guy Eddie shares his enthusiasm for Seventies music with Mr Pink, a friend of his father's since childhood. This slight, goatee-bearded veteran works with Mr White to wrest the diamonds from the manager of Karina's, shooting his way out and hijacking a car when everything goes wrong.

Mr Pink is perhaps the most reprehensible character in Joe Cabot's line-up. As if his constant whining wasn't enough (most famously over his allocation of code name) the list of his character defects seems never-ending - he refuses to tip waitresses on principle, is overtly racist in accusing his colleagues of bickering 'like fucking niggers', regards cops as cannon fodder because they're not 'real people', dismisses the dying Mr Orange, changes sides during an argument between Mr White and Mr Blonde primarily to suit himself and relishes beating the bound Marvin Nash - even though he clearly doesn't know how to throw a punch.

Despite all this Mr Pink proves himself the most professional criminal in the gang. While his volatile temperament prevents him from seeing through the cold logic of his reasoning, he is uniquely successful in escaping the scene of the crime with any diamonds, later having the good sense to hide the bag before returning to the warehouse. 'I stashed it till I could be sure this place wasn't a police station', he tells Eddie.

It is a keen sense of self-preservation that sees Pink as the only character to escape the warehouse alive, although he skulks away from the triangular shoot-out straight into the waiting policemen. Whether that sense of self-preservation is keen enough to avert a lengthy jail sentence is never discovered.

(See also: Buscemi, Steve; Morality; Race)

PLUMMER, AMANDA (1957 -)
Honey Bunny, *Pulp Fiction*

The daughter of thespians Christopher Plummer and Tammy Grimes, New Yorker Plummer studied theatre at the Neighborhood Playhouse, marking time as - variously - an usherette, a jockey, and a switchboard operator. A noted and award-winning presence on Broadway led to her film debut in Universal's 1981 *Cattle Annie and Little Britches*; many quirky supporting roles, in such as *The World According to Garp* and *The Hotel New Hampshire*, followed. She joined the *Pulp* gang

at the instigation of Tim Roth (qv), with whom she'd appeared in a student short. Roth had apparently suggested to Tarantino that they'd make a fine gun-toting pairing; the notion stuck. Noted also for her stint in TV series *LA Law*, her other credits include: *Joe Versus the Volcano* (1990), *The Fisher King* (1991), *So I Married an Axe Murderer* (1993), *Butterfly Kiss* (1995).

PULP

'A magazine or book containing lurid subject matter . . .'

Tarantino's well-documented love affair with 'hardboiled' crime fiction has persistently underlined themes, characters and situations in his screenplays. This literary sub-genre is usually credited as having commenced in the early Twenties with America's *Black Mask*. 'The

'It ain't the giggle it used to be. Too many foreigners own liquor stores': Honey Bunny (Amanda Plummer) and Pumpkin (Tim Roth) review their careers.

He-Man's Magazine', *Black Mask* was a Depression-influenced mass-market short story anthology which published early works by such as Dashiell Hammett, Carroll John Daly and Raoul Whitfield, and introduced the original 'private dicks' (Hammett's Sam Spade, and Race Williams, Daly's proto-Mike Hammer). *Pulp Fiction*'s 'jumping-off point was *Black Mask*', confirmed Tarantino in 1994. 'Of course, it's not like *Black Mask* at all now, but that was the starting point.' In fact, Tarantino and Roger Avary's original 1989-90 conception of what would later become *Pulp* - a strictly regimented, tripartite anthology of overdone pulp premises with a modern twist, including Avary's *Pandemonium Reigns* and a much shorter version of Tarantino's *Dogs* - initially bore the title *Black Mask*. Post-WWII, with the ascendancy of the cheap paperback pocket book and publishing companies such as Gold Medal, Ace, Signet and Dell, the hardboiled genre became predominantly associated with the novel: texts such as Kenneth Fearing's *The Big Clock*, Geoffrey Homes's *Build My Gallows High*, and works by Raymond Chandler, James M Cain and the obligatory Hammett posited the urban USA as a violent, brutal dystopia, and its practitioners soon became a target for the attentions of Senator Joseph McCarthy's UnAmerican Activities Committee. This strand would, thanks to the 1941 collision between Gregg Toland's deep focus cinematography for *Citizen Kane* and the themes in John Huston's oblique version of Hammett's *The Maltese Falcon*, give rise to a new genre of cinema: *film noir*, whose *femmes fatales* - Lana Turner, Rita Hayworth, Barbara Stanwyck *et al* - would later find expression in their archetypal grand-daughter, Uma Thurman's objectified and oh-so-dangerous Mia Wallace. Significantly, too, black novelist Chester Himes would accrue a reputation as a writer of angry, polemicised hardboiled fiction during this era; Himes's *Cotton Comes to Harlem* would later be instrumental in defining the early Seventies blaxploitation boom, another genre dear to Tarantino. Reactionary, explicitly right-wing

writers such as Mickey Spillane, creator of anti-hero Mike Hammer, rose to prominence during the Cold War post-McCarthy: the Fifties would also publish writers such as Dolores Hitchens, Jim Thompson and Lionel White, notable for having inspired some of Tarantino's directorial idols to make movies which would massively inform his work. Hitchens's *Fool's Gold* was adapted by Jean-Luc Godard (qv) to become his 1964 *Bande a Part*; White's *Obsession* became *Pierrot le Fou*, made by Godard the following year; and, in 1956, White's *Clean Slate* was adapted, with input from Thompson, as Stanley Kubrick's *The Killing*, with all its attendant bearing upon *Reservoir Dogs*.

Note also that Tarantino allegedly read Leigh Brackett's *No Good From a Corpse* while writing the *Pulp* screenplay. Brackett, a woman, had been a preferred screenwriter of director Howard Hawks's (she had a hand in both *The Big Sleep* and *Rio Bravo*, this latter Tarantino's favourite film of all time). The latter-day (post-Fifties) school of hardboiled writers include Tarantino favourites such as Elmore Leonard (qv) and Charles Willeford, whose novel *The Cockfighter* was filmed by Monte Hellman in 1974. 'I don't do neo-*noir*', says Tarantino. 'I see *Pulp Fiction* as closer to modern-day crime fiction, a little closer to Charles Willeford . . . [who] is doing his own thing with his own characters, creating a whole environment and a whole family . . . My stuff so far has definitely fallen into what I consider pulp fiction. I think *Reservoir Dogs* fits in that, *True Romance* fits in that . . . *Pulp* sneaked in through the cracks, it was made for a certain brand of reader. The pulps weren't put under any kind of critical light except in retrospect.'

(See also: Dialogue; Heist movies; *Kiss Me Deadly*)

PULP FICTION
(See appendix)

q

QUARTERPOUNDERS

'One minute they're havin' a Denver Omelette, next minute someone's stickin' a gun in their face' - Pumpkin, *Pulp Fiction*.

Food, and places to eat it in, are integral elements in the lives of Tarantino's characters. While film-makers before him traditionally relied on such locations as bars to establish characters and develop their relationships, Tarantino rarely has his characters drink, preferring instead to sit them in a donut shop, pancake house, burger bar, coffee shop or a diner as the ideal setting for plot and character exposition. In keeping with the predominance of naturalistic dialogue, the proliferation of such an everyday indulgence as food goes some way towards fostering the audience's empathy for his characters.

Some of the most important sequences of character exposition are conducted over meals. 'I love to get pie after a movie', *True Romance*'s Alabama tells Clarence, and the couple's mutual attraction burgeons over a few slices in Rae's Diner. Mickey and Mallory are similarly introduced to us in a diner at the beginning of *Natural Born Killers*, the pie motif again explored as Mickey asks what kinds are on the menu. From the wide selection offered, he opts

for the bright green key lime, despite the waitress's warning that 'it's an acquired taste'. Uncle Bob's Pancake House is the location for the lengthy pre-credits sequence of *Reservoir Dogs*. Immediately prior to the jewellery heist, the gang are treated to breakfast by Joe Cabot. The setting of a shared meal is again employed by Tarantino as an opportunity for us to glimpse each character before the gang, and the narrative, are fractured. Later in the film, when Holdaway (the only principal not present in the pancake house at the beginning) is first seen, he is introduced in a diner, digging into 'a bacon, cheese and avocado burger'.

Fast food is employed elsewhere as a yardstick or comparative in everyday conversation. When Mr White attacks Mr Pink for not tipping his waitress, he tells him 'This is a hard job'. Pink retorts, 'So's working at McDonald's, but you don't feel the need to tip them do you?' In *Pulp Fiction*, Lance takes exception to Vincent's suggestion that his heroin may not be up to the same standard as the narcotics on sale in Holland. 'I'll take the Pepsi challenge with that Amsterdam shit any ol' day of the fuckin' week,' he tells him. 'That's a bold statement,' says Vincent. Towards the end of the film, when Pumpkin and Honey Bunny confront Jules in

Dogs food:

the predators feast.

(where else?) a diner, Jules spares Pumpkin's life, telling him, 'Normally both your asses would be dead as fuckin' fried chicken.' Most famously, Vincent expounds the difference between Europe and the USA by describing the variations in cheeseburger culture between the two continents. 'You know what they call a quarterpounder with cheese in Paris? . . . They call it a "Royale with cheese".' 'What do they call a Whopper?' Jules enquires. 'I don't know,' Vincent replies. 'I didn't go in Burger King.'

Characters who enjoy a special fondness for donuts include Wayne Gale's right hand man Roger. The absence of his chocolate cream-filled donuts tempts him to add a Mexican store owner to the already considerable list of casualties in *Natural Born Killers*. In *Pulp Fiction*, Marsellus is returning from the donut store near Butch's apartment when he 'bumps into' his old friend. Needless to say, events overtake him and he doesn't get the chance to enjoy his take-away. Finally, Chester Rush has a special request of the Mon Signor Hotel's room service. 'A donut,' he beams, taking the snack from Ted. 'That's for me.'

Elsewhere, fast food is less significant but nonetheless prolific - Clarence makes several visits to buy hamburgers, cops Gerald and Dale are parked outside Alfie's Donuts when they are attacked in *Natural Born Killers*, Mr Blonde brings a fast-food Coke back to the warehouse and Vincent's death is synchronised with the arrival of a pair of toaster pastries. In keeping with the imaginary brand of cigarettes Tarantino has his characters smoke (see Red Apple), Brett in *Pulp Fiction*, Chester in *Four Rooms* and Seth in *From Dusk Till Dawn* buy their fast food from 'Big Kahuna Burger'. Jules approves - 'If you like burgers, give 'em a try some time.'

Precisely why Tarantino consistently serves up food as a controlling image deserves speculation: throughout *Pulp Fiction* especially, conspicuous consumption underlines virtually every key scene, suggesting that the young *auteur* is attempting to construct an allegory above and beyond merely the use of a common cultural vocabulary shared between his viewers and his characters. Predatory desires are suggested in Jules's appropriation of Brett's Big Kahuna breakfast; hawk-like, he swoops to deprive a creature lower in the pecking-order/food chain than he - first of his burger, next of his life (likewise, in *Dogs*, Mr Blonde's feral tendencies are pre-empted by his detour for a snack). In *Pulp*, Vincent and Mia's dinner-date is loaded with an appetite far beyond that which can be satisfied in their stomachs alone: Vincent's carnality is surely emphasised by his choice of a bloody steak, and no cod-Freudian analysis

would miss the opportunity to establish an iconographic link between Mia's vanilla milk-shake and semen (particularly given Mrs Wallace's playfulness with her straw). Fabienne's desire for homely blueberry pancakes might reflect a little girl's desire to run home to Mom and Pop (or Knoxville, anyhow); Butch's lust for toaster pastries signals - and literally triggers - his lust for blood. Later/earlier, the psychological rift between Jules and Vincent is heavily signposted by their disagreement on the ethics of pork consumption. And surely no clearer indication of this tendency is given than in the pet-names granted to one another by Tarantino's two loved-up stick-up artistes? As 'Pumpkin' and 'Honey [Bunny]'s hunger for easy money is ignited, so too is their hunger for one another ('I love you, Pumpkin.' 'I love you too, Honey Bunny'). However, it is Big Don, in *True Romance*, who makes the sex/food link as explicit as can be: 'I eat the pussy. I eat the butt. I eat every motherfuckin' thang.' A more political interpretation of Tarantino's food preoccupations would note that his 'trash' characters, between mouthfuls of junk food, spout references to pulp culture, often retiring to 'waste'/be wasted by others (cf *Reservoir Dogs*'s opening scene). Is this, therefore, an elaborate critique of the inherent worthlessness of American consumer culture in the late twentieth century? Pop, after all, will eat itself . . .

r

RACE

'You know what you've done?' an admirer
told Tarantino after *Reservoir Dogs* was first
screened at the 1992 Sundance Festival.
'You've given white boys the kind of movies
black kids get.' Tarantino's directorial debut,
with its reverential stance towards Pam Grier
(qv)and authoritarian black cop Holdaway certainly betrayed its director's enthusiasm for the
stars and style of early Seventies blaxploitation
(qv) movies. Whether this proved a strong
enough counterbalance for the racist sneerings
of such characters as Joe, Nice Guy Eddie and
Mr Pink remained debatable in some quarters.
'You fucking guys are acting like a bunch of
fucking niggers,' Mr Pink tells the squabbling
Mr White and Mr Blonde. 'You worked with
niggers, huh? Just like you two - always saying
they're gonna kill each other.'

The racism the characters in *True Romance* display is principally directed towards the Sicilian
gangsters, or 'wops', who trail Clarence and
Alabama. Most famously explored in Cliff's
protracted taunting of Coccotti ('here's a
fact . . . Sicilians were spawned by niggers')
the potentially controversial tone of such dialogue was overshadowed by the violence in
Tony Scott's film.

The issue of racism only really came to a head
in *Pulp Fiction*. Whereas previous scripts had
seen liberal use of the word 'nigger' by white
racists and a white character who considered
himself black (*True Romance*'s Drexl), *Pulp
Fiction* featured the first prolific use of the
insult by leading black characters. Jules and
Marsellus's frequent use of the word 'nigger'
significantly defuses its racial overtones. 'No
word should have so much power', Tarantino
told *Village Voice*'s Lisa Kennedy in 1994. 'I kind
of refuse to deal with it as this white guy talking about black guys or a black wannabe guy or
a white wannabe black guy thing. In my heart
of hearts I know where I'm coming from.'

Although *Pulp Fiction* featured racist characters
such as heroin dealer Lance ('Am I a nigger?'
he indignantly asks Vincent. 'White people
who know the difference . . . this is the house
they come to.') it is the portrayal of blacks that
nagged at *Village Voice*'s Devon Jackson. 'In
essence, Tarantino uses blacks the way Arizona
Cardinals football coach Buddy Ryan does: as
men who are big, cool, macho, not to be
fucked with, able to wreak havoc on folk
because it's in their "nigger" genes . . .
Tarantino can say "nigger" all he wants, but
until he really comes to terms with race and

racial issues . . . [he's] not really saying much of anything.'

It is clearly simple-minded to assume that Tarantino sympathises with the racist characters in his scripts. The fact that race is never pushed to the forefront of his films (for example, the intriguing origin of Mia and Marsellus's interracial marriage is never divulged in *Pulp Fiction*) reveals nothing more than a reluctance to tackle it as a political or dramatic issue. Its presence can be better explained as another element in the director's 'cool by numbers' approach to film-making - an element borrowed from blaxploitation sitting alongside elements taken from the cinema of Hong Kong or Japan. The racial stereotypes paid homage to in characters such as Jules and Marsellus have their roots in a genre that celebrated its characters' blackness and portrayed them as powerful, influential figures. The fact that other, overtly racist characters, proliferate in Tarantino's scripts is an issue that looks unlikely to be forgotten by future critics and may continue to muddy the water.

Samuel L Jackson, who played *Pulp Fiction*'s Jules, remains on Tarantino's side over the issue: 'Oh Quentin, he's above that shit.'

RED APPLE

Characters in early Tarantino scripts favour Chesterfields as their preferred smoke. 'Could I have one of those Chesterfields now?' asks Cliff of his torturer Coccotti in *True Romance*. It proves to be the condemned man's final request. In *Reservoir Dogs*, Mr White asks an agitated Mr Pink, 'Want a smoke?' and produces a packet of Chesterfields. Despite having apparently quit, Mr Pink finds it impossible to resist. Stress might account for this lapse, but the chance of gaining something for nothing also fits with the character's make-up.

The careful and protracted preparation of *Pulp Fiction* gave Tarantino the opportunity to rein-

force his genre 'neverland' with a number of imaginary brands for his characters to consume. Among these were the curiously named 'Red Apple' cigarettes bought by Butch in Sally LeRoy's ($1.40 for twenty) and carried by Mia to Jack Rabbit Slim's. The packet's lurid design featured a cheeky motif of a grinning maggot emerging from a fresh apple with a cigarette clinched between its teeth.

The custom-made cigarettes briefly reappeared in *Four Rooms*, the distraught bellboy Ted keeping a packet nearby to calm his increasingly frayed nerves. It's possible that we also briefly catch sight of a pack of the same brand when Johnny Destiny first arrives at the Casino in *Destiny Turns On The Radio* (qv). The references to Big Kahuna Burger in *Pulp Fiction* and *Four Rooms* similarly helped ensure that 'real world' references rarely infringed on the films' genre-contrived characters and situations.

REDEMPTION

Reservoir Dogs and *Pulp Fiction*, while sharing many aesthetic similarities, remain diametrically opposed in their differing sub-texts. The characters in *Reservoir Dogs* are preoccupied with, or victims of, revenge. Most of Joe's gang are seeking vengeance over the 'rat' who betrayed them to the police. Even Mr Orange, the undercover policeman, is a state avenger against the perpetrators of crime. While the theme of revenge motivates certain characters in *Pulp Fiction*, the film is more obviously concerned with the journeys its characters make to earn or learn redemption. '*Pulp Fiction* is ultimately a film about forgiveness and mercy, albeit in a hard and brutal world,' Tarantino claimed upon its release. 'Things seem to be building to an explosion, but every incident ends with forgiveness or compromise or a shaking of hands.'

The *Vincent Vega and Marsellus Wallace's Wife* segment literally does end with the couple shaking hands, Mia having learnt the folly of her decadence after being pulled back from the brink. Mia almost dies, and is seen to be reborn following Lance's adrenaline shot. In *The Gold Watch*, Butch kills a man in the ring and redeems himself by going back to the pawnshop to save the life of Marsellus, his arch-enemy. An appreciative Marsellus learns the value of mercy, and Butch leaves the scene of the crime on a chopper called Grace. Jules is spiritually reborn when the Fourth Man's bullets miss him in *The Bonnie Situation*. While he struggles to come to terms with the revelation, he takes the first steps towards a new life by letting Pumpkin and Honey Bunny go free when they hold up the Hawthorne Grill. A sequence ultimately cut from the film illustrated the path stretching before Jules when, in a 'parallel' reality, he imagines shooting Pumpkin - an innocent bystander dies in the ensuing chaos. Vincent remains cynical about redemption and the value of forgiveness - he saves only his own skin by reviving Mia, and itches to kill Honey Bunny in the hold-up. He never empathises

with Jules after the 'miracle' of the missed bullets - the result being that he is unable to wash Marvin's blood from his hands in Jimmie's house, only reluctantly allows himself to be cleansed by Winston Wolf, and meets a meaningless end when he is machine-gunned by Butch.

The bloodbath that closes Reservoir Dogs shows us how the ignorance of revenge is ultimately self-destructive. The end of *Pulp Fiction* sees Jules an enriched man, having learned the value of redemption.

(See also: Inferno; Morality)

RESERVOIR DOGS
(See appendix)

RHAMES, VING
Marsellus Wallace, *Pulp Fiction*
A veteran of Tarantino's De Palma-helmed

Redemption. Butch leaves the 'Pit of Hell' by way of Grace.

Vietnam favourite, 1989's *Casualties of War*, Ving Rhames read, unsuccessfully, for the role of Holdaway in *Reservoir Dogs*. He did not, however, blow his audition for *Pulp*, subsequently turning down a more lucrative appearance in the Danny De Vito comedy *Renaissance Man* to play crime lord Marsellus. The characteristic sticking-plaster on the nape of Marsellus's neck was intended to cover a scar of Rhames's; looking apt, it stayed. Rhames had Marsellus cry tears during several takes of the notorious 'butt-fucking' scene; Tarantino elected not to use these. Rhames's other credits include: *Patty Hearst* (1988), *Jacob's Ladder* (1990), *Homicide* (1991), *Dave* (1993), *Mission: Impossible* (1996) and *Striptease* (1996).

RICHARD GECKO

Seth's unbalanced brother is very much like the backward Lennie in *Of Mice and Men* - indeed, just as George is protective of Lennie in John Steinbeck's novel, Seth overlooks Richard's most heinous crimes in *From Dusk Till Dawn*.

Richard Gecko is a known armed robber and sex offender who spectacularly liberates Seth during a parole hearing. The Geckos have already killed thirteen people between Seth's escape and our first sight of them at the raid on Benny's World of Liquor. On one hand, Richard is an endearing if occasionally annoying kid brother: 'Do they have cable?' he asks Seth upon their arrival at the Dew Drop Inn. 'Do they have an X-rated channel? Do they have a waterbed?' On the other hand, the flipside of Richard's manic character is a dangerous schizophrenic prone to alarming hallucinations - he imagines the clerk at Benny's is mouthing for help, and later thinks Kate asks him 'Richard, will you do me a favour and eat my pussy?' Richard delights in the clerk's fiery death and can't help himself from raping and murdering his bank raid hostage.

It's not difficult to imagine Richard's thoughts when, like a kid in a sweet shop, he tastes the sexual delights the Titty Twister has to offer. It takes a woman with the stamina of Santanico Pandemonium to avenge the lecherous lizard's victims.

(See also: Men; Seth Gecko; Tarantino, Quentin [as actor])

ROCKWELL, ALEXANDRE (1956 -)
Executive producer, *Four Rooms*
Writer/director, *Four Rooms: Room 404: The Wrong Man*

Boston-born writer-director Rockwell has been working the arthouse circuit since 1981: his early directorial efforts include *Lenz* (1981), *Hero* (1983), *Cheat 'n' Heart* (co-directed, 1985) and *Sons* (1989). Tarantino and Rockwell first met at the 1992 Sundance Festival where *Reservoir Dogs* was screened, but it was Rockwell's second feature, *In the Soup* - which, like *Dogs*, featured Steve Buscemi (qv) - that won the Grand Jury Prize. Tarantino and Rockwell were the first of *Four Rooms*'s four directors to collaborate on the core concept: Allison Anders and Robert Rodriguez (both qv) also exhibited at Sundance in 1992.

Rockwell's segment, *Room 404: The Wrong Man* - which he describes as 'a weird psychodrama . . . like *Days of Our Lives* on crack' - was part-inspired by a rumour he'd heard that a jealous Sean Penn had tied his then-wife Madonna up on New Year's Eve (Madonna, of course, featured in Anders's segment, *Honeymoon Suite: The Missing Ingredient*). The three-hander bore the working titles *Two Sides To a Plate* and *No-one Here But Us Chickens*; Rockwell cast his actress wife, Jennifer Beals (*Flashdance*, etc), alongside David Proval. Rockwell's third feature, *Somebody to Love*, was actually shot in 1994 immediately prior to *Four Rooms*: Tarantino made a cameo appearance as a bartender alongside Eddie Bunker,

Steve Buscemi, and Harvey Keitel (all qv). Rockwell's follow-up, *The Button Man*, was slated for 1996 production, with the omnipresent Tarantino executive-producing.

RODRIGUEZ, ROBERT (1968 -)
Writer/director/editor, *Four Rooms: Room 309: The Misbehavers*
Director/editor/co-executive producer, *From Dusk Till Dawn*

Born in San Antonio, Texas, and raised in Austin, the teenage Rodriguez - one of nine children - made umpteen amateur Super 8mm movies; he cites John Carpenter's 1981 *Escape From New York* as his spur. Upon being refused admittance to the University of Texas's film course, the self-taught film-maker submitted three of his previous works to a small film festival under the title *Austin Stories*. He won, and the college felt obliged to take him on. (Rodriguez would make somewhere in the region of thirty shorts as a student).

'If you're creative and technical, you're unstoppable'. Robert Rodriguez directing *Desperado*.

Rodriguez's formative work also included a self-created comic strip, *Los Hooligans* (from which he'd later take the name of his production company) for *The Daily Texas* newspaper, and another festival-screened short, *Bedhead*. Rodriguez's feature debut, *El Mariachi*, was made for a mere $7,000, a full two thousand dollars less than he'd budgeted for. Notoriously, the film, shot on 16mm with a cast of untrained amateurs on location at Acuna, just over the Mexican border, was part-financed by Rodriguez volunteering his body for medical trials into a new cholesterol-inhibiting drug. The writer/director planned to sell his film to a Hispanic video label; when the projected deal failed to materialise, he sent a videocassette of *El Mariachi* to LA's ICM talent agency. Hollywood was duly impressed; he signed with Stephanie Allain, Columbia Pictures's vice-president, to remake the film for $5 million. Meanwhile, Rodriguez's original was exhibited at film festivals; it played at the 1992 Sundance event alongside *Reservoir Dogs* (Rodriguez won the audience prize), but it wasn't until a festival in Toronto that Rodriguez first met Tarantino and Alexandre Rockwell (qv). Duly recruited into the *Four Rooms* fold, Rodriguez was intrigued by Tarantino's previously sold, but unproduced 1991 *From Dusk Till Dawn* screenplay; eventually, Tarantino would be persuaded to rewrite his original script if Rodriguez directed the movie. During 1994, Rodriguez wrote, directed, edited and produced two pictures: *Desperado*, his *El Mariachi* reworking starring Antonio Banderas with a cameo appearance from Tarantino, and *Road Racers*, an hour-and-a-half long TV movie in Showtime's *Rebel Highway* series.

From Dusk Till Dawn, set in Rodriguez's beloved Mexico, with a correspondent dose of Hispanic vampire lore, was shot during the summer of 1995; Rodriguez's wife, Elizabeth Avellan, produced. Noted for his speed on set - on a typical day, he'll complete around thirty set-ups - Rodriguez told *Cinescape*: 'I'm shooting it completely the way I shot *Desperado* - by just grabbing the camera and running around really fast - so it's very hyper-kinetic . . . It's almost like the kind of movie you'd do in your backyard with your friends - with a little bit bigger budget . . .' Rodriguez's scheduled future projects include a mooted new version of *Modesty Blaise* starring Uma Thurman (qv), *Zorro* for Amblin Entertainment, and a screenplay for the second *Predator* sequel.

ROLE PLAYING

'Let's get into character' - Jules Winnfield, *Pulp Fiction*.

The prevalence of characters acting behind assumed identities, especially in Tarantino's most autobiographical work, reflects his own background and formal training as an actor. Drawing on these experiences, Tarantino has always featured role-playing on various levels throughout his scripts. In *True Romance*, while Dick and Elliot are both actors, Clarence is living out something that feels altogether more real. When he isn't being spiritually directed by Elvis Presley, it seems nearly all his actions are inspired by movies and television. His gun-toting drug-dealing whirlwind romance is certainly a far cry from life in the Heroes For Sale comic shop. His aspirations are unequivocally outlined during the opening scene, when he eulogises Elvis to the nonchalant girl he's trying to pick up. 'I watch that hillbilly,' he tells her, 'and I wanna be him so bad . . .'. He gets to live out some of the less cheesy aspects of The King's movie persona during the remainder of the film.

Perhaps the most obvious role-playing member of the *True Romance* cast is drug-dealing pimp Drexl Spivey (qv) - a white man who not only shares the slang and colloquialisms of his black colleagues, but also seems to genuinely believe he is a negro. His exchange with Clarence, more fully expounded in the

script than the film, includes the taunt 'It ain't white boy day, is it? . . . Next time you bogart your way into a nigger's crib, an' get all in his face, make sure you do it on white boy day.' Clarence's response of 'Wannabee nigger' is an accurate, if politically incorrect, description of perhaps the most intriguing character Tarantino has yet devised. We never establish the truth of Alabama's report that Drexl is apparently half-Apache, but this has little bearing on the dramatic validity of his obvious identity confusion. Clarence's role-playing is mirrored in that of his arch-nemesis Drexl - that both aspire to such bizarre and unattainable ideals (Clarence to be Elvis, Drexl to be black) accentuates the friction between them. When Clarence raises his gun to Drexl, Elvis Presley is seeking vengeance from Moses Gunn.

Tarantino's construction of a situation where a white man aspires to be black is his first use of 'blackness' to represent power and superiority. A more sophisticated reworking of this inverted racism would later feature in *Pulp Fiction*.

This interest in role-playing was developed further in *Reservoir Dogs*, where nearly all the principal characters assume colour-coded names in order to preserve their anonymity from each other, should any of them get arrested. Of all the members of the diamond heist gang, Mr Orange presents perhaps the most complex character. Freddy Newendyke is an undercover cop, role-playing a criminal who then assumes a false name. However noble his intentions, his deceit is multi-layered and rewarded with death when he comes clean to Mr White in the film's closing moments. Newendyke's deception must be so naturalistic that he is even seen to take acting lessons from Holdaway in order to perfect it.

Role-playing became such a prominent facet of *Pulp Fiction* that the characters themselves recognise their own pretence on screen. Jules, concerned that his hitman persona is slipping, following a protracted conversation about foot massage, advises Vincent that they should 'get into character' before they 'collect' Marsellus's briefcase from Brett and his friends. When they return from the job they have to rely on Winston Wolf to resolve *The Bonnie Situation*. When contacted on the phone by Marsellus, the Wolf asks 'Give me the principals' names . . .'. His behaviour at Jimmie's house further reinforces his role as director to Jules, Vincent and Jimmie's repertory company of actors.

A yet more sinister style of role playing is witnessed in Marsellus's sexual tormentor, Zed. Just as Drexl masquerades as a negro, this sadistic homosexual rapist masquerades as a straight policeman. He suffers a similar fate to Drexl when his balls are blown to bits.

Characters forced into role-playing include Elliot in *True Romance*, who is 'persuaded' by the police to catch Lee Donowitz in an incriminating situation, and Pete, the Benny's World of Liquor manager in *From Dusk Till Dawn*. Under pressure from the Geckos while they wait for the local ranger to emerge from his toilet, Pete snaps: 'Look, you asked me to act natural, and I'm acting as natural - in fact, under the circumstances, I think I ought to get a fuckin' Academy Award for how natural I'm acting.'

Tarantino's development of more committed role playing characters came to a natural conclusion in an early draft of his *Four Rooms* script: action film star Connie Bakalinkoff was by no means the first actor to appear in one of his scripts. Perhaps aware that the story was parodying enough of his themes already, Tarantino excised the character from the finished screenplay.

The prevalence of such role playing should come as no surprise, informed as it is by Tarantino's extensive personal experience and his reliance on dramatic friction being

generated by genre characters operating in 'real world' situations. In movies better informed by other movies than reality, all Drexl, Jules and Connie are reminding us is that life is only a movie . . .

(See also: Alter egos; *Badlands*; *Deliverance*; Elvis Presley; *My Best Friend's Birthday*; Race; Tarantino, Quentin [as actor])

ROLLING THUNDER

The formation of this Tarantino-controlled film distribution label was announced in January 1995. Established as a sub-division of Miramax, the company is intended as an opportunity for Tarantino to bring the work of some of his favourite directors to a wider audience. 'He's looking for movies that don't have a chance,' claims Miramax boss Harvey Weinstein, who has agreed to exhibit four Tarantino-chosen films every year. Rolling Thunder's first release was the acclaimed *Chunking Express* (1994), an examination of the emotionally troubled personal lives of two Hong Kong cops by Wong Kar-Wai, a man Tarantino described as 'the most exciting director to emerge on the film scene in the last two years.'

At the end of 1995, Tarantino hoped to persuade Weinstein to take on 'Beat' Takeshi Kitano's *Sonatine* (1993), as well as older work by directors such as Jack Hill and Jean-Pierre Melville. In 1996, Miramax pledged 25 per cent of the label's profits to film preservation efforts.

Rolling Thunder takes its name from a 1977 movie directed by John Flynn and written by key Scorsese collaborator Paul Schrader. Starring William Devane and Tommy Lee Jones, it concerns a Vietnam vet's bloody revenge against those that murdered his family. The film also features a performance by James Best, the founder and guiding light of the acting school attended by Tarantino as a teenager.

ROTH, TIM (1961 -)
Mr Orange [Freddy Newendyke],
Reservoir Dogs
Pumpkin, *Pulp Fiction*
Ted, *Four Rooms*

Born in London's Dulwich, Roth, the son of a
left-wing journalist and a teacher, first plied
his later trade at 16 on the stage of his Tulse
Hill comprehensive: he played Dracula in the
school's revue. He enrolled at the Camberwell
School of Art, but dropped out after a term in
favour of fringe theatre, which kept him occasionally occupied until, in 1983, he won a
lead role in playwright Alan Clarke's skinhead
TV movie, *Made In Britain*. Later that year, on
Clarke's recommendation, he was cast in
improvisational director Mike Leigh's Channel
4 production, *Meantime*, opposite Gary
Oldman (qv). More TV movies - including
Stephen Frears's 1984 *The Hit* - followed; he
made his big screen debut in the 1987 British
film, *A World Apart*. He played the
lughole-bereft Van Gogh in the Robert Altman
biopic *Vincent et Theo*, was reunited with
Oldman in the 1990 two-hander *Rosencrantz
and Guildenstern Are Dead*, and, shortly thereafter, made his US debut in *Jumpin' at the
Boneyard*, playing an unemployed
Irish-American; Alexis Arquette (qv) played his
crackhead brother.

Roth was, and is, a huge admirer of Harvey
Keitel, and was asked to audition for both
Keitel and Tarantino for *Reservoir Dogs*. 'One of
the reasons I became an actor,' he says, 'is
because I thought guys like Nicholson, Pacino
and Keitel were amazing - especially Keitel . . .
Knowing he had casting approval on *Reservoir
Dogs* and chose me was fantastic enough.
Working with him was hysterical.' Roth was
cast as Orange - his preferred choice - but was
initially considered as a Pink or a Blonde. The
actress playing the woman shot by Orange was
actually Roth's American dialogue coach,
Suzanne Celeste. Like other of the *Dogs*, Roth
later turned down a role in Oliver Stone's *NBK*.

Tim Roth in Robert
Altman's *Vincent et Theo.*

Pumpkin, Roth's *Pulp Fiction* character, was
devised after Roth introduced Tarantino to
actress Amanda Plummer (qv), with whom
he'd made a 1992 student short, *Monkey Park*.
He told *Premiere*: 'I said [to Tarantino], "I want
to work with Amanda in one of your films,
but she has to have a really big gun." And he
went, "OK . . .".'

On *Four Rooms*, Roth was required to play
bellhop Ted, the only character to link the
quartet of stories. He replaced Steve Buscemi,
who'd been envisaged for the role. 'It's a
weird experiment trying to get four directors
to make a film that is complete and isn't just
four segments . . . on some levels it works
really well and not so well on others . . . To
be honest, I said "yeah" even before I read
the script,' he told *Sky*. Other credits include:
The Cook, the Thief, His Wife and Her Lover
(1989), *Farendj* (1990), *Backsliding* (1991),
Bodies, Rest and Motion (1993), *Little Odessa*
(1995), *Captives* (1995) and *Rob Roy* (1995),
for which he was Oscar-nominated the
following year.

(See also: Orange)

S

SAVINI, TOM (1948 -)
Sex Machine, *From Dusk Till Dawn*

Horror make-up designer Savini (*Friday the 13th*, etc) graduated from gory effects work for such as director George Romero to cameo film appearances and eventually to directing a remake of Romero's *Night of the Living Dead* (once, at a horror convention, Tarantino had tried - unsuccessfully - to persuade Savini to make a PA at Video Archives, qv). Savini was originally intended to play *Dusk*'s Frost, but, upon reading the script, chose to send back an audition videotape reading Sex Machine's lines. Savini performed his own stunts, instigating the expansion of a small altercation involving a pool cue to a 10-minute Jackie Chan homage. Sex Machine's 'crotch gun' had been devised by director Robert Rodriguez (qv) for his own *Desperado*, but was not to be used in the latter. (Savini also handled effects work on Roger Avary's *Killing Zoe* (qv), and made a cameo appearance in Avary's TV pilot *Mr Stitch*.) Other acting credits include: *Martin* (1977), *Dawn of the Dead* (1979), *Knightriders* (1981), *Creepshow* (1982), *Two Evil Eyes* [with Harvey Keitel, qv] (1990).

SCOTT, TONY (1944 -)
Director, *True Romance*

Younger brother to director Ridley (*Blade Runner*, etc), Scott was born in Newcastle and attended the Sunderland Arts School, graduating with a Fine Arts degree in painting. On a postgraduate course in Leeds, Scott made a half-hour short, *One of the Missing*, based on an Ambrose Bierce short story. Later, at the Royal College of Arts, he directed his second film, *Loving Memory*; like his first, it was backed by the British Film Institute. In 1973 he formed a commercials production company, RSA, with Ridley; their advertising slots earned them a reputation as formidable stylists, creating a template for much of their later feature work. During this time, Scott also made a number of TV movies. His feature debut, 1983's *The Hunger*, was an oblique and elegiac vampire picture starring David Bowie, Susan Sarandon, and Catherine Deneuve; 1986's *Top Gun*, his first in partnership with archetypal Eighties producers Don Simpson and Jerry Bruckheimer, would be mercilessly spoofed for its alleged homosexual subtext by Tarantino as Sid in 1994's *Sleep With Me* (see Tarantino, Quentin [as actor]).

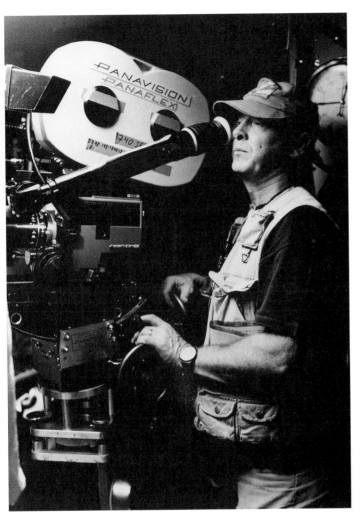

Director Tony Scott. According to Tarantino, Scott's direction of *True Romance* 'captured my world, but he captured my world through his eyes . . .'

Alex McGregor: 'Normally I fall in love with a story or the action or a twist or turn in the story. This is very much an actor's piece and it is the first time I had fallen in love with a piece like that. No matter how dark or violent or strange the scene, you were always left with a smile because you fell in love with these guys.' Principal photography on *True Romance* commenced in September 1992; during post-production, several scenes ran foul of the Motion Picture Association of America (see X-rated). The film was a box-office flop.

Despite Tarantino and Scott's directorial styles being the apparent antithesis of one another's - Tarantino loves long, static shots, Scott close-ups and fast cutting; Tarantino prefers flat, naturalistic lighting, Scott garish filters and atmospheric smoke effects - Tarantino was well pleased with the end results. Citing Scott's 1990 *Revenge* as a particular favourite of his, Tarantino has called Scott 'the Douglas Sirk [qv] of action movies': 'Tony captured my world but he captured my world through his eyes. And that's really cool.' Tarantino went on to perform an uncredited rewrite on Scott's 1995 *Crimson Tide* (qv). Other credits include: *Beverly Hills Cop II* (1987), *Days of Thunder* (1990), *The Last Boy Scout* [with Bruce Willis, qv] (1991).

(See also: Arquette, Patricia; *Badlands*; Fictional film and television; Pinchot, Bronson)

Tarantino's first full feature screenplay *True Romance* was optioned by producer Stanley Margolis in 1990, who then proceeded to fix a production deal with Samuel Hadida's Davis Films; exploitation director Bill Lustig (*Maniac Cop*, etc) was originally assigned to the project. The film's ending was rewritten by Roger Avary (qv) shortly thereafter, but Tarantino and Hadida were not convinced that Lustig was necessarily the right choice for the film. In 1991, Scott was sent the script via Tarantino associate Catalaine Knell; his assent attracted production company Morgan Creek and distributors Warner Brothers, and the film's budget was duly inflated. Scott told *Time Out*'s

SEKULA, ANDRZEJ
Director of photography, *Reservoir Dogs*
Director of photography, *Pulp Fiction*
Director of photography, *Four Rooms: Penthouse: The Man From Hollywood*

Originally a stillsman, Polish-born cinematographer Sekula learned his craft when, upon being conscripted into the Polish army, he served as a cameraman and shot Communist military exercises for propaganda films. Demobbed, he worked briefly as a cameraman on television documentaries, before enrolling at the British National Film and Theatre School in 1985, where he was tutored by the Oscar-winning Oswald Morris (*Fiddler on the Roof*, etc). Graduating in 1988, he shot a number of British commercials and TV movies before touting for work in LA. Recommended for *Dogs* by executive producer Monte Hellman (qv), he first met Tarantino at 3am one morning while preparing to fly to Poland for his father's funeral.

In preparation for *Dogs*, Tarantino had Sekula watch Kubrick's *The Killing* (see Heist movies, qv) and *A Bout de Souffle*, directed by Jean-Luc Godard (qv). The director, a self-confessed 'stickler about framing', generally handled composition, leaving lighting to Sekula; he required Sekula to maintain a large depth of field and sharp focus throughout. *Dogs* was shot on Eastman 50 ASA 5245 stock, a slower film than would normally be expected for interiors; the main camera used was a Panavision Gold (the title sequence's strut to camera used a 600mm Canon lens). Sekula added to the opening 'Madonna' scene: he told American Cinematographer, 'Quentin was originally going to just cut back and forth, but I suggested we should do a circular move to reveal the characters gradually.' According to Tarantino, 'Andrzej brought a quality to the images exactly as I had imagined.' Re-hired for *Pulp Fiction*, Sekula spent much of the shoot wheelchair-bound after a car accident. Other credits include: *Three of Hearts* (1993), *Bank Robber* (1993), *Sleep With Me* [with Eric Stoltz and Quentin Tarantino, both qv] (1994), *Across the Room* (1994), *Oleanna* (1994) and *Hackers* (1995).

SETH GECKO

A lengthy jail sentence has given the 'hero' of *From Dusk Till Dawn* time to plan a lucrative bank robbery down to the finest detail - he masterminds the perennial getaway favourite (crossing the border into Mexico) and is smart enough to rent rooms either side of his at the Dew Drop Inn to prevent eavesdropping. A less predictable problem, however, is posed by his psychotic brother Richard. While grateful for Richard's help in releasing him, Seth nevertheless thinks his brother is 'a fuckin' nut' and struggles to keep him under control during the journey to El Ray (sic). He is appalled when his brother rapes and murders their hostage at the Inn. 'This is not me!' he tells him. 'I am a professional fucking thief. I steal money. You try to stop me, God help you. But I don't kill people I don't have to, and I don't rape women. What you're doin' ain't how it's done. Do you understand?'

'How it's done' includes raising Benny's World of Liquor to the ground (burning its clerk alive in the process) and breaking Chet Pussy's finger when he insults Kate outside the Titty Twister. During the mayhem inside the biker bar, Seth discovers God just as his uncomfortable ally, Jacob, rediscovers Him. 'If there is a hell, and these monsters are from it, then there's got to be a heaven,' he surmises, before asking Jacob 'Which are you, a faithless preacher or a mean, motherfuckin' servant of God?'

Seth is one of the few to emerge from the Titty Twister alive, and quickly admonishes his Mexican contact Carlos for arranging to rendezvous at vampire central. A ten per cent reduction in Carlos's cut of his ill-gotten gains seems scant compensation for such a traumatic night.

(See also: Clooney, George; Fingers; Richard Gecko)

SIRK, DOUGLAS (1900-1987)

After emigrating to Hollywood, Danish director Douglas Sirk made his name in the Fifties as a purveyor of wry 'women's picture' melodramas characterised by a slavish attention to detail; an architect of *mise-en-scene*, Sirk's most renowned films - *Magnificent Obsession, All*

That Heaven Allows, *Written on the Wind*, and *Imitation of Life* - were stylised, richly-coloured critiques of middle-class American mores. Tarantino's arch, cryptic inclusion of a 'Douglas Sirk steak . . . burnt to a crisp, or bloody as hell' on the Jack Rabbit Slim's menu in *Pulp Fiction* might be interpreted as either a general ironic comment on his own use of obsessive background detail and design (particularly bearing in mind the strange, retro, kitsch setting of the scene), as a critique of the unevenness of Sirkian melodrama in general, or as a more specific reference to Sirk's 1956 *Written on the Wind*. Starring Robert Stack as oil heir Kyle Hadley, *Written on the Wind* opened with Kyle being shot and falling dead to the ground; the remainder of the film, told in flashback, concerned itself with the events leading up to Kyle's death - the first flashback scene showing Kyle and family friend Mitch (Rock Hudson) flying to New York in order that Kyle might buy a steak sandwich, oddly enough. Sirk himself claimed that Kyle's early death was a device used to imbue the narrative with 'an underlying theme of hopelessness', one that asked the film's audience 'to turn its attention to the how instead of the what - to structure instead of plot'. Of course, *Pulp*'s Vincent Vega will, shortly after tucking into his 'bloody as hell' Sirk steak, be suddenly gunned down - and later 'resurrected'.

(See also: Jack Rabbit Slim's)

SIZEMORE, TOM
Cody Nicholson, *True Romance*
Jack Scagnetti, *Natural Born Killers*

Detroit-born Sizemore graduated in theatre arts from Wayne State and Temple universities before moving to New York, where he appeared in several off-Broadway productions. He landed his first film role in Oliver Stone's *Born on the Fourth of July*. Blown away as Detective Nicholson in *True Romance*, he met a similarly premature end when re-hired by Stone to play the lecherous Detective Scagnetti in *NBK*. Other credits include: *Heart and Souls* [with Robert Downey Jr, qv] (1993), *Striking Distance* [with Bruce Willis, qv] (1993), *Wyatt Earp* [with Michael Madsen, qv] (1994), *Strange Days* [with Juliette Lewis, qv] (1995), *Devil in a Blue Dress* (1995).

SLATER, CHRISTIAN (1969 -)
Clarence Worley, *True Romance*

The son of an actor and a casting director, it's unsurprising to learn that Christian Slater made his acting debut at seven years of age in a daytime soap; he made other television appearances throughout his early teens, and made his first film - *The Legend of Billie Jean* - in 1985. The following year he was cast opposite Sean Connery in *The Name of the Rose*; after his performance as the psychotic 'JD' in 1989's *Heathers* he found himself oft-compared to the young Jack Nicholson. Cast in *True Romance* as Tarantino alter ego Clarence, Slater met Tarantino prior to principal photography in order to better get the measure of his character. Regarding Clarence's blurred, murky morality, he told *Empire*: 'He was just confused . . . He loved the movies. He always wanted to be a part of them in some way, and Alabama opened the door . . . it sorta picks up where *Taxi Driver* left off.' As a surrogate Travis Bickle, an ersatz James Dean via Martin Sheen in *Badlands* (qv), Slater was required to play perhaps one of the single most dysfunctional (anti-) heroes in mainstream Hollywood cinema: a film fan-cum-vigilante. Clarence's cold-blooded murder of Drexl is justified only because that's the way things happen in the movies. Other credits include: *Pump Up the Volume* (1990), *Robin Hood: Prince of Thieves* (1991), *Mobsters* [with Chris Penn, qv] (1991), *Untamed Heart* (1993), *Interview With the Vampire* (1994), *Murder in the First* [with Gary Oldman, qv] (1995).

(See also: Alter egos; Clarence Worley)

Dusty Springfield

was *Son of a Preacher Man*. I can't even imagine it without *Son of a Preacher Man*. I probably would have cut it out if I couldn't get *Son of a Preacher Man*.'

One of Britain's most popular female vocalists of the Sixties, Dusty Springfield (real name Mary O'Brien) was experimenting with a mature sound that better reflected her own taste when she recorded *Dusty in Memphis* (1968). The album featured the single *Son of a Preacher Man*, a track previously turned down by Aretha Franklin, who disapproved of the suggestive lyrics. Springfield's version was released in November 1968 and reached top ten on both sides of the Atlantic, prompting a rethink from Franklin who later covered the song. Despite this success, audiences were unenthusiastic about *Dusty in Memphis* - the highest chart position it attained was 99 in the US. It signposted a halt in Springfield's career, and she had little further success until The Pet Shop Boys brought her talents to the fore on records such as *What Have I Done To Deserve This?* (1987) and *Nothing Has Been Proved* (1989).

Springfield wholeheartedly approved of *Son of a Preacher Man* being included in *Pulp Fiction* and still hangs the soundtrack's commemorative silver disc in her home. The film also engendered fresh interest in *Dusty in Memphis*, already rediscovered and reappraised as her finest album.

Mia isn't the only Tarantino character touched by Dusty's unique voice - in *Natural Born Killers*, Wayne Gayle tells Mickey that his similarly jailed wife, Mallory, has been repeatedly singing *I Only Want To Be With You* in her cell.

SPOOFS

Satires and pastiches of Tarantino's films have been especially prevalent in Britain, where *Reservoir Dogs* in particular has had a far-reaching impact upon pop culture consciousness. One of the earliest was a comedy

SON OF A PREACHER MAN

Mia Wallace chooses the sultry sounds of vintage Dusty Springfield as her preferred easy listening. As the record plays, Vincent explores Mia's living room, searching for the intercom and waiting for the Big Man's wife to make an appearance.

In 1994, Tarantino explained why that particular record was essential to *Pulp Fiction*: 'That sequence in the movie . . . where a guy goes to a house to pick up a date and he's waiting for her, and there's all this tension . . . That whole idea for a story I've had in my head for six or seven years, and it always was scored to *Son of a Preacher Man*. The key to the sequence sketch on TV's *Newman and Baddiel in Pieces*: in the skit, transmitted October 1993 on BBC2, the Dogs are joined by a pseudo-Mr Man, Mr Wobbly Tickle (the Mr Men being a luridly-coloured series of children's cartoon characters). Cue 'Mr Mauve': 'At least I'm a goddamn fuckin' professional. At least when the bullets started flyin', I didn't start goin', "wobbly-do, wobbly-day". What is it with this "wobbly-do, wobbly-fuckin'-day" crap, anyway?' The same channel's *Game On* sitcom of 1995 featured a *Dogs* homage in the episode *Matthew: a Suitable Case for Treatment*, wherein agoraphobic and border-line psychotic Matthew, alone in his flat, dresses up as Blonde and slices the ear off a teddy-bear with a flick-comb to the strains of *Stuck In The Middle With You*. BBC2's 1995 late-night comedy talent show *Don't Give Up Your Day Job* spoofed the *Dogs* titles in its own credit sequence, and in January 1996, viewers of Channel 4's *Jo Brand Through the Cakehole* were treated to the Littlecock Amateur Players' version of *Dogs*, wherein a troupe of terribly nice, Laura Ashley-wearing Home Counties women performed a village hall rendition of the closing moments of Tarantino's script verbatim. Directed by one 'Celia Mortimer', this for-one-night-only staging was accompanied by a tune-free tinkling 'silent movie' piano score.

Pulp Fiction was satirised in the titles to ITV's *Jack Dee's Saturday Night*; in an autumn 1995 edition of ITV's *Hale and Pace*, the comedy duo played an ersatz Jules and Vincent in 'Quentin Tarantino's Pub Luncheon', wherein the pair blew away hostelry waitresses offering them amusingly-termed comestibles ('Two faggots?'). Similarly, in February 1996, BBC1's female double-act French and Saunders dragged up as the fast-talking hitmen, assigned to protect Scots entertainer Lulu. A cruel, torpedo-chinned puppet of Tarantino featured as a character in the final season of ITV's *Spitting Image*; MTV slackers

Beavis and Butt-head, meanwhile, made reference to *Pulp* in the episode *Party* (Butt-head: 'Quit actin' like a damn wuss Beavis, or I'm gonna get medieval on your ass.')

Starting in 1994, Britain's fortnightly satirical magazine *Private Eye* ran a semi-regular one-panel cartoon taking off Tarantino's predilection for smutty language, commencing with 'Quentin Crispantino' ('Hello, fucking sweetie') and continuing via such gems as 'Pulp Classic Fiction' (*Pride and Prejudice*: 'Drop dead, Darcy, you fucking fuck'). In November 1995, issue 9 of DC Comics's quirky title *Animaniacs* was given over totally to three Tarantino parodies, including 'Reservoir Mice' and 'Pulped Fractions', which featured 'hot new director Squintin Tarantella'. That same month, America's Rhino Films announced a forthcoming comedy in the *Airplane!/Naked Gun* mould. Entitled *Plump Fiction*, this *Dogs/Pulp* take-off would be shot for a 1996 release with 'a low-profile cast and no-frills budget' by writer/director Bob Koherr.

And Tarantino has taken the rip out of himself on screen: in the sitcom *All-American Girl*, and in a 1995 edition of *Saturday Night Live* (see Tarantino, Quentin [as actor]).

STONE, OLIVER (1946 -)
Director/co-writer, *Natural Born Killers*

Oliver Stone served in the US army between 1967 and 1968; as a specialist infantryman, fourth class, he came under fire in Vietnam, and subsequently received the Purple Heart and Bronze Star with Oak Leaf Cluster. After service, he worked briefly as a New York taxi driver; in 1974, he wrote and directed a bizarre Canadian horror flick, *Seizure*. He founded his production company, Ixtlan, in 1977; his screenplay for *Midnight Express* won an Oscar in 1979. After directing another throwaway shocker, *The Hand*, in 1981, he made *Salvador*, the first of the

Gathering no moss: Oliver Stone at work on *Natural Born Killers*.

Tarantino was now busy developing *Reservoir Dogs*, and Vossler appears to have been nominated as director himself. Murphy and Hamsher interested first the Motion Picture Corporation of America, who later passed; Vossler, meanwhile, planned to shoot the film's twenty-minute 'American Maniacs' segment to interest potential investors. However, Vossler would be sidelined when Murphy and Hamsher interested Oliver Stone in the film (Vossler would receive a credit as the film's co-producer, but had no substantive input from this point on). Stone, in association with David Veloz and Richard Rotowski, rewrote Tarantino's screenplay; their alterations transformed the script from an in-your-face pulp satire to an apocalyptic parable for the breakdown of American society in the late twentieth century. Substantially, they added two completely new scenes to the screenplay: Mickey and Mallory's encounter with the Indian mystic (a similar scene was in Stone's 1991 rock biopic *The Doors*) and the *I Love Mallory* sit-com, which revealed the story of Mallory's sexual abuse through TV-tinged flashback. 'There's so much pain in her', Stone told *Time Out*, 'she distances herself, filters it as a memory so that it just becomes part of the TV channel surf trip . . . I'm being ironic, yes, but also imagining how she might deal with that.' Mickey's less believable portrayal as a potential rapist muddied the water in a film dominated by a clear polemic - newspaper headlines read '666 Death' and the Knoxes have slogans such as 'too much TV' projected onto their t-shirts. Hearing characters say lines such as 'This is the 1990s, all right?' distances the film yet further from its original author's style, and *Natural Born Killers* remains an incoherent mix of Tarantino and Stone's polarised intentions.

Stone attempted to involve several of the *Dogs* cast in the movie, including Steve Buscemi, Michael Madsen and Tim Roth (all qv); Tarantino, however, was deeply unhappy with Stone's spin on on his screenplay, and all bar

heavily polemicised drama-documentaries for which he'd become best known. In 1986, he wrote and directed *Platoon*, the first in a trilogy of films concerning the Vietnam war; it won him a second Academy Award, this time as best director.

Tarantino's *Natural Born Killers* - his second screenplay - was derived from an earlier piece, *The Open Road* (qv). Completed in September 1989, it was sent to Rand Vossler, who'd helped out on *My Best Friend's Birthday* (qv) and then had connections with MGM. Vossler set himself up as the project's producer, intending to shoot it 'guerrilla-style'. Late in 1990, producers Don Murphy and Jane Hamsher bought an option on the project;

Kirk Baltz and Steven Wright (both qv) would refuse.

NBK, with a budget in the region of $35 million, wrapped in August 1993; its frantic mix of film stocks and tone, although partly indicated in the original screenplay, had been a feature of Stone's earlier *The Hand*. Two endings were shot; the alternative to Mickey and Mallory's driving off into the sunset was their being suddenly shot dead by a random psycho on the loose. Thereafter unfolded a very public slanging match between variously Tarantino, Stone, Murphy and Hamsher, and Vossler. For Tarantino, speaking in UK *Premiere*, Stone's 'obviousness' had tainted the film, which he described as no longer his movie, but '"Oliver Stone Takes On Serial Killers And Violence In America"'. Stone dismissed Tarantino's complaints: 'The way Tarantino wrote it, it was a Roger Corman homage. This was used material.' The director believes his film to be of far greater significance: 'I am celebrating . . . a *Beavis and Butt-head* crimescape in the 1990s - enormous crime, violence and the celebration of that in the media,' he told *Premiere*. 'When I started the movie, honestly the events in the picture were surreal . . . Over the year-and-a-half of shooting and editing there was a transformation in the American landscape, and what we were shooting was no longer surreal. Bobbitt, Menendez, Buttafuoco, the King case, Tonya Harding . . . The glamorization of crime that we were satirising was happening repeatedly. So by the time I finished the movie, it seemed to me that the Mickey and Mallory case could happen as we speak.' (Indeed, NBK was accused of inspiring several such crimes itself: see Causality and imitation, qv.) NBK went on to become a sizeable commercial hit and net Stone a Golden Globe nomination as best director. Other directing credits include: *Wall Street* (1987), *Talk Radio* (1988), *Born on the Fourth of July* (1989), *JFK* [with Tommy Lee Jones and Gary Oldman, qv] (1991), *Heaven and Earth* [with Tommy Lee Jones, qv] (1993).

(See also: Arquette, Patricia; Avary, Roger; Downey Jr, Robert; Harrelson, Woody; Lewis, Juliette; Sizemore, Tom; X-rated)

STOLTZ, ERIC (1961 -)
Lance, *Pulp Fiction*

Born in American Samoa, Eric Stoltz has accrued a reputation for eclectic and idiosyncratic character roles; latterly, he has made some headway as a producer. He first came to attention as Rocky Dennis, the gruesomely

Eric Stoltz as Zed in *Killing Zoe*.

disfigured teenager at the heart of 1985's *Mask* - and was again smothered beneath layers of latex as the eponymous changeling in *The Fly II*. He gained his first producing credit on 1993's *Bodies, Rest and Motion*, in which he starred alongside Tim Roth (qv); he was promoting the film at the 1992 Sundance Festival when Roth introduced him to Tarantino. Simultaneously, Roger Avary was considering Stoltz for the key role of Zed in his debut picture, *Killing Zoe* (qv); Zed being something of an Avary alter-ego, the director was keen to cast somebody with whom he shared a passing resemblance. Stoltz was duly affirmed for the role after Tarantino had told him of it during a later chance meeting; by way of return, Tarantino agreed to make a cameo in the upcoming *Sleep With Me* (see Tarantino, Quentin [as actor]), which Stoltz again produced and starred in. He made *Killing Zoe* in early 1993; in *Pulp Fiction*, he appeared as drug dealer Lance. Other credits include: *Fast Times at Ridgemont High* (1982), *Some Kind of Wonderful* (1987), *The Waterdance* (1991), *The Heart of Justice* [TVM, with Dennis Hopper, qv] (1992), *Singles* (1992), *Grace of My Heart* [director Allison Anders, qv] (1996).

STUCK IN THE MIDDLE WITH YOU

The 1973 Stealer's Wheel hit helped Tarantino achieve his aim to 'accomplish two effects with one thing' during the notorious ear-slicing scene in *Reservoir Dogs*. 'The music was supposed to be reacting as somewhat of an ironic counterpoint to what you were seeing on the screen . . . How it works is that this sugary, bubblegum song comes on and you go, "Hey, that's a really catchy song", and your body just starts moving. So you're getting in with the beat of the song, and Michael Madsen [Mr Blonde] stars dancing, and he's having a good time, and you enjoy what he's doing, and the next thing you know he's committing these incredible acts of violence. But it's too late, you're already hooked into the beat of the song. It almost makes you a co-conspirator in what's being portrayed on the screen.'

In *Reservoir Dogs* DJ K-Billy dates the song from April 1974, and describes how it 'reached up to number 5' in the charts. In actual fact, the single made its debut in the US top twenty in April 1973, peaking at number 6. In the UK it reached number 8 in May 1973.

Stuck in the Middle With You was the first, and most successful, of Stealer's Wheel's three major hits. The duo comprised Gerry Rafferty and Joe Egan, whose uneasy alliance fell apart while 'Stuck in the Middle With You' was at the height of its success. Rafferty left the group only to return soon after, but the duo were never again able to recapture the popularity of their earliest recordings. They split two albums later, Rafferty going on to considerable solo success with the singles *Baker Street* (1978) and *Night Owl* (1979). Aside from being one of the highlights of the *Reservoir Dogs* soundtrack, *Stuck in the Middle With You* can be found on Stealer's Wheel's eponymous debut album (1973) and the recent compilation *One More Dream - The Very Best of Gerry Rafferty* (1996).

'When you take the right songs and put them in a sequence in a movie right, it's about as cinematic a thing as you can do', Tarantino asserts. 'It really works in this visceral, emotional, cinematic way that's just special. And when you do it right, the effect is you can never really hear that song again without thinking about that image from the movie. 'Personally, I don't know if Gerry Rafferty appreciated the connotations that I brought to *Stuck in the Middle With You*. There's a good chance he didn't.'

(See also: Ears)

SUITS

The black tie and suit has become one of the most readily identifiable elements of *Reservoir Dogs*, *Pulp Fiction* and, to a degree, Quentin Tarantino himself. The stark sartorial chic of

Tarantino's best-known characters is a look he has personally adopted at a number of high profile events, including the 1995 Oscars.

The sharp-suited dress code adopted by Joe Cabot's jewel thieves and Marsellus's hit men is a variation on the gangster gear immortalised in such seminal films as William A Wellman's *The Public Enemy* (1930) and Howard Hawks's *Scarface* (1932). However, the black suits that appear in *Reservoir Dogs* and *Pulp Fiction* owe a greater debt to post-war Italian fashion than pre-war American gangster movies.

When Jules and Vincent leave their blood-stained suits for Otto the garbage man, Tarantino ensures that the 'dorkish' clothes they swap them for prove as contrasting as possible. The difference between the t-shirts and shorts they reluctantly don ('You guys going to a volleyball game or something?' - Raquel) and the suits they were formerly identified by is as great a difference as that between Nice Guy's Eddie's shell suit and the Dogs's apparel. The contrasting clothes serve to accentuate the importance of the criminals' 'uniform', a uniform we are led to believe Jules has taken off for the last time. In *Reservoir Dogs*, the morgue-like setting of the film's principal location is made all the more poignant by the warehouse's occupants dressing like funeral attendees. For ease of identification, the script of *From Dusk Till Dawn* labels the as yet unnamed Gecko brothers as 'Black Suit # 1' and 'Black Suit # 2'.

Aside from Tarantino's employment of such suits as genre reinforcers, they also form an integral expression of his characters' motivations. 'It has a basis in reality', Tarantino claims. 'A lot of times, when robbers commit a robbery they'll want to adopt a uniform . . . the idea is that they go in and they do the robbery and they all look alike. So when they leave and the cops come back later and ask "What did they look like?" [you'd say] "I don't know, they look like a bunch of black suits. How do I know?"' The director was also influenced by another, more immediate, factor: 'It looks neat.'

The importance of the black suit as a *Reservoir Dogs* icon is perhaps best illustrated by the efforts undertaken to underline its prominence. The photographs that appeared on the film's UK and US posters were carefully manipulated - Nice Guy Eddie's casual look was replaced in both of them by a skilfully doctored illustration of a black suit.

SUNDANCE INSTITUTE

Reservoir Dogs's shooting script was refined during a fortnight's preparation in the summer of 1991 at workshops at Utah's Sundance Film Institute, a college for young film-makers set up by Robert Redford. There, Tarantino experimented with techniques - such as long takes, distant framing, and hand-held camerawork - that he'd use in his feature debut; actor Steve Buscemi (qv) would be on hand. Although his work was less than rapturously received in seminars with other would-be directors, professional tutors such as Terry Gilliam were encouraging. *Reservoir Dogs* was premiered at the Institute's annual film festival in 1992 - an event which led Tarantino to contemporaries Allison Anders and Alexandre Rockwell (both qv), and thus the anthology project *Four Rooms*.

(See also: Hellman, Monte; Rodriguez, Robert)

t

TARANTINO, QUENTIN [as actor] (1963 -)
Clarence Pool, *My Best Friend's Birthday*
Mr Brown, *Reservoir Dogs*
Jimmie Dimmick, *Pulp Fiction*
Chester Rush, *Four Rooms: Penthouse:*
The Man From Hollywood
Richard Gecko, *From Dusk Till Dawn*

Quentin Tarantino's acting career was forged at the Torrance Community Theater Workshop in 1979; he won a role in a version of the adult play *Two and Two Makes Sex*. In the early Eighties, he enrolled briefly as a part-timer at the James Best Theater Center; there, he met Rich Turner (later cast in a minor role in *Reservoir Dogs*) and Craig Hamann (with whom he'd collaborate on the short film *My Best Friend's Birthday*, qv). Aspiring thespian Tarantino signed on with agent Cathryn James shortly thereafter; despite many auditions, no parts were forthcoming (a fallow era recalled in *True Romance*'s depiction of Dick Ritchie's reading for an episode of *TJ Hooker*). Circa 1988, Tarantino restarted drama lessons under the tutelage of former Lee Strasberg Institute tutor Allen Garfield; he won his first significant role as an Elvis Presley impersonator in an instalment of TV sitcom *The Golden Girls* transmitted on 19 November that year (see Elvis, qv).

Tarantino cast himself as Mr Brown in 1992's *Reservoir Dogs*, having stood in for White during rehearsals at the Sundance Institute (qv); at an early stage, he'd planned to play Pink opposite Lawrence Bender's (qv) Nice Guy Eddie. 1993's *The Coriolis Effect* featured a voice-only cameo courtesy Tarantino, here playing DJ Panhandle Slim; directed by Louis Venosta, this 35-minute short putting a contemporary spin on *The Wizard of Oz* headlined Dana Ashbrook and Jennifer Rubin. That same year, he appeared as an orderly in Jeff Burr's *Eddie Presley*, a film concerning an overweight security guard's attempt to revive his one-time career as an Elvis impersonator. In 1994, once again, he cast himself as *Pulp Fiction*'s Jimmie; as a favour to *Pulp* actor Eric Stoltz (qv), he featured as Sid in 1994's *Sleep With Me*, reciting the notorious *Top Gun* monologue sometimes credited to Roger Avary (qv). Also in 1994, he shot a small cameo as a bartender in *Somebody to Love*; directed by Alexandre Rockwell, the film also featured Eddie Bunker, Steve Buscemi and Harvey Keitel (all qv). Shortly afterwards, Tarantino directed himself as egomaniac hotshot director Chester Rush in the *Four Rooms* segment, *Penthouse: The Man from Hollywood*. His largest film role to date was as the pivotal Johnny Destiny in *Destiny Turns On the Radio* (qv); shot in the autumn of 1994,

Jack Baran directed this metaphysical comedy-drama. On 22 March 1995, he guest-starred in an instalment of the TV comedy *All-American Girl*; playing videostore clerk Desmond Winocki, Tarantino's episode would be wantonly peppered with thinly-veiled references to portions of *Pulp Fiction*. For Robert Rodriguez (qv), he made a minor appearance in 1995's *Desperado*, and a major one as the psychotic Richard Gecko in Rodriguez's film of Tarantino's script, *From Dusk Till Dawn*. Also in 1995, he appeared as himself in an instalment of comedy show *Saturday Night Live*, and as the lecherous 'QT' ('America's hottest director') in Spike Lee's *Girl 6*. Some reference guides claim that Tarantino took a role in the 1987 version of *King Lear* directed by idol Jean-Luc Godard (qv); the fledgling actor falsely put the film on his CV in a misguided attempt to impress casting directors.

(See also: Alter egos; Brown; Richard Gecko; Yuppie scum)

TELEVISION

'TV should never be ignored in Quentin's whole scheme of things,' claims co-director and friend Allison Anders. Indeed, Tarantino has donated some of his recent earnings to the UCLA television archive - a measure of the medium's importance to him. 'I'm 30. We grew up through the Seventies', he explained to *The Guardian*'s Clancy Sigal in 1993. 'The number one thing we all shared wasn't music, that was a Sixties thing. Our culture was television, and movies too. TV is what we all shared completely, passionately. It's a shared memory and language.'

Not least of television's influences on Tarantino's films is the pre-credit sequence. A practise pioneered by such shows as *The Avengers* (1961-69) and *Star Trek* (1966-69), the concept of beginning programmes with teasing extracts of action to lure viewers was especially popular on American television in the Seventies. With the obvious exception of

Tarantino's most significant screen role to date: Richard Gecko in *From Dusk Till Dawn*. George Clooney (left) co-stars as Richard's brother Seth.

his *Four Rooms* segment, all Tarantino's screenplays, from *My Best Friend's Birthday* to *From Dusk Till Dawn*, have employed a similar device.

In *Natural Born Killers*, Mickey Knox cites watching television as his second favourite pastime after serial killing. *Pulp Fiction* dwells on Mia's short-lived foray into television drama with several protracted examinations. Like the mention of films throughout Tarantino's scripts, the extent and variety of television references baffle clear insight into their deployment. The following record of mentions should, however, go some way to illustrating the degree to which television flavours Tarantino's scripts and screenplays:

My Best Friend's Birthday
'I'll watch *The Partridge Family*, then I'll kill myself', Clarence tells Lenny, recounting a childhood trauma.

True Romance
Inside the dingy hotel room where Drexl convenes his meeting, a television plays an episode of *Bewitched*. In Tony Scott's film, two televisions appear to be tuned into MTV.

Alabama wears only a long t-shirt with a picture of Bullwinkle on the front.

The script describes how 'Clarence and Alabama immediately start singing *Hello My Baby* like the frog in the old Chuck Jones cartoon.'

Clarence and Alabama watch a modern gangster movie in their apartment.

When Clarence visits Drexl, *The Mack* is playing on the television screen behind them. The pimp is wearing a Farrah Fawcett t-shirt.

Dick auditions for a bit part in William Shatner's *TJ Hooker* series. 'Did you meet Captain Kirk?' asks Clarence.

Nicholson and Dimes are described as 'Starsky and Hutch-type police detectives.'

'This is Crockett and Tubbs all the way', says Dimes, comparing him and Nicholson to the heroes of *Miami Vice*.

Natural Born Killers
Mickey writes a letter to the similarly imprisoned Mallory, recalling how they used to watch David Letterman.

The script describes how one sequence is filmed in '16mm color, *cinema-verite à la Cops*.' Mickey has a bit of fun with the swarming reporters by telling them his favourite show is *Have Gun Will Travel*. 'I was on the set of *Dukes of Hazzard* once,' Wurlitzer tells the deputies, prior to Mickey's television interview. 'It was a much bigger deal than this.' He later repeats the claim to Wayne Gayle, telling him it happened 'about eight years ago'.

Reservoir Dogs
Joe tells Larry that his new wife was a regular on the television show *Hee-Haw*. Holdaway tells Freddy to imagine he's stand-up comic Don Rickles to help him tell the commode story as if it were a joke. 'You're fucking Baretta,' Freddy tells himself in the mirror, attempting to pluck up courage. '*Christie Love* was like a Pam Grier [qv] TV show without Pam Grier,' Nice Guy Eddie claims. (The star of *Get Christie Love* was actually Teresa Graves.)

Pulp Fiction
In discussing the fictional show *Fox Force Five*, Jules tells Vincent about the television industry's preference for producing 'pilot' shows before beginning full-scale production on a series.

When Vincent visits Lance to buy the heroin, the dealer is wearing a *Speed Racer* t-shirt. Later in the script, the young Butch Coolidge has just begun watching an episode of the cartoon when Captain Koons visits him. In the film, he is seen watching an episode of *Clutch Cargo*.

'First question, *Brady Bunch* or *The Partridge Family*?' Mia asks Vincent in attempting to establish his personality.

Answering a later question, Vincent tells Mia that he fantasises about being beaten up by Emma Peel from *The Avengers*.

An Ed Sullivan impersonator introduces the entertainment at Jack Rabbit Slim's in the same manner as the Sixties' light entertainment show host.

Lance is watching *The Three Stooges* on television when he receives a frantic phone call from Vincent.

Jody, his wife, is wearing a long t-shirt with a picture of Fred Flintstone on the front.

The script describes the ensuing scene as being 'frantic, like a documentary in an emergency ward'.

'Ever seen that show *Cops?*' Vincent asks Jules.

'Mmm', approves Winston, contributing the coffee commercial scenario developing in Jimmie's kitchen.

'If they ever do *I Spy: The Motion Picture*, you guys'd be great.' Raquel tells the comically dressed Jules and Vincent.

TV influences: Emma Peel (Diana Rigg) goes to work in *The Avengers*.

In defending his reluctance to eat pigs, Jules tells Vincent that for any swine to change his mind, 'He'd have to be ten times more charming than that Arnold on *Green Acres*, you know what I'm saying?'

He later compares his intended lifestyle to that of Caine (David Carradine) in the television series *Kung Fu*. 'Just walk from town to town, meet people, get in adventures . . .'

During the tense stand-off in the Hawthorne Grill, Jules tells Pumpkin that everyone's going to be cool. 'We're gonna be like three Fonzies,' he says, referring to the smooth character played by Henry Winkler in the sit-com *Happy Days*.

Four Rooms: Penthouse: The Man From Hollywood

In the original script Toby tells Chester, 'Isaac on *The Love Boat* was a Ted,' adding to his list of famous Teds.

'Stop playing *Beat the Clock*,' Chester tells the nervous Ted, referring to the Sixties game show.

'We now return you to *The Man from Rio*', says Chester in the style of a television continuity announcer. This is just one of many references to the *Alfred Hitchcock Presents* episode *The Man from the South*.

The script describes how Chester 'now plays *Beat the Clock*', as he gives himself one minute to persuade Ted to wield the meat cleaver.

From Dusk Till Dawn

Bored with watching a news report detailing the injuries he received in the Benny's raid, Richard Gecko changes channel and watches a *Casper the Friendly Ghost* cartoon instead.

Richard Gecko claims to be Don Cornelius, but 'not the Don Cornelius from *Soul Train*'.

Kate (sharing Alabama's taste in clothing, if not her wardrobe) wears a Bullwinkle t-shirt.

(See also: *Crimson Tide*; Fictional films and television)

THURMAN, UMA (1970 -) Mia Wallace, *Pulp Fiction*

A former model, Boston-born Uma Karuna Thurman - named after a Hindu goddess, apparently - made her film debut in 1987's *Kiss Daddy Goodnight*; two subsequent film appearances - as Cecile in Stephen Frears's *Dangerous Liaisons*, and in the dual role of Venus and Rose in Terry Gilliam's *The Adventures of Baron Munchausen* - won her the oft-quoted epithet, 'most beautiful woman in the world'. Casting Mia Wallace was an open book; actresses as diverse as Rosanna Arquette (qv), Holly Hunter, Brigitte Nielsen, Meg Ryan and Alfre Woodard had been considered before Thurman met Tarantino over dinner. She auditioned initially for the part of Honey Bunny; legend, however, dictates that Tarantino knew he'd found his Mia there and then. Thurman needed some persuading. While shooting she -with John Travolta (qv) - would be required to study the dance sequence from *Bande a Part* (and she, especially, Anna Karina in *Vivre Sa Vie*), for their winning Jack Rabbit Slim's twist contest turn (see Godard, Jean-Luc). It was Thurman, too, who provided the impetus to alter Tarantino's initial conception of Mia's adrenaline-induced revival from a shuddering, zombie-esque rise to a sudden animal shriek and leap. Oscar-nominated as best supporting actress for *Pulp*, Thurman's next major role was to have been as Marlene Dietrich in the planned Louis Malle biopic, *Marlene*; the film was put on hiatus after Malle's sudden death late in 1995. In May of that year, however, Screen International reported that Thurman was to take the eponymous lead in Miramax's new version of *Modesty Blaise*, alongside Sean Pertwee as Willie Garvin; the film was due to be helmed by Robert Rodriguez (qv). Her planned casting in the role formerly played by Monica Vitti in Joseph Losey's 1966 version is somewhat uncanny; in *Pulp*, Mia's character in TV pilot *Fox Force Five* is so clearly based on Blaise that the besotted Vincent takes to reading one of Peter O'Donnell's Modesty novels on trips to the bathroom. Formerly married to Gary Oldman (qv), Thurman's other credits include: *Johnny Be Good* (1988), *Henry and June* [with Maria de Medeiros, qv] (1990), *Where the Heart Is* (1990), *Robin Hood* (1991), *Final Analysis* (1992), *Mad Dog and Glory* (1992), *Jennifer 8* (1992), *Even Cowgirls Get the Blues* (1993).

(See also: Comics; Drugs; Fictional films and television; Mia Wallace)

TIERNEY, LAWRENCE (1919 -)
Joe Cabot, *Reservoir Dogs*

Brother to the late - and often-similarly cast - Scott Brady (*Canon City*, TV's *Shotgun Slade*, etc), Lawrence Tierney has forged a successful screen career as a take-no-prisoners tough. Rightly famed for the title role in 1945's *Dillinger*, itself invoked in *Dogs* - Mr Blue is, we are told, 'dead as Dillinger' - Tierney had become a Tarantino favourite for both that and his portrayal of a homicidal psychopath in Robert Wise's 1947 'B' noir, *Born To Kill*, aka *Lady of Deceit* - to the extent that Tierney was one of the heroes to whom Tarantino dedicated the first draft of *Reservoir Dogs*. Unaware that he was still alive until a mutual acquaintance informed him otherwise, Tarantino eagerly cast Tierney as gangland kingpin Joe Cabot; reportedly, there was some friction between the *ingenu* director and the veteran actor on set. Tierney featured heavily in the *Bell Jar* scene which was cut from the movie - Sylvia Plath's estate refused Tarantino the rights - and was apparently considered for the role of outgoing bellboy Sam in *Four Rooms* (the part eventually went to Marc Lawrence). Other credits include: *San Quentin* (1947), *The Hoodlum* (1951), *Prizzi's Honor* (1985) and *Tough Guys Don't Dance* (1987).

(See also: Joe Cabot)

John Travolta and Nancy Allen in *Blow Out*.

TRAVOLTA, JOHN (1954 -)
Vincent Vega, *Pulp Fiction*

Travolta's mould-breaking *Pulp Fiction* appearance as a short-tempered heroin-addicted hitman led to the revival of an acting career which had shone most brightly some fifteen years earlier. Born in Engelwood, New Jersey, he made his film debut in 1975's occult-themed horror *The Devil's Rain*; it was his regular TV role as Vinnie Barbarino in the ABC series *Welcome Back, Kotter* (1975-1979) which made his name. He became a Seventies icon after his portrayal of Tony Manero in 1977's *Saturday Night Fever*, and capitalised upon his fame as Danny Zucco in 1978's *Grease*; these two roles, however, would eclipse his later work and, despite some substantial character roles - most notably in 1980's *Urban Cowboy* and 1981's *Blow Out* - prior to *Pulp* he'd be best known for a returning role in the *Look Who's Talking* series, playing second fiddle to a baby voiced by Bruce Willis (qv).

Pulp's Vincent Vega had, of course, been written for Michael Madsen (qv), who'd played brother Vic in *Reservoir Dogs*; Madsen, however, passed on the role. Tarantino, who'd been hopelessly devoted to Travolta since *Blow Out*,

145

contacted the actor in January 1993 ostensibly with a view to a possible role in the under-development *From Dusk Till Dawn*; they met, and, after a session playing - among others - the *Welcome Back, Kotter* board game, Tarantino asked Travolta to read for Vincent. Despite having appeared as a hitman in a 1987 Robert Altman-directed TV version of Harold Pinter's *The Dumb Waiter*, Travolta had never killed anyone on-screen before: the actor -a noted Scientologist - wrestled with his conscience while the director attempted to persuade sceptical aides that Travolta was the one that he wanted. 'There are a lot of other guys who wanted that role,' Travolta told the *Calgary Herald* in October 1994, 'a lot of them hotter and in more demand than myself. They shall remain nameless, but . . . I understand why [Miramax] would have liked these other guys. It made better business sense.' The director's choice prevailed: '[I] cast John because he's a terrific actor, not because he's a trash culture icon . . . when he's in that booth with Uma [Thurman], he's not John Travolta, he's Vincent Vega . . . But when he steps up to dance, it's like, "Wow! That's John Travolta!". He's in a restaurant where the waiters are dressed like icons - and he is an icon!'. Such casting fits in perfectly with Tarantino's obsession with jarring, Continental realist techniques: see Godard, Jean-Luc (qv).

Travolta's performance had the effect, as many have pointed out, of creating an utterly sympathetic quasi-hero from the antisocial, drug-dependent killer scripted; its consequent effect on Travolta's career was near incalculable. Jonathan Krane, Travolta's business manager, told the *Los Angeles Times*: 'It has been the most direct and immediate response I have ever seen in my life . . . From the moment [*Pulp Fiction*] was seen at Cannes, people have been coming to John with offers.' Oscar-nominated as best actor for Vincent, Travolta's next film role, as would-be film producer Chilli Palmer in *Get Shorty* (see Leonard, Elmore, qv) reportedly netted him $3.5 million dollars.

Says Travolta of Tarantino, 'It's like this young man comes into my life and gives me the opportunity to rekindle the kind of career people expected from me and that I expected from myself . . . It's funny, one movie can make you, and one movie can remake you. It's like I went to the moon, then came back down to Earth, and now I get to go to Mars . . .' Other credits include: *Carrie* (1976), *Staying Alive* (1983), *Chains of Gold* [as actor and writer] (1990), *Broken Arrow* [with Christian Slater, qv] (1996), *White Man's Burden* (1996).

(See also: Vincent Vega)

TRUST AND BETRAYAL

'Being loyal is very important,' Vincent tells the bathroom mirror in *Pulp Fiction*. Indeed, trust, loyalty, and their betrayal, underpin much of Tarantino's most successful work. The roots of their predominance are possibly personal, and undoubtedly echoed in such admired influences as Japanese cinema and the films of Howard Hawks. 'What I respond to in Hawks is all the sub-text of friendship and camaraderie,' Tarantino once claimed.

It has been speculated that Tarantino's absentee father aroused feelings of abandonment which are addressed in the collapse of the relationship between Mr Orange and Mr White in *Reservoir Dogs*. Mr Orange's punishment for the abuse of Mr White's trust is no less than murder. We see an actual father/son relationship in ruin during *True Romance* - Clarence's meeting with Cliff is their first communication in three years. Whatever the reasons behind the inclusion of such dramatic scenes, Tarantino undoubtedly regards loyalty to his closest friends as very important. Director Allison Anders (qv) told *Premiere*'s Peter Biskind how Tarantino supported her following Hugh Grant's decision not to appear in her film *Peter Is Dead*. 'Hugh dropped out for no reason,' she said. 'At Cannes, Quentin told me

Trust and betrayal. Early on in *True Romance* Clarence tells Alabama 'I want you to know that you can count on me to protect you.'

a woman was talking about how Hugh was beyond reproach. So Quentin goes, "Oh yeah? Lemme tell you something. Hugh Grant fucked me over. Cause he fucked over my friend Allison Anders. She's green-lit, and then he balls. Your actor doesn't have the balls to tell her he doesn't want to do the film any more. He fucked her over, and then he fucked me over, because when you fuck one of us, you fuck us all."'

Broadly speaking, the maintenance of trust is seen as an admirable trait in Tarantino's scripts - exhibitions of disloyalty are common to reprehensible characters. Our first glimpse of Drexl Spivey has him murdering a group of his colleagues and stealing a suitcase full of their cocaine. Minutes later, Clarence tells Alabama 'I want you to know that you can count on me to protect you', thus establishing himself as trustworthy in contrast. Even the murderous gangster Coccotti demonstrates a strict personal code when giving hitman Virgil the benefit of his doubt after he goes missing. Coccotti tells how he admired Virgil for keeping his mouth

shut during a jail sentence he served following his arrest in a warehouse. 'Anybody who clams up and does his time, I don't care how I feel about him personally, he's OK.' The scene never made it into Tony Scott's film, but bears a remarkable similarity to Joe and Eddie's demonstration of faith in Vic Vega during *Reservoir Dogs*. The climactic shoot-out at the end of *True Romance* is of course triggered by Lee's realisation that Elliot has betrayed him to the police. Blinded by anger at this deceit ('You stabbed me in the heart!') he is seemingly oblivious to the powder keg he ignites by attacking his two-faced assistant.

The original script of *True Romance* featured a soliloquy from Clarence that clearly defined its author's feelings on trust. It never appeared in the final screenplay, but was partially recycled for *Pulp Fiction*. Following Alabama's beating by Virgil, Clarence tells the camera: 'It's very easy to be enraptured with words, but to remain loyal when it's easier, even excusable, not to - that's a test of oneself. That's true romance.'

Moral laxity is a trademark of nearly every character in *Natural Born Killers*, but Wayne Gayle is seen to deserve Mickey Knox's later contempt for him when he lies to the serial killer, saying the network won't run another Mickey and Mallory edition of *American Maniacs* unless it features a new Mickey interview. Wayne later tells Scott the truth: 'They wanted a follow-up episode and would've taken anything I had given them. I'm not gonna tell Mickey Knox that. I'm gonna make him think his grey matter depends on it.'

Reservoir Dogs concentrates on betrayal and loyalty more than any of Tarantino's other scripts - the search for the 'rat' who betrayed Joe's gang to the police occupies the characters and their audience for much of the film. The traditional villains of the piece stick together - Joe trusts his debtor enough to allow him extra time to pay him back, and looks after the imprisoned Vic Vega ('What the hell did you expect me to do? Just forget about you?'): Eddie tells his dad that they 'damn sure' know they can trust Vic, and Mr White is all too eager to believe that Mr Orange is innocent of betrayal - his primary motivation being a suspicion of Mr Blonde's unprofessional (and therefore disloyal) behaviour during the robbery. Even Mr Pink's 'every man for himself' philosophy about the heist doesn't extend to ultimately walking out on his colleagues. When he tells Mr White that he's abandoning the rendezvous plan, it's not for good - 'I'm gonna check into a motel for a few days. I'll lay low and call Joe.'

Unsurprisingly, undercover cop Freddy Newendyke (aka Mr Orange) is the only character in the film who seems to struggle with the concept of loyalty. After unseen criminal Long Beach Mike makes a deal with the police and recommends Freddy to Joe Cabot, Freddy is appreciative of the referral. 'Do right by him,' he tells his police contact Holdaway, 'he's a good guy. I wouldn't be inside if it weren't for him.' Holdaway doesn't share the same

respect for the defecting criminal. 'Long Beach Mike is not your fucking amigo,' he snaps. 'Long Beach Mike is a fucking scumbag. He is selling out his amigos, that's what kind of a nice guy he fuckin' is, all right?'

It is the strength of conflicting loyalties - Eddie's to Mr Blonde, and Mr White's to Mr Orange - that catalyses the climax of *Reservoir Dogs*. In the closing seconds of the film, Mr Orange's exploration of honour seals his fate - he rewards Mr White's loyalty with the truth about his identity, and dies as a result.

Nowhere is the importance of loyalty better verbalised by a Tarantino character than in *Pulp Fiction*. Suppressing his attraction towards his boss's wife, Vincent Vega wrestles with his conscience in the bathroom mirror: 'This is a moral test of oneself,' he says.

Whatever Butch's motivation for going back to the pawnshop to save arch-enemy Marsellus, The Big Man (who doubtless doesn't feel quite so big after his rape ordeal) values the rescue attempt. He acknowledges their uneasy new alliance with a raised hand and a simple 'We're cool'.

A similarly delicate bond develops between Seth and Jacob in *From Dusk Till Dawn*. On the way to The Titty Twister, Jacob promises not to escape and to help get the Geckos over the Mexican border. In return, Seth promises to release the Fuller family in the morning, and to ensure his brother Richard doesn't sexually assault Kate. Many of the men's exchanges from here on are dominated by the maintenance of that trust, and reluctant cooperation becomes hard-earned mutual respect. In Tarantino's hands the Fullers, of course, have nothing to fear - as an endearing anti-hero, Seth Gecko knows the rules. 'I give you my word,' he tells Jacob, as if speaking for all honourable men. 'My word's my law.'

(See also: Inferno; Morality; Redemption)

U

UNFILMED PROJECTS

Talents as scattergun and prodigious as Tarantino's are bound to give rise to a multiplicity of unseen projects: speculation concerning the nature of his follow-up to *Pulp Fiction* led him to remark several times, 'I've got 16 ideas, any one of them I could do. You could say I'm dating them, but I'm not in love with any of them . . .' Uncompleted, *Captain Peachfuzz and the Anchovy Bandit* was the teenage Tarantino's first attempt at a screenplay. A comedy-adventure in the vein of *Smokey and the Bandit*, 1977's successful Burt Reynolds vehicle, *Captain Peachfuzz* was an extended car chase which used then-fashionable CB radio argot. Tarantino's version - which never got beyond its first 20-30 pages - replaced Reynolds's bootlegger with a protagonist who robbed pizzerias. Having pointedly retained copyright on them, all of *Pulp Fiction*'s double-acts have been nominated by Tarantino, albeit semi-seriously, as suitable characters for sequels/prequels: hence the sometimes-mooted titles *The Further Adventures of Butch and Fabienne*, *The Adventures of Pumpkin and Honey Bunny*, *Jules and Vincent Meet Frankenstein*, and *Jules and Vincent Meet the Mummy* (these latter two suggested after the 1940s 'Abbot and Costello meet the Universal monsters'

comic-horrors, particular Tarantino favourites). Also once mooted was a Vega Brothers movie: Mr Blonde visiting Vincent's Amsterdam club. Post-*Ed Wood*, Tarantino suggested a biopic of Budd Boetticher, the 1950s bullfighter-turned-director (*Ride Lonesome*, *The Rise and Fall of Legs Diamond*, etc), and has apparently had an idea for a storyline for *Die Hard IV*. Especially pernicious was the suggestion that Tarantino might direct the big-screen version of 1960s television spy series, *The Man From Uncle*; he was allegedly offered 1994's *Speed*, and suggested by none other than Sean Connery as a suitable helm for 1995's James Bond revival, *GoldenEye* (eventually handled by Jan de Bont and Martin Campbell respectively). Once reportedly linked to a project entitled *Rock All Night*, possibly a remake of the 1957 AIP feature starring Dick Miller (qv), Tarantino did, however, make some progress on a screenplay for Hong Kong action director John Woo. The Woo actioner never saw fruition - likewise, Tarantino collaborator Roger Avary (qv) penned a script for Woo entitled *Hatchetman* - but many other projects beckoned: an uncharacteristically romantic piece about 'how a guy feels about his ex-girlfriend'; 'a guys-on-a-mission movie', in the vein of *Where Eagles Dare*; a Western; and a straightforward adaptation of a novel.

V

VIDEO ARCHIVES

The now-legendary video rental store where, from 1984 to 1989, Tarantino worked as a clerk and ultimately as manager. Once widely thought to have been the equivalent of a 'film school' where Tarantino discovered his hobby, the director has since protested that it was his encyclopaedic knowledge of film that originally earned him a job in the store. 'It's been blown up as being more important to my film education than it was', he told *Premiere*. 'What was great about it is that it just stopped me from having to work for a living.'

Video Archives had its roots in a rental shop called Video Outtakes, located in Redondo. While a customer there, Tarantino made the acquaintance of staffers Scott McGill and Eddie Karpinsky (sometimes called 'Nice Guy' - Tarantino would borrow the nickname for a *Reservoir Dogs* character). When Outtakes closed, Tarantino took his business to a store called Video Archives which opened on North Sepulveda Boulevard, Manhattan Beach, in October 1983. Owned by manager Lance Lawson and local entrepreneurs Rick and Dennis Humbert, Video Archives soon earned a reputation for the breadth and quality of its stock. Tarantino was so taken with the store

and its staff, who included his friend Scott McGill, that he persuaded Lawson to give him a job in 1984.

Tarantino found kindred spirits among many of the people who worked alongside him - his first film-making attempt, *Lovebirds in Bondage*, had already been partially shot with the help of McGill. Tarantino co-wrote *My Best Friend's Birthday* and a treatment called *Criminal Mind* with colleague Craig Hamann who, in 1985, also collaborated on a storyline called *The Open Road. The Open Road* was originated by fellow clerk Roger Avary (qv), whose influence directly and indirectly informed much of Tarantino's writing during the Video Archives years and beyond. Elsewhere, other staff-members proved catalytic towards some of Tarantino's key scenes - the reaction of Sicilian Stephen 'Stevo' Poliy to Tarantino's theory on his countrymen's origin helped the emerging writer realise the full dramatic potential of a scene which found its way into *True Romance*. While working at Video Archives, Tarantino and Poliy shared a house with a character known as 'Dave the British guy'. The label 'English Dave' was much later applied to the genial barman at Sally LeRoy's in *Pulp Fiction*.

Other Video Archives colleagues included Gerald Martinez, Russell Vossler and Rowland Wafford, as well as Lance Lawson, who lent his name to Clarence's benevolent boss in *True Romance* and Vincent's less benevolent heroin dealer in *Pulp Fiction*.

While at Video Archives, Tarantino attempted to liven the shop up by organising 'seasons' of highlighted films, typified by particular themes. It was his season of heist movies that prompted him to write a script concerning a bungled robbery, and his misinterpretation of a customer's request for *Au Revoir Les Enfants* as 'Reservoir Dogs' that gave that script its name. At other times Tarantino tried to convince film industry celebrities to make personal appearances in the shop - he once unsuccessfully asked special effects maestro Tom Savini (qv) to come along. Prestigious Hollywood people who did visit the shop included customer Jeff Maguire (who wrote the screenplay for *In The Line Of Fire*). Maguire would read and comment on the staff's scripts in return for free video rental.

Towards the end of his time at the shop, Tarantino had been promoted to manager and had started dating regular customer Grace Lovelace. He later used his influence to secure her a position at the store. By this stage, *The Open Road* had developed into *True Romance* and *Natural Born Killers*. *True Romance* was under development by British producer Stanley Margolis, and progress was beginning to look promising when Tarantino was fired from Video Archives by Dennis Humbert in 1989. Although he soon returned on a part-time basis, Margolis's optimism and Tarantino's desire to move closer to Hollywood's film-making community prompted his ultimate departure. He went on to a job as a roving salesman for video distributors Imperial.

Such were Tarantino's fond memories of Video Archives and its staff that he never quite left it, or them, behind. Around 1990 he began work on a novel inspired by his experiences working at the store, although he abandoned the project after several months intensive work and a mere two chapters. When shooting *Reservoir Dogs*, he cast Rowland Wafford and Gerald Martinez as extras in the diner where Newendyke makes his rendezvous with Holdaway. While Newendyke relates his phoney story to Joe Cabot, 'Stevo' Poliy can be seen as 'Sheriff # 4' in the bathroom flashback. Craig Hamann provided the voice of one of the cops trailing Nice Guy Eddie outside Freddy Newendyke's apartment. Gerald Martinez and Russell Vossler both lent their names and talents to the visuals of *Pulp Fiction*, Craig Hamann offered advice on the portrayal of Mia's overdose, and Grace Lovelace lent her Christian name to Zed's chopper. Craig Hamann is also said to have had crucial input to the structure of *Reservoir Dogs*, while the exact nature of co-writer Roger Avary's contributions to both *Dogs* and *Pulp* is still the subject of some controversy.

Tarantino has even cast Video Archives employees who began working at the shop after he left - redheads Laura Rush and 'Unruly' Julie McClean make brief appearances at the party in *Four Rooms*.

Notable return visits to Video Archives included the press launch for the US video of *Reservoir Dogs*, held in the store on 7 April 1983. Tarantino made his final visit to the shop's original premises on 11 August 1994 to record a sequence for the BBC's *Omnibus* documentary *Quentin Tarantino: Hollywood's Boy Wonder*. Shortly after the cameras stopped, the store's sign was torn down. On the same day, the documentary crew accompanied him to a reunion with Lance Lawson and Gerald Martinez at Video Archives' new premises in nearby Hermosa Beach. Lawson had moved the store to a location opposite the old Bijou Theater, adding 2,000 extra titles (bringing the library up to 10,000) and constructing a coffee bar to host the punters' debates. Sadly, the expansion was over-ambitious and the move poorly publicised. A private screening of *Pulp Fiction* for Video Archives employees proved to by the final landmark in the shop's illustrious history. It closed, weeks later, at the end of November 1994.

When the huge library was auctioned soon after, Tarantino bought around 600 video tapes, and Roger Avary bought many of the laserdiscs.

(See also: *Crimson Tide*; Names)

VINCENT VEGA

Wallace employee and assassin Vincent has spent three years in Amsterdam, leaving his beloved Malibu behind in storage; maybe his burger and drug-fuelled sabbatical has left him sloppy (he accidentally shoots Marvin dead, carries the heroin which nearly kills Mia in his coat pocket, and will make a more profound miscalculation which will cost him his life). Of his family background, we learn nothing:

in a cut section of *Pulp Fiction*'s script, we discover that his cousin is named Suzanne, but she's no relation to the singer (according to a *Melody Maker* interview with Tarantino, Suzanne Vega's eponymously-titled debut is one of the director's favourite albums of all time. Other interviews have confirmed that Vincent is the brother of the equally ill-fated Vic, *Reservoir Dogs*'s Mr Blonde). Marsellus trusts Vincent with his wife, although he may have a low opinion of Vincent otherwise (to The Wolf, Marsellus describes Vincent in terms of comedian Dean Martin). Vincent lives in suburban Redondo Beach (where Tarantino's former haunt, Video Outtakes, once stood), and 'don't watch TV'; his bootlace tie marks him out as an unreconstructed Fifties man. He knows his drugs: he buys three hundred dollars' worth of Choco, a vivacious German heroin, from his regular dealer, Lance. Vincent injects. (He knows his guns, too, recognising the Fourth Man's .357 at a glance.)

More substantially, Vincent's quick-tempered: he's prepared to face off Butch in Sally Leroy's

Vincent stands firm: 'Jules, you give that fuckin' nimrod fifteen hundred dollars, and I'll shoot her on general principle . . . '

for being over-familiar, and takes offence when Winston Wolf omits the requisite Ps and Qs. He's developed a personal moral code: loyalty figures highly. It is Vincent's loyalty to Marsellus, rather than his fear of him, that prevents him from making a move on Mia (note also Vincent's other key maxim: 'You don't fuck another man's vehicle'). Nevertheless, he's clearly attracted to Mia (he even blows her a discreet, rueful little kiss) and is so taken by her *Fox Force Five* persona that - for the remainder of his short life - he carries a *Modesty Blaise* novel about him as an *aide-memoire* (which he, er, 'reads' in the toilets of both the Hawthorne Grill and Butch's place). Whether it's his carelessness (in leaving his machine-gun on Butch's kitchen worktop), or his ignorance (in 'blowin' off' the divine intervention which may, like Jules, have given him the chance to be redeemed) which kills him is a matter open to conjecture. Nevertheless, he dies the death of a true Elvis man: on the john.

(See also: Blonde; Elvis Presley; Mia Wallace; Morality; Travolta, John)

VIOLENCE

Tarantino's scripts are punctuated by violence - without exception, his drama is hallmarked by instigating, catalysing and redeeming acts of brutality. No other writer or director active in contemporary cinema shares such an indelible reputation for visceral film-making, although many are more melodramatic and few are more accountable.

At the heart of Tarantino's liberal deployment of violence throughout his work is his firm belief in its function as a pure cinematic aesthetic (a function that initially dominates, and ultimately overwhelms, his screenplay of Robert Kurtzman's SFX showcase *From Dusk Till Dawn*). As he frequently argued in the wake of the *Reservoir Dogs* ear-cutting controversy, in purely cinematic terms the idea of a

film containing 'gratuitous' violence is comparable to a musical featuring gratuitous song-and-dance numbers. And just as there are classic musical routines, Tarantino clearly favours a few set-pieces of his own. Chair-bound torture visits Cliff in *True Romance*, Marvin in *Reservoir Dogs* and, to a degree, Brett in *Pulp Fiction*. Drexl in *True Romance* and Zed in *Pulp Fiction* both have their genitals blasted off in acts of revenge. The severing of fingers features in *Natural Born Killers* and *Four Rooms: Penthouse Suite: The Man From Hollywood*, while Mr White recommends it as a method of crowd control in *Reservoir Dogs*. That Tarantino has been able to serve up so many variations from such a relatively limited menu proves he is an imaginative cook, if nothing else.

The other foundation for Tarantino's depiction of violence is his adherence to authentic examinations of brutality. In *Reservoir Dogs*, when he shoots something as commonplace in film as a fight between two men, he shows Mr White and Mr Pink kicking and scratching at each other like catty girls. The cliched and unrealistic jaw-punches of action film fisticuffs are refreshingly absent from his work. Alabama's retaliation against Virgil in *True Romance* is desperate and animalistic - a factor which caused problems for director Tony Scott when the film was submitted for American certification.

Where much of Tarantino's violence differs more significantly from the carefully choreographed blood ballets of John Woo or the comic-book banality of James Cameron is in its unrelenting concentration on violence as something that has long-term effects on its victims and those around them. In *Reservoir Dogs* we share Marvin's post-torture anguish, but we never directly witness the severing of his ear. The drawn-out demise of Mr Orange, meanwhile, serves to accentuate the gravity of his suffering not just for the purposes of a single scene, but for practically the duration of the entire film. In *Pulp Fiction*, the Bonnie Situation segment treats the aftermath of Marvin's accidental murder with far more attention than the accidental shooting itself. Bullets maim, kill, and are messy. This inversion of the traditional approach to GBH as a finite dramatic device is a twist Tarantino relies upon to evoke poignancy or humour.

One of the ways in which the non-sequential narrative of *Reservoir Dogs* serves its director is in increasing the impact of a key violent consequence. Provided with no establishing information about the predicament of Mr Orange following *Reservoir Dogs*'s opening credits, audiences are forced to address the moral questions over his shooting in a way the film's characters never do. In the same way that the film's pre-credit sequence defines so many thematic parameters in Tarantino's dialogue, the sequence of Mr Orange bleeding to death in the back of Mr White's car encapsulates Tarantino's approach to violence as he continues to set out his stall in the opening minutes of his first film.

It is perhaps significant that *Natural Born Killers* (by its author's own admission, 'the worst script I ever wrote') suffers from the most ill-defined and cursory stance towards violence in all of Tarantino's writing. While *True Romance* inspires only empathy for Clarence and Alabama during the course of their self-improvement, the killings perpetrated by Mickey and Mallory Knox were always intended to make the audience question their initial loyalty to, and enjoyment of, these characters. That this bridge was never effectively crossed in either Tarantino's script or Oliver Stone's film is at least partly due to the extent and nature of the couple's murders and the relatively brief attention each individual act of brutality is accorded. The enormity of the Knoxs' actions never sinks in, and Tarantino's

most intentionally moral story becomes his most seemingly amoral script. It is testimony to Tarantino's developing writing skills that he was able to achieve this audience interactivity more effectively during the single ear-cutting scene in *Reservoir Dogs* than he was able to during the entire course of *Natural Born Killers*.

Although preoccupied with the crucial functions of violence as dramatic catalyst and visual garnish, Tarantino also finds space to voice his own repellence of real-life brutality through the mouths of his characters. Virgil's speech to the concussed Alabama ('Now I'll just do it to watch their fucking expression change . . .') reveals his utter desensitization to slaughter in a way that almost evokes sympathy for the pathetic hitman. While one of the least 'cool' characters from *True Romance* is certainly the most violent, one of the coolest characters in *Pulp Fiction* earns our respect (and the right to leave the film alive) when he decides to renounce his murderous lifestyle. Jules's spiritual awakening at the end of *The Bonnie Situation* segment sees him turn his back on the killing that has previously defined him.

This reclamation of meaningful cinematic brutality has been recognised by the chairman of the British Board of Film Classification, James Ferman, who passed *Reservoir Dogs* for theatrical and video release uncut with an 18 certificate. Sadly, in the aftermath of Jamie Bulger's tragic death and several murders in France allegedly inspired by *Natural Born Killers*, the BBFC delayed granting video certification to *True Romance* and *Reservoir Dogs*. This wariness over violence in Tarantino's films was largely responsible for the current misreadings of its portrayal.

(See also: Blood; Ears; Fingers; Morality; *Stuck In The Middle With You*; X-rated)

W

WALKEN, CHRISTOPHER (1943 -)
Vincent Coccotti, *True Romance*
Captain Koons, *Pulp Fiction*

Born in New York, Roland Walken changed his Christian name to assume a number of different guises in films from 1968 on; he won an Oscar as best supporting actor for 1979's *The Deer Hunter*. Seemingly thereafter cast as a cold, Aryan villain - notably as the Maxes, Zorin and Schreck, in *A View to a Kill* and *Batman Returns* respectively - Walken was allegedly proposed for the role of *Dogs*'s Mr Blonde by Harvey Keitel, but, despite an announcement of Walken's casting in a

January 1991 edition of *Screen International*, Walken was unable to appear (the *Dogs* budget was consequently reduced; Walken had previously acted alongside its producer, Lawrence Bender, in a private performance of *A Midsummer Night's Dream*). Walken was central to Tarantino's two longest monologues, the first as Vincent in *True Romance* (a role once earmarked for Michael Madsen, qv). He has fond memories of being on the receiving end of Dennis Hopper's (qv) Sicilians polemic: 'I was really enjoying this guy, and then I shoot him anyway,' he told *Empire* magazine. 'And the same is true of him - he really enjoyed telling me that story. And you could see it was delightful . . . It happens to end with me shooting him in the head. But up until then, wasn't it delightful?' Less amusing was the prop gun director Tony Scott asked him to fire against Hopper's forehead. When Walken refused, Scott asked him to demonstrate its safety by firing it agaist his own forehead. The hapless director still bears the scar.

Walken made an even greater impression with his next Tarantino monologue - the astonishing 'gold watch' speech that remains a highlight of *Pulp Fiction*. Other credits

Wayne Gayle and his mute assistant Unruly Julie interview the incarcerated Mickey Knox.

include: *The Anderson Tapes* (1971), *Annie Hall* (1977), *Heaven's Gate* (1980), *The Dead Zone* (1983), *At Close Range* [with Chris Penn, qv] (1986), *Things to Do in Denver When You're Dead* [with Steve Buscemi, qv] (1996), *Funeral* [with Chris Penn] (1996).

WAYNE GAYLE

Described as a 'young, energetic, commando journalist' in the mould of talk show host Geraldo Rivera (who secured a sensational interview with Charles Manson in the Eighties) Wayne Gayle is the obnoxious Yuppie at the helm of television show *American*

Maniacs. 'Everyone knows who you are', Mickey tells him in a generous moment of ego-massage. 'You're famous.'

Not averse to hoodwinking Mickey into getting an interview, or hoodwinking his audience into thinking the next edition of *American Maniacs* will comprise entirely new material, Gayle's Machiavellian instincts know no bounds. After all, as he claims, 'Am I God or what?'.

Gayle's delivery is sometimes melodramatic, sometimes mournful, but never less than cliched, especially in sensationalising the

Knoxs' 'candy lane of murder and mayhem' for his forty million viewers. Gayle shares the sentiments of *Four Rooms*'s similarly loud-mouthed Chester Rush concerning video. 'Fuck video', he snaps, while discussing the importance of using 16mm film stock during Mickey's interview. 'This is just too damned important.' Gayle's arrogance extends to thinking his stature will make him a more valuable hostage during the climactic prison stand-off, and to thinking that Mickey and Mallory will leave him alive to tell their tale. Ultimately, however, Mickey will make him a bigger star dead than he ever was alive.

(See also: Downey Jr, Robert)

WHITE [LAWRENCE DIMICK]

Possessor of perhaps the most complex personality among the *Reservoir Dogs*, Mr White spends much of the film 'barking up the wrong tree' (as Mr Blonde observes) with his loyalty towards the wounded Mr Orange.

Tarantino's original script for *Reservoir Dogs* reveals much more than the finished film about Mr White's true personality. White's real name is Lawrence 'Larry' Dimick, although criminal records also indicate that he goes by the names Lawrence Jacobs and Alvin 'Al' Jacobs. Jodie at police headquarters prefers to call him 'Mr Joe-Armed-Robbery', and with good reason. The first of Dimick's two convictions came at the age of 21, when he was arrested staging an armed robbery at a lumber yard payroll office in Milwaukee. Dimick remained a Milwaukee Brewers fan after moving to Los Angeles in 1977, where he was next convicted following an arrest in a routine vice squad bust in 1983. Dimick was wearing a diamond ring known to have been taken from a jewellery store robbery a year earlier, and served two years in prison as a result.

Moving forward in time, we next discover that Larry teamed up with a girl called Alabama (could this be following the death of her husband and partner in crime Clarence?) and the two worked as a team. 'Hell of a woman - good little thief,' Larry tells Joe, after explaining why the two split up. 'You push that woman/man thing too long and it gets to you after a while.' Around 18 months before the *Reservoir Dogs* raid, Dimick enrolled for a four-man bank job and discovered that one member of the gang was an undercover cop. The policeman, John Dolenz, was murdered on his birthday in front of a crowd of surprise party guests, three of whom were killed by the escaping assassin. The police suspected Dimick of the murders, but were unable to bring charges. The proposed bank robbery was cancelled.

Two jobs later, and Larry Dimick is specially called in from out of town by Joe Cabot to carry out a vital role in the diamond heist - he is entrusted with taking the diamonds from the store manager. However, while Mr White is clearly experienced in handling uncooperative staff members and customers, the prospect of defending himself against the trigger-happy Mr Blonde takes him by surprise. He is driven to nearly shooting his psychotic colleague, and escapes the chaos with Mr Orange. On the way, Mr White callously murders a number of pursuing cops without any hesitation or sign of remorse. When Mr Orange is shot, however, he becomes increasingly paternal towards his young friend and blames himself for the injury. 'I think I'm jinxed,' he tells Mr Pink.

Such is Larry's loyalty to the injured Mr Orange that he is prepared to kill Mr Pink to defend his honour, and later shoots both Eddie and Joe following the accusation that Orange is an undercover cop. Larry's primal scream upon discovering the truth betrays all the pain of betrayal in a man who seems to have abandoned faith in everything but honour amongst thieves.

(See also: Keitel, Harvey; Morality; Names; Trust and betrayal)

John Travolta and Bruce
Willis share a joke (and a
Red Apple?) between
takes on *Pulp Fiction*.

WHO DO YOU THINK YOU'RE FOOLING? (THE STORY OF A ROBBERY)
(See: *City on Fire*)

WILLIS, BRUCE (1955 -)
Butch Coolidge, *Pulp Fiction*
Leo, *Four Rooms: The Man From Hollywood*
[uncredited]

Born Walter Willison in Germany, welder's son
Willis grew up in New Jersey, studied his craft
at Monclair State College, and endured several
years as a Dick Ritchie-esque struggling actor
from 1978 on - interspersed with day jobs at a
chemical company, a nuclear power plant, and
as a barman at New York's Kamikaze and Cafe
Central - before securing the part of David
Addison, male lead in TV series *Moonlighting*
(1985-1989), for which he was awarded a
best actor Emmy in 1987. A noted Republican,
his most successful on-screen persona - as

New York cop John McClane in the action-ori-
ented *Die Hard* series -would overshadow his
leading roles in two of the most publicised
Hollywood failures of the 1990s, *The Bonfire
of the Vanities* and *Hudson Hawk*. Willis was
cast as *Pulp*'s Butch after Harvey Keitel (qv)
had introduced him to Tarantino at a barbecue
in July 1993; the part had allegedly been
considered for actor Matt Dillon. Willis -
reportedly delighted to play a credibility-
enhancing role - worked a grand total of 18
days on *Pulp*; he followed this up with an
uncredited appearance as Chester Rush's manager Leo in *Four Rooms*. Other credits include:
Blind Date (1987), *Look Who's Talking* [voice
only; with John Travolta, qv] (1989), *The Last
Boy Scout* (1991), *The Player* (1992), *National
Lampoon's Loaded Weapon 1* [uncredited; with
Samuel L Jackson, qv] (1993), *Die Hard With a
Vengeance* [with Samuel L Jackson] (1995),
Twelve Monkeys (1996).

WINSTON WOLF

'I'm Winston Wolf, I solve problems' - *Pulp Fiction*.

Meticulous Marsellus employee The Wolf ('Call me Winston') has the automatic respect of those in the Wallace organisation (bar Vincent, who's been out of circulation for a while) and appreciates it, too: he's got a clear head, he makes notes, and is curt under pressure. We first meet The Wolf in a hotel suite-cum-casino: so cool is The Wolf, he's wearing the unmarked tux of the night before at eight-thirty in the ay-em. He drives 'real fuckin' fast', and is consequently able to make a thirty-minute journey in nine minutes and thirty-five seconds (a cut portion of the script reveals that The Wolf lacks tardiness behind the wheel of his Porsche because he likes driving so). He takes his coffee with 'lotsa cream, lotsa sugar' and he 'don't smile in pictures' (again, a cut line). He's got a useful link to ask-no-questions scrap merchant Monster Joe (with whom he's dealt many times in the past); he's occasionally dating Joe's surely-too-young daughter, Raquel. And if his speediness seems divine, he also cleanses Jules and Vincent of their Earthly sins (albeit with a garden hose). Believe us, it's a pleasure watchin' him work . . .

(See also: Keitel, Harvey)

WOMEN

'I gotta go pee. I wanna go home' - Honey Bunny, *Pulp Fiction*.

The evidence thus far suggests that, as a writer, Tarantino shares little affinity with his female characters. While his key male characters are often sophisticated, complex and sensitive people (Clarence, Mr White, Jules etc) what relatively few female characters there are in his scripts are superficially sketched women, often defined by their relationships to men. For example, Jody, Lance's body-pierced wife in *Pulp Fiction*, has a stud in her tongue because 'it helps fellatio'.

While Alabama Whitman (qv) has a fully fleshed background as American white trash turned hooker, her role in *True Romance* is as fairy tale princess to Clarence. Tarantino has admitted that, at the time of writing *True Romance*, his experience of women was limited and that he devised the character very much as a 'dream girlfriend'. She remains the most self-reliant and perhaps the most endearing of Tarantino's female characters, but by the end of the film we still know little about her, her actions and motivations inseparable from Clarence's influence.

Unsurprisingly, given how *Natural Born Killers* shared the same origins as *True Romance*, Mallory Knox (qv) comes across in a similar vein. Self-reliant, if hardly endearing, the serial killer likewise lives for her husband Mickey. We learn far more about the girl in Oliver Stone's film that Tarantino's screenplay, the director taking pains to redress what he saw as an omission in the original script by making her more independent of Mickey and clearly defining her motivation. Her flashbacks to her father's repeated sexual abuse are some of the most effective sequences, adding depth to a character left decidedly one-dimensional in Tarantino's script.

In *Reservoir Dogs*, women are practically absent from the entire picture, although their presence is certainly felt by Mr Orange - he takes pains to find his wedding ring before he leaves his flat and is later shot by one of the only women glimpsed in the picture. We learn a lot about women from various characters (especially the politically incorrect Mr Pink - 'learn to fuckin' type') but these comments illustrate only a group of men who see women's roles as waitresses, typists and sexual providers.

In following genre stereotypes, *Pulp Fiction* gave us the gangster's tough moll (Mia), the boxer's cute girlfriend (Fabienne) and a mysterious South American beauty (Esmarelda). Sadly, the briefly glimpsed Esmarelda fawns towards Butch and the more prominent women, Fabienne and Mia (both qv), have little identity beyond their relationship to their prospective partners and both blunder into catastrophes which male characters need to extricate them from. Fabienne's forgetting of Butch's precious watch forces him to return to his apartment, leading him into 'the single weirdest fuckin' day of my life.' Towards the end of the *Gold Watch* segment, Butch is forced to talk to her as if she were a child simply to cultivate a sense of urgency. Mia, while initially appearing self-confident and assertive, accidentally overdoses on heroin, forcing Vincent and Lance to save her life with an adrenaline shot. Her ultimate fate as someone who needs rescuing by the men around her is a disappointing end to the only character in any of Tarantino's scripts who even looks as though she may be hold her own against her male peers.

As a director, however, Tarantino imbues Fabienne and Mia with genuine expressiveness and sensuality. Fabienne, while never anything other than utterly submissive, is able to invest her requests for everything from blueberry pancakes to oral sex with a sensuality that Butch finds impossible to demolish, even in his deepest rage. Mia is similarly established as a manipulative of a sex kitten, her moist lips tightly framed against the intercom microphone as she manoeuvres the surveillance camera's joystick. Tarantino continues to tease us, building up our expectations of the predatory Mia - before we see her face we are treated to a sensual shot of her stalking feet, the upturning of a bare sole accompanying her assertive 'Let's go'. Despite this, Vincent fails to make it with Mia, and we are again denied a realistic relationship conceived under 'real' circumstances in 'genuine' surroundings. *From Dusk Till Dawn*, a script that makes

virture of the way its genre characters operate in 'unreal' surroundings, presents the feisty Kate Fuller. While undeniably a resourceful and independent character, her origins are as clearly rooted in B-movie stereotypes as the vampires that threaten her life. Kate obeys all the traditional expectations of teenage girls who start out horror films as straight-laced Christians - she soon rebels against her repression, as well as the undead. Alongside many other characters in *From Dusk Till Dawn*, Kate reacts to much while instigating little.

If Tarantino is to realise his wish to make a film about 'how a guy feels about his ex-girlfriend' (see Unfilmed projects, qv) then his female characters must first achieve the sophistication of his male leads in order to be as effective.

(See also: Arquette, Patricia; Foot fetishism; Lewis, Juliette)

WRIGHT, STEVEN (1955 -)
K-Billy DJ, *Reservoir Dogs* [voice only]
Dr Emil Reingold, *Natural Born Killers*
In 1979, New York-born writer-comedian Steven Wright tried his hand on the stand-up comedy circuit after menial stints parking cars and working in a warehouse; in 1982, he broke into television, making appearances on *The Tonight Show* and *Saturday Night Live*, among others. His first straight acting role was as a dentist in 1985's *Desparately Seeking Susan*, opposite Rosanna Arquette (qv) and Madonna; he followed this with a role in 1986's *Coffee and Cigarettes*, from his own screenplay. In 1989, his television play *The Appointments of Dennis Jennings* garnered an Oscar for best live action short. His *Dogs* voiceover as the so-laid-back-he's-catatonic DJ led to a small part as a psychiatrist in Oliver Stone's *NBK*. Other acting credits include: *Stars and Bars* (1988), *Men of Respect* (1990), *Speechless* (1994).

XYZ

X-RATED

Strangely enough, for such a - to some - controversial director, matters of censorship have been but rarely pertinent to Tarantino's *oeuvre*. The Motion Picture Association of America objected to certain sequences in *True Romance*, demanding trims to make the film suitable for an 'R' [Restricted] certificate, other than a box-office-poison 'NC-17' [No-one under 17 admitted]. Much of the 'cunnilingus' dialogue between Drexl, Floyd and Don was cut (virtually eliminating Don, played by Samuel L Jackson, qv, from the film altogether); the end of the Virgil/Alabama scene, wherein - according to the script - Alabama, after despatching Virgil with several blasts from the shotgun, 'runs at him, hitting him in the head with the butt' while reciting the prayer of St Francis of Assisi; and Officer Dimes would be shot by one of the Mafia hoods, rather than Alabama (see Penn, Chris). The cuts were made after three weeks of negotiations between Tony Scott and the MPAA; in the UK, some of the sequences would not be so severely trimmed. *Natural Born Killers*, meanwhile, would be treated far more harshly by the MPAA; it was submitted ten times in total, and some 150 cuts made to it, before being granted an 'R' (much of the excised material depicted the cli-

mactic prison riot; see Jones, Tommy Lee). '[It] was a demeaning process', Oliver Stone reflected, 'humiliating, because I much preferred the rhythms of my original'. A director's cut has been promised. The UK video release of *Reservoir Dogs* was put on hiatus for some two years in the wake of a media-induced outcry over video violence in the wake of the James Bulger case; it was eventually released uncut on 14 June 1995 (long after Channel 4, which had purchased the film, vowed to screen it likewise uncut). By November of 1995, the British Board of Film Classification announced that no complaints had been received since its release (according to the *Evening Standard*, a recent survey of 69 juvenile delinquents' viewing habits prompted a mention of the film from only one). *Pulp Fiction*'s video release, however, would be subject to a minor alteration: BBFC director James Ferman confirmed to *The Guardian* that there is 'one tiny change in the panning and scanning of a shot showing the needle of the syringe going into Travolta's arm' ('this sort of image is known to be hypnotically seductive' to would-be addicts, apparently). Two consecutive shots - one showing the needle penetrating the skin, one showing the syringe's plunger descending - were cropped, the first to eliminate a drop of blood from the puncture, the second eliminating details of the syringe itself (the letterboxed widescreen version was subject to similar adjustments in framing). After taking advice and concluding that *Natural Born Killers* was unconnected to several crimes allegedly inspired by it, the BBFC granted the film a theatrical release despite an hysterical, high-profile campaign against it; to date, *NBK* has not received a video release (like *Reservoir Dogs* before, it continues to do brisk business in the bootleg trade). Tarantino himself seems remarkably unconcerned by the fate of his films on video, telling the BBC's *Kaleidoscope* programme: 'To be truthful, I could care less about [*Reservoir Dogs* being put on hiatus in the UK] . . . If they were to cut a frame of the theatrical, I might be banging at the doors of Parliament. But as far as the video is concerned, the easiest way to kill the excitement and cult of something is to make it readily accessible . . .' When preparing the bloody *From Dusk Till Dawn*, Tarantino, producer Lawrence Bender, and director Robert Rodriguez were all well aware of the problems that the film might have with such as the MPAA: 'We can't do an NC-17,' Tarantino told *Fangoria*, 'because this is going out with a big 2,000-screen release. I'm not worried about cuts, though, because I have a good relationship with the MPAA. We're going to have to go back a few times, but one of the things I've learned is that I usually get them released exactly the way I want them to.' Before production finished, there was talk of a longer version for laserdisc, and the possibility was raised that the film would be released simultaneously in both a no-holds-barred NC-17 version and a trimmed R: the box-office failure of Paul Verhoeven's *Showgirls*, the first major studio NC-17, may have scuppered the notion. Strangest of all, in Australia - according to an *Empire* reader - the published script of *Reservoir Dogs* was - astonishingly - altered by university librarians in Perth before being judged fit for student consumption. Among the casualties were: the Madonna scene - '*Like a*

Virgin is all about a guy who digs big bucks. The whole song is a metaphor for big bucks'; 'Now I know I'm no piece of shit' became 'Now I know I'm no piece of liver'; and 'Someone's stickin' a red hot poker up our asses' was bowdlerized into 'Someone's stickin' a red hot poker up our noses'.

(See also: Causality and imitation; Morality; Violence)

YOU NEVER CAN TELL

Mia and Vincent's entry in Jack Rabbit Slim's 'world famous' twist contest is loosely choreographed to Chuck Berry's *You Never Can Tell*, one of the most memorable tunes from the *Pulp Fiction* soundtrack.

Charles 'Chuck' Berry, one of rock 'n' roll's most influential founding fathers, wrote *You Never Can Tell* in prison during 1962/63, following his conviction for 'transporting an under-age girl across state lines for immoral purposes'. It later reached number 23 in the UK in August 1964. Berry's recording career began with the legendary *Maybellene* in 1955, and went on to produce such quintessential anthems as *Johnny B Goode*, *Sweet Little Sixteen* and *No Particular Place To Go*. Despite the enduring popularity of his best work, Berry only scored one UK chart-topper - the infamous comedy number *My Ding-A-Ling*, which was released near the end of his singles career in 1972. Now in his seventies, the tempestuous Berry continues performing live, and continues to attract controversy.

It was Berry's characteristically crisp lyrics that attracted Tarantino to the song: 'It doesn't have a French sound at all, but [the mention of] "Pierre" and the "mademoiselle" gives it a cool Fifties French New Wave dance sequence feel.'

It is fitting that the song should conjure up such imagery for the director - in advising

Followed footsteps:
Bande a Part, inspiration
for *Pulp Fiction's*
twist contest.

Uma Thurman and John Travolta on how to
play the scene, he showed them its inspiration
- Anna Karina, Sami Frey and Claude Brasseur's
impromptu musical shuffle from Jean-Luc
Godard's *Bande a Part* (1964). 'My favourite
musical sequences have always been in
Godard, because they just come out of
nowhere,' he enthuses. 'And the fact that it's
not a musical, but he's stopping the movie
to have a musical sequence, makes it all the
more sweet.'

YUPPIE SCUM

Tarantino usually shows the most loathsome
of characters in at least a semi-sympathetic
light. *Reservoir Dogs's* Pink (qv) may be a racist
misanthrope - and tight-fisted to boot - but at
least he's 'a fuckin' professional'; likewise,
Vincent Vega (qv) may be a randy drug-
peddling assassin with an attitude problem,
but his wrestling with his conscience and the
sheer scale of the predicament he finds himself in during his date with Mia makes him

possibly the most likeable character in *Pulp Fiction*. Such concessions to audience empathy serve to blur and obfuscate any editorial pontificating on the side of the auteur; the amorality of his characters is studied, if nothing else. However, besides - possibly - cops, there's one group of characters whom Tarantino clearly holds in the lowest of possible regard: young, upwardly-mobile, urban professionals or, as the name of the character played by Lawrence Bender (qv) in both *Pulp* and *Four Rooms* has it, 'yuppie scum'.

In *Reservoir Dogs*, Daddy's boy Nice Guy Eddie (qv) bears all the hallmarks of the *arriviste*: an obsession with his 'take', appalling taste in leisurewear, and he's clearly so in love with his prominently-displayed cellular phone that he blabs details of the heist over its easy-to-monitor channels. He's the LA equivalent of an East End barrow-boy done good in the family firm. Likewise, *True Romance*'s duplicitous and craven Elliot Blitzer - 'a real *GQ* blow dry boy', according to the script's directions - has a highly-overestimated sense of his own worth, a recreational interest in cocaine, and, when it comes to cops or his boss, the equally *nouveau* carphone-using Lee Donowitz, kisses ass bigtime. And the sharpsuited, egomaniac media vulture Wayne Gayle, as written in *Natural Born Killers*, hires a PA, Unruly Julie, who was 'born without a tongue', presumably so she can't answer back (the same script also suggests class hatred between mass murderers:

Mickey dismisses serial killer Ted Bundy as a 'yuppie piece of shit'). Eddie, Elliot, Lee and Wayne all meet violent ends. And, Tarantino appears to be saying, quite rightly so.

But note two further examples of this sub-species: *Pulp Fiction*'s Jimmie Dimmick and *Four Rooms*'s Chester Rush, both portrayed on screen by Tarantino himself. Jimmie appears to have forsaken a life of 'gangsta' shit' for a professional wife, Bonnie (qv), and a two-bedroom suburban house in Toluca Lake; the entire *Bonnie Situation* segment of Pulp revolves around an effort to maintain the lifestyle to which he has become accustomed, and not get 'fucking divorced'. Jimmie buys the very best coffee - 'gourmet expensive stuff' - worries about his bed linen, and is prepared to put aside familial pride for an oak bedroom ('Oak's nice', after all). Vulgar, Cristal-guzzling hotshot director Chester Rush, like Jimmie, believes in conspicuous consumption: he's portrayed lovingly with his 1964 Chevy Chevelle on the cover of *Hot Classic Cars*, and peels off banknotes like leaves from a tree. Although clearly a monstrous caricature, Chester is surely a Tarantino alter ego: if that's the case, has the young auteur become 'yuppie scum' himself?

(See also: Alter egos)

ZED

Zed's dead, baby. Zed's dead.

APPENDIX

This appendix lists cast and key production credits for the films directed, co-directed, written or significantly co-written by Quentin Tarantino. Names in square brackets are credited in scripts, but absent from on-screen credits and/or dialogue.

MY BEST FRIEND'S BIRTHDAY
produced 1985-1987, never completed

An attempt at screwball comedy originated by Craig Hamann. Produced in 16mm black-and-white by Hamann and his colleagues at the Video Archives store, impoverished resources dictated that sequences be shot as and whenvolunteer actors and suitable locations became available. A laboratory accident when developing the final two reels of film finally led to the abandonment of Quentin Tarantino's first serious attempt at directing. ' We were shooting this thing for three years,' he recalled in 1994, 'and I thought we were making something really special. It was kind of embarrassing when I started looking at it again.'

The following cast and credits list is the fullest yet compiled from what little is known about the project.

CAST

Clarence Pool	Quentin Tarantino	**Mickey Burnett**	Craig Hamann
Misty Knight	Crystal Shaw	**Lenny Otis**	Rowland Wafford
Pimp	Al Harrell	**Ex-girlfriend**	Linda Kaye
Her new boyfriend	Rich Turner	**DJ**	Stevo Poliy
'An entertainment impressario'	Allen Garfield	**Screenplay**	Craig Hamann and Quentin Tarantino

Sound	Dov Schwarz	Director of	Scott McGill,
		Photography	Rand Vossler
Editor	Quentin Tarantino	Producer	Rand Vossler
Director	Quentin Tarantino		

(Other crew responsibilities were handled by
Roger Avary, Craig Hamann and Quentin Tarantino.)

RESERVOIR DOGS
produced 1991
US premiere 18 January 1992 certificate 'R'
UK release 8 January 1993 certificate '18'

Shot in only five weeks from July to September 1991, *Reservoir Dogs* cost a mere $1.5 million. Relatively more popular in Europe than the US, the film's modest success ensured its budget was recovered many times over, but more importantly secured the reputation of its talented young director. 'I thought *Reservoir Dogs* was gonna play for four weeks and be gone,' Tarantino told *What's On In London* in October 1994. The reality is that many cinemas continue to play the film on a regular basis, business boosted by the film's formidable cult status.

A stylish and sophisticated debut, many critics were caught unawares on *Reservoir Dogs*'s low-key release. 'The story of a group of criminals who fall foul of each other's suspicions when a diamond robbery goes fatally wrong, it features neither reservoirs nor dogs,' exclaimed a bemused Howard Maxford in January 1993. The film's reputation soon spread, based largely on misconceptions about its most notorious scenes. 'A startling story of betrayal, violence, loyalty, violence, friendship and violence,' wrote *The Times*. *The Mail on Sunday* were more succinct: '[This is] possibly the greatest film ever made.' Detractors focused mainly on the film's supposed amorality. 'I felt sickened by the coldness of the picture's visual cruelty,' claimed *The Wall Street Journal*'s Julie Salamon. 'Mr Tarantino is a good writer and shows promise of being a clever showman. But he's taken the easy route. Doesn't he know that it's easy to get people to gasp at the sight of blood?'

Following the British Board of Film Classification's delay in granting a video certificate (much to Tarantino's delight - it kept the film in the cinemas) *Reservoir Dogs* was finally made available to rent in June 1995. It was released to the sell-thru market in November, only available as two box sets featuring widescreen tapes. The less expensive one featured such gifts as 'Joe Cabot's little black book' and 'Dress Groovier [geddit?] hair gel'. Mr Blonde's Deluxe Edition, on the other hand, featured a booklet about the making of the film, together with a replica Zippo lighter, a pair of shades and some of Vic Vega's trademark toothpicks. The video cassette in the deluxe box set also contained a specially recorded interview with Tarantino. The interview reappeared on the widescreen and pan-and-scan versions of the film issued as standalone cassettes in February 1996. 'Robbery, blood, violence, torture,' ran one of the advertisements for the tapes, 'all in the comfort of your own home.'

Let's go to work: Tarantino on location in *Reservoir Dogs*.

Live America Inc Presents
A Lawrence Bender Production
In Association with
Monte Hellman and Richard N Gladstein
A Film by Quentin Tarantino

Casting	Ronnie Yeskel, CSA	**Music Supervisor**	Karyn Rachtman
Costume Designer	Betsy Heimann	**Editor**	Sally Menke
Production Designer	David Wasco	**Director of Photography**	Andrzej Sekula
Co-Producer	Harvey Keitel	**Executive Producers**	Richard N Gladstein Ronna B Wallace and Monte Hellman
Produced by	Lawrence Bender		

CAST

Mr White/Larry [Dimick]	Harvey Keitel	**Mr Orange/ Freddy [Newendyke]**	Tim Roth
Mr Blonde/Vic [Vega]	Michael Madsen	**Nice Guy Eddie [Cabot]**	Chris Penn
Mr Pink	Steve Buscemi	**Joe Cabot**	Lawrence Tierney
[Jim] Holdaway	Randy Brooks	**Marvin Nash**	Kirk Baltz
Mr Blue	Eddie Bunker	**Mr Brown**	Quentin Tarantino
Sheriff # 1	Rich Turner	**Sheriff # 2**	David Steen
Sheriff # 3	Tony Cosmo	**Sheriff # 4**	Stevo Poliy
Teddy	Michael Sottile	**Shot Cop**	Robert Ruth
Young Cop	Lawrence Bender	**Shocked Woman**	Linda Kaye
Shot Woman	Suzanne Celeste	**K-Billy DJ**	Steven Wright
Voices for background radio play	Laurie Lathem Maria Strova Burr Steers Craig Hamann Lawrence Bender	**Written and Directed by**	Quentin Tarantino
Production Manager	Paul Hellerman	**1st Assistant Directors**	Jamie Beardsley Francis R Mahoney III
2nd Assistant Director	Kelly Kiernan	**2nd 2nd Assistant Directors**	Andy Spilkoman Steven K Thomas
Stunt Coordinator	Ken Lesco	**Stunt Players**	Marian Green Marcia Holley Ken Lesco Pat McGroarty
Script Supervisor	Martin Kitrosser	**Location Manager**	Billy A Fox
Dialect Coach	Suzanne Celeste	**2nd Unit Director of Photography**	Alan Sherrod
Steadicam Operator	Mark Moore	**Production Sound Mixer**	Ken Segal
Makeup Artist	Michelle Buhler	**Hair Design**	Iain Jones
Hairdresser	Rachelle Tanner	**Costume Supervisor**	Mary Claire Hannan
Set Costumer	Jacqueline Aronson	**Set Decorator**	Sandy Reynolds-Wasco
Unit Photographer	Linda Chen	**Music Supervisor for MCA**	Kathy Nelson

Extras Casting	Star Casting Service	**Production**	Wendy Baker
	Mary Santiago	**Assistants**	Moses Robinson
			Scott Sampler
			Elizabeth Treadwell
Special Effects	Larry Fioritto	**Key Special Effects**	Pat Domenico
Coordinator			
Special Effects	Steve DeLollis	**Special Makeup**	KNB EFX Group
	Rick Yale	**Effects by**	
Supervising Sound	Stephen H Flick	**Sound Editors**	Curt Schulkey
Editors	Geoffrey G Rubay		Chuck Smith
			Dave Stone
Rerecording Mixer	Ron Bartlett	**Negative Cutter**	Innovative Cutting
			Enterprises
			Boyd Steer
			Mark Lass
Background Radio	Quentin Tarantino		
Dialogue Written by	and Roger Avary		

Special Thanks	Greta Vosteinbauer	Michelle Satter	Todd Thaler
	Tony Safford	Becka Boss	Stephen Sacks
	Cathryn Jaymes	Laurie Post	Mike Carlon
	Alison Howard	Merry Cheers	Kenneth McGreggor
	Peter Flood	Lily Parker	Harry Nilsson
	Sundance Institute	Terry Gilliam	Ulu Grosbard
	Tony Scott	Bill Unger	Stacy Sher
Promotional Thanks	Judy Garland	**Dog Eat Dog Logo**	Roger Avary
	& Associates	**Created by**	
	Quaker Oats		
	Mr John Lieberman		
	NBA Properties, Inc		
	Pepsi-Cola		

TRUE ROMANCE
Produced 1992
US release 10 September 1993 certificate 'R'
UK release 15 October 1993 certificate '18'

Tarantino's first major screenplay finally made it to the screen under the directorship of Tony Scott, who rearranged the narrative into a linear structure and hired Roger Avary to write a new beginning and radically alter the end. Principal shooting took place between September and December 1992, Tarantino granting his seal of approval to the finished product. 'I dig the movie,' he told *Time Out*. '[Tony] did a much better job than I ever could have done.'

The release of *True Romance* benefited from the stir surrounding Tarantino's directorial debut (one critic renamed Tony Scott's film *Reservoir Snogs*) but failed to capitalise on the attention. Theatrically released in September 1993, its US takings fell slightly short of its $12.5 million budget. Critical reaction was nonetheless generally positive, *Rolling Stone* describing the film as 'a savagely funny thrill ride'. Scott maintains the film to be his finest, partly blaming what he felt to be inappropriate marketing for its box-office performance.

Following a BBFC delay similarly imposed on *Reservoir Dogs*, *True Romance* was released on sell-thru video in the UK in December 1994, heavily promoted as 'The first Tarantino to own'. A widescreen box set followed in autumn 1995, packaged with a t-shirt bearing the slogan 'Sex Drugs Gratuitous Violence - *True Romance*'. Both video releases featured the UK print of the film - at 113 minutes, slightly longer than its US counterpart.

James G Robinson Presents
A Morgan Creek Production
A Tony Scott Film

Casting	Risa Bramon Garcia Billy Hopkins	**Costume Designer**	Susan Becker
Music by	Hans Zimmer	**Edited by**	Michael Tronick Christian Wagner
Production Designer	Benjamin Fernandez	**Executive Producers**	Bob and Harvey Weinstein Stanley Margolis
Director of Photography	Jeffrey L Kimball ASC	**Written by**	Quentin Tarantino
Produced by	Samuel Hadida	**Produced by**	Steve Perry
Produced by	Bill Unger	**Directed by**	Tony Scott
Executive Producers	James G Robinson Gary Barber	**Produced in association with**	Davis Film

CAST

Clarence Worley	Christian Slater	**Alabama Whitman**	Patricia Arquette
Clifford Worley	Dennis Hopper	**Mentor [Elvis Presley]**	Val Kilmer
Drexl Spivey	Gary Oldman	**Floyd (Dick's roommate)**	Brad Pitt
Vincenzo [Vincent] Coccotti	Christopher Walken	**Elliot Blitzer**	Bronson Pinchot
Big Don	Samuel L Jackson	**Dick Ritchie**	Michael Rapaport
Lee Donowitz	Saul Rubinek	**Mary Louise Ravencroft**	Conchata Ferrell
Virgil	James Gandolfini	**Lucy**	Anna Thomson
Lenny	Victor Argo	**Marty**	Paul Bates
Nicky Dimes	Chris Penn	**Cody Nicholson**	Tom Sizemore

Burger Man	Said Faraj	**Burger Stand Customer**	Gregory Sporleder
Kandi	Maria Pitillo	**Frankie**	Frank Adonis
Marvin	Kevin Corrigan	**Luca**	Paul Ben-Victor
Wurlitzer	Michael Beach	**Police Radio Operator**	Joe D'Angerio
Detective	John Bower	**Boris**	Eric Allan Kramer
Squad Cop # 1	John Cenatiempro	**Lobby Cop # 1**	Dennis Garber
Monty	Patrick John Hurley	**Running Cop**	Hilary Klym
Lobby Cop # 2	Scott Evers	**Floyd 'D'**	Laurence Mason
IA Officer	Steve Gonzales	**Stunt Coordinator**	Charles Picerni
Stunts	Todd Adelman	Joni Avery	Ken Bates
	Steve Boyum	Keith Campbell	Steve Hulin
	Eric Mansker	Noon Orsati	SH Perry
	Chuck Picerni, Jr	Paul Picerni	Steve Picerni
	Tony Rich	Robby Robinson	Big Daddy Wayne
	Nancy Young	Ric Waugh	
Unit Production Manager	SH Perry	**First Assistant Director**	James W Skotchdopole
Key Second Assistant Director	Carey Dietrich	**2nd Second Assistant Director**	Craig Pinckes
Co-Producers	Don Edmonds	**Associate Producers**	Lisa Cogswell
	James W Skotchdopole		Spencer Franklin
			Gregory S Manson
Art Director	James J Murakami	**Camera Operator**	Michael A Genne
Camera Operator/ Steadicam	Gregory Lundsgaard	**Still Photographer**	Ron Phillips
Post Production Supervisor	Jody Levin	**Supervising Sound Editor**	Robert G Henderson
Music Editor	Thomas Milano	**Re-recording Mixers**	Kevin O'Connell
			Rick Kline
Costume Supervisor	Hugo Pena	**Make-Up**	Ellen Wong
Prosthetic Make-Up Designs	Frank Carrisosa	**Hair Stylist**	Ron Scott
Wigs	Mary Barnard	**Script Supervisor**	PR Tooke
Special Effects Coordinator	Mike Meinardus	**Special Effects**	Robert Henderson
			Larry Shorts
Casting Associates	Mary Vernieu	**Negative cutting**	Boyd Steer
	Suzanne Smith		Jay Wiechman
Music Supervisor	Maureen Crowe	**Additional music**	Jay Rifkin

Special Thanks To	August Entertainment, Inc
	Michael A Mendelsohn/Douglas Hansen,
	Banque Paribas, Los Angeles Agency
	Bruce STJ Lilliston
	Roger Avary
	Marc J Federman,

Near North Insurance Brokerage
Vista Group/GMC
Coca-Cola USA
Norm Marshall and Associates
Walker Location Services
California State Film Commission
Los Angeles County Film Office
Norfolk Southern Corporation
Michigan Film Office
Mayor's Office - City of Detroit

© 1993 Morgan Creek Productions, Inc

NATURAL BORN KILLERS
Produced 1993
US release 26 August 1994 certificate 'R'
UK release 24 February 1995 certificate '18'

Although undoubtedly a radical revision of Tarantino's 1989 script, Oliver Stone's $35 million film of *Natural Born Killers* added more than it took away. While Tarantino's script concentrated on TV anchorman Wayne Gayle, Stone shifted the emphasis onto serial killers Mickey and Mallory Knox, fleshing out their characters and motivation in the process. Tarantino was unimpressed: 'My script was pure,' he lamented. 'I wish he'd left it alone'.

Principal shooting wrapped in August 1993 and was followed by many months of complex post-production and editing. Following a tortuous classification process, *Natural Born Killers* was finally released in the US on 26 August 1994. Despite initial reluctance on the part of the BBFC, the same version was released in the UK six months later. Reviews were mixed, often criticising the director's aggressive stance: '*NBK* is a lazy, immature, simplistic work camouflaged by a whole lot of bluster', complained *Premiere*. The resulting controversy nevertheless ensured it became a popular attraction. By 1996 its cinema takings alone had earned it approximately $100m worldwide, although the film itself was largely eclipsed by the controversy surrounding it and Tarantino's *Pulp Fiction* released soon after.

In 1994 the screenplay inspired a novelisation: 'Natural Born Killers - The Strange, Wild Ride of Mickey and Mallory Knox' by John August and co-producer Jane Hamsher. The book, which featured an introduction by Oliver Stone, was published in the US by Signet.

The UK rental video release of the film was originally scheduled for 22 March 1996, but delayed out of respect for the victims of the Dunblane shooting tragedy.
On 16 May 1996, Warner Bros Home Video announced that the release of the tape had been postponed 'indefinitely'.

Warner Bros Presents
In Association with

**Regency Enterprises
and Alcor Films
An Ixtlan/New Regency Production
In Association with
JD Productions**

Casting	Risa Bramon Garcia	**Costume Designer**	Richard Hornung
	Billy Hopkins		
	Heidi Levitt		
Edited by	Hank Corwin	**Production Designer**	Victor Kempster
	Brian Berdan		
Director of Photography	Robert Richardson ASC	**Co-Producer**	Rand Vossler
Executive Producers	Arnon Milchan	**Story by**	Quentin Tarantino
	Thom Mount		
Screenplay by	David Veloz &	**Produced by**	Jane Hamsher
	Richard Rutowski		Don Murphy and
	& Oliver Stone		Clayton Townsend
Directed by	Oliver Stone	**Unit Production Manager**	Lee Ann Stonebreaker
First Assistant Director	Herb Gains	**Second Assistant Director**	Noga Isackson
Second Assistant Director	Scott Senechal	**Associate Producer**	Risa Bramon Garcia
			Richard Rutowski
Post-Production Supervisor	Bill Brown	**Executive Music Producer**	Budd Carr
Supervising Art Director	Alan R Tomkins	**Art Director**	Margery Zweizig
Set Decorator	Merideth Boswell	**2nd Unit Director**	Philip Pfeiffer
Still Photographer	Sidney Baldwin	**Supervising Sound Editors**	Michael Wilhoit
			Wylie Stateman
Optical Effects Coordinator	Alex Olivares	**Music Editors**	Alex Gibson
			Carlton Kaller
Second Second Assistant Director	David Venghaus Jr	**Stunt Coordinator**	Phil Neilson
Special Effects Coordinator	Matt Sweeney	**Special Effects Foremen**	Bob Stoker
			Larry L Fuentes
Special Effects	Steve Luport	**Special Effects Make-Up and Key Make-Up**	Matthew W Mungle
	Frank L Pope		
	Jim Schwalm		
	Lucinda Strub		
Make-Up Artist	John E Jackson	**Special Effects Make-Up**	Gordon J Smith
Hair Designer	Cydney Cornell	**Visual Effects by**	Pacific Data Images
Visual Effects Supervisor	Rebecca Marie	**Visual Effects Producer**	Daniel Chuba

Lead Animator	Wendy Rogers	**Animator**	Cathy Wagner
Animation Sequences by	(Colossal) Pictures	**Animation Designer**	Mike Smith
Animation Producers	Paul Golden	**Set Designers**	John Perry Goldsmith
	Richard Quan		Stella Furner
Sound Editors	Jeff Watts	**Dialogue Coach**	Nadia Venesse
	Robert Batha		

CAST
(in order of appearance)

Mabel	O-Lan Jones	**Mickey [Knox]**	Woody Harrelson
Mallory [Knox]	Juliette Lewis	**Pinball Cowboy**	Ed White
Sonny	Richard Lineback	**Earl**	Lanny Flaherty
Short-Order Cook	Carol-Renee Modrall	**Mallory's Dad**	Rodney Dangerfield
Mallory's Mom	Edie McClurg	**Kevin**	Sean Stone
Work Boss # 1	Jerry Gardner	**Work Boss # 2**	Jack Caffrey
Work Boss # 3	Leon Skyhorse Thomas	**Wayne Gale**	Robert Downey, Jr
TV Mallory	Corey Everson	**Dale Wrigley**	Dale Dye
Gerald Nash	Eddy 'Doogie' Conna	**David**	Evan Handler
Roger	Kirk Baltz	**[Unruly] Julie**	Terrylene
Deborah	Maria Pitillo	**Soundman**	Josh Richman
Kid # 1	Matthew Faber	**Kid # 2**	Jamie Herrold
Kid # 3	Jake Beecham	**Japanese Kid # 1**	Saemi Nakamura
Japanese Kid # 2	Seiko Yoshida	**London Boy**	Jared Harris
London Girl	Katharine McQueen	**French Boy # 1**	Salvator Xuereb
French Girl	Natalie Karp	**French Boy # 2**	Emmanuel Xuereb
Young Girl	Jessie Rutowski	**Mickey's Mom**	Sally Jackson
Mickey's Dad	Phil Neilson	**Young Mickey**	Brian Barker
Emily (hostage in motel)	Corinna Laszlo	**Gas Station Attendant**	Balthazar Getty
Jack Scagnetti	Tom Sizemore	**Cowboy Sheriff**	Red West
Indian Cop	Gerry Runnels	**Young Indian Boy**	Jeremiah Bitsui
Old Indian	Russell Means	**Pinky**	Lorraine Ferris
Druggist	Glen Chin	**Japanese Reporter**	Saemi Nakamura
Kavanaugh	Pruitt Taylor Vince	**Dwight McClusky**	Tommy Lee Jones
Wurlitzer	Everett Quinton	**Dr Emil Reingold**	Steven Wright
Intense Cop	Peter Crombie	**Black Inmate**	John M Watson, Sr
Duncan Homolka	Joe Grifasi	**Mallory's Guard # 1**	Douglas Crosby
Mallory's Guard # 2	Carl Ciarfalio	**Deputy # 1**	Marshall Bell
Antonia Chavez	Melinda Renna	**Smithy**	Jim Carrane
Napalatoni	Bob Swan	**Sparky**	Louis Lombardi
WGN Newscaster	Robert Jordan	**Stunt Double**	Timothy P Trella
Stunt Double	Janet Paparazzo		

Photography by	Wayne Goldwyn
Negative Cutting	D Bassett & Assoc

©1994 Warner Bros Productions Ltd, Monarchy Enterprises CV

PULP FICTION
Produced 1993
World Premiere Cannes May 1994
UK premiere 18 June 1994
US premiere 23 September 1994
US release 14 October 1994 certificate 'R'
UK release 21 October 1994 certificate '18'

'After the murderous violence and dark tension of his debut film, the question now is where does Quentin Tarantino go next?' asked the *Evening Standard* in February 1993. Amsterdam was the answer, to write an anthology movie based on pulp crime stories. Originally titled *Black Mask*, and conceived with considerable input from Roger Avary, *Pulp Fiction* went before the cameras in September 1993, principal shooting wrapping in November.

Officially opening at the New York Film Festival on 23 September 1994 (the screening was interrupted when one diabetic audience member went into shock during Mia's revival scene) *Pulp Fiction* had already made an unexpected world debut at Nottingham's Shots In The Dark film festival in June 1994. Special guest Tarantino brought the recently completed film with him as a surprise treat for the appreciative audience of fellow film buffs. Reviews on the official UK release were generally enthusiastic: '*Pulp Fiction* is a roller-coaster ride of a movie not containing one ounce of slack in its entire 153 minutes,' said *Q* magazine's Sue Elliott. 'The entire cast inhabits Tarantino's wacky little world to perfection, and there are signs that the young genius is fast developing his own desperate, frazzled visual style to match his subject matter.' The film was a huge success, grossing $107 million worldwide by autumn 1995 - a healthy profit against a relatively meagre budget of $8.5 million. *Pulp Fiction*, while marking Tarantino's commercial coming of age, also saw his first major recognition at the world's award ceremonies - highlights included the Palme d'Or and an Oscar for its screenplay. Plans to novelise the screenplay in the wake of this success came to nothing when author Will Self rejected Miramax's suggestion that he might be interested.

Pulp Fiction was released on sell-thru video in September 1995, the pan-and-scan tape featuring a comic strip showing key scenes on the reverse of its sleeve, the widescreen version carrying brief production notes.

Miramax Films Presents
A Band Apart
and Jersey Films Production
A Film by Quentin Tarantino

Casting by	Ronnie Yeskel CSA	**Music Supervisor**	Karyn Rachtman
	Gary M Zuckerbrod		
	CSA		

The Japanese press book for *Pulp Fiction* included this handy guide to the characters' complex inter-relationships . . .

Costume Designer	Betsy Heimann	
Editor	Sally Menke	
Co-Executive Producers	Bob Weinstein	
	Harvey Weinstein	
	Richard N Gladstein	
Stories by	Quentin Tarantino & Roger Avary	
Written and Directed by	Quentin Tarantino	

Production Designer	David Wasco
Director of Photography	Andrzej Sekula
Executive Producers	Danny De Vito
Michael Shamberg	
Stacey Sher	
Produced by	Lawrence Bender

CAST

(in order of appearance)

Pumpkin	Tim Roth	**Honey Bunny [Yolanda]** Amanda Plummer	
Waitress	Laura Lovelace	**Vincent Vega**	John Travolta
Jules Winnfield	Samuel L Jackson	**Marvin**	Phil LaMarr
Brett	Frank Whaley	**Roger**	Burr Steers
Butch Coolidge	Bruce Willis	**Marsellus Wallace**	Ving Rhames
Paul ['English Dave']	Paul Calderon	**Trudi**	Bronagh Gallagher
Jody	Rosanna Arquette	**Lance**	Eric Stoltz
Mia Wallace	Uma Thurman	**Ed Sullivan**	Jerome Patrick Hoban
Phillip Morris Page	Michael Gilden	**Ricky Nelson**	Gary Shorelle
Marilyn Monroe	Susan Griffiths	**James Dean**	Eric Clark
Dean Martin	Josef Pilato	**Jerry Lewis**	Brad Parker
Buddy Holly	Steve Buscemi	**Mamie Van Doren**	Lorelei Leslie
'Hold Hands You	Emil Sitka	**Butch's Mother**	Brenda Hillhouse
Love Birds'			
Captain Koons	Christopher Walken	**Young Butch**	Chandler Lindauer
Klondike	Sy Sher	**Sportscaster # 1**	Robert Ruth
Sportscaster # 2	Rich Turner	**Esmarelda Villalobos**	Angela Jones
Wilson's Trainer	Don Blakely	**Dead Floyd Wilson**	Carl Allen
Fabienne	Maria De Madeiros	**Gawker # 1**	Karen Maruyama
Herself	Kathy Griffin	**Pedestrian**	Vanessia Valentino
Shot Lady	Linda Kaye	**Maynard**	Duane Whitaker
Zed	Peter Greene	**The Gimp**	Stephen Hibbert
Fourth Man	Alexis Arquette	**Jimmie [Dimmick]**	Quentin Tarantino
Bonnie [Dimmick]	Vanessia Valentino	**The Wolf [Winston]**	Harvey Keitel
Raquel	Julia Sweeney	**Coffee Shop**	Robert Ruth
Long Hair	Lawrence Bender		
Yuppie-Scum			
Production Manager	Paul Hellerman	**Post Production**	Heidi Vogel
		Supervisor	
1st Assistant	Francis R 'Sam'	**2nd Assistant**	Kelly Kiernan
Director	Mahoney III	**Director**	
2nd-2nd Assistant	John 'Crash'	**Add'l 2nd-2nd**	William Paul Clark
Director	Hyde, Jr	**Assistant Director**	
Script Supervisor	Martin Kitrosser	**Camera Operator**	Michael Levine
Steadicam Operator	Robert Gorlick	**Second Unit**	Alan Sherrod
		Photography	
Production Sound	Ken King, CASKey	**Makeup Artist**	Michelle Buhler
Mixer			
Key Hair Supervisor	Audree Futterman	**Hair Designer**	Iain Jones
Wigmaker	Bill Fletcher	**Hair Extensions**	Designed by Piny
			of Beverly Hills
Costume Supervisor	Jacqueline Aronson	**Art Director**	Charles Collum
Set Decorator	Sandy Reynolds-Wasco	**Set Designers**	Daniel Bradford
			Jacek Lisiewicz

Chief Graphic Designer	Gerald Martinez	Graphic Designer	Chris Cullen
Character Artist	Russell Vossler	Music Editor	Rolf Johnson
Unit Photographer	Linda R Chen	Stunt Coordinator	Ken Lesco
Stunt Players	Cameron	Special Effects Coordinator	Larry Fioritto
	Chris Doyle		
	Marcia Holley		
	Terry Jackson		
	Melvin Jones		
	Linda Kaye		
	Hubie Kerns, Jr		
	Scott McElroy		
	Dennis 'Danger' Madalone		
Special Effects	Wesley Mattox	Special Make-Up Effects by	Kurtzman, Nicotero and Berger EFX Group, Inc
	Stephen DeLollis		
	Pat Domenico	Re-recording Mixers	Rick Ash
Supervising Sound Editor	Stephen H Flick, MPSE		Dean A Zupancic
Negative Cutter	ICE Negative Cutting		

Special Thanks To:	Scott Spiegel	Agnes b	Chequered Flag Slot Car Raceway
	Emporio Armani	Hama Design	Rozann Newman,
	The Warner Drive Warehouse	Lou Arkoff Inc	Ringside Products,
	Cindy Jo Stanberry	Emanuel Steward	Jim Hannafan
	Jamie Toscas	Cathryn Jaymes	Linda Chen
	Jennifer Beals	Cindy Lou Johnson	Steven Martinez
	Bill Unger	Ricardo Mestres	John Logigian
	Mike Simpson	Lee Stollman	Video Archives

© 1994 Miramax Films

FOUR ROOMS
Produced 1994
US release 26 December 1995 certificate 'R'
UK release 26 December 1995 certificate '18'

'Four friends telling four stories making one film' began the script for this light-hearted anthology movie which united Tarantino with three other directors dubbed part of the 'American New Wave'. The project was conceived by producer Doug Lindeman, who approached Tarantino to become one of the contributors to a film called *Five Rooms* after *Reservoir Dogs* made an impact at the 1992 Sundance Festival. It was two years before Tarantino returned to the project, slimming it down and enlisting Allison Anders, Robert Rodriguez and Alexandre Rockwell as company. Each director wrote and shot their

The four directors behind *Four Rooms:* Robert Rodriguez, Allison Anders, Quentin Tarantino and Alexandre Rockwell.

segment in isolation, a chaotic schedule allowing only one week's filming for each story. The end result came in under budget ($4 million) but over length. Upon viewing a rough cut some two-and-a-half hours long, Rockwell was despondent: 'Quentin said, "No way, man, come on. We all just have to go back and rethink this thing."' Tarantino duly cut short a high-profile publicity tour to the UK in January 1995 to begin re-editing the film. Missing its intended premiere at the Venice Film Festival in September 1995, a 96 minute version of *Four Rooms* was finally given a limited release by Miramax in December.

Even taking into account a growing Tarantino backlash, the reviews were universally savage. Los Angeles based internet reviewer Scott Renshaw shared common misgivings: 'If the segments in *Four Rooms* are mostly bad individually, they are even worse in combination. There is no thematic connection between them, unless excess counts; only Tim Roth's manic bellhop unites the four stories. The very least the directors could have done is get together to agree on an arc for Ted's character, but Roth is given wildly uneven direction, and wings it with a truly depressing performance. He ricochets through the Hotel Mon Signor completely out of control, like most everything else about *Four Rooms*. This is the very definition of a one star hotel.'

Miramax Films Presents
A Band Apart
A film by
Allison Anders
Alexandre Rockwell
Robert Rodriguez
Quentin Tarantino

Costume Designers	Susan L Bertram	**Music by**	Combustible
	Mary Claire Hannan		Edison
Music Produced by	Mark Mothersbaugh	**Production Designer**	Gary Frutkoff
Co-Producers	Paul Hellerman	**Executive Producers**	Alexandre Rockwell
	Heidi Vogel		Quentin Tarantino
	Scott Lambert		
Produced by	Lawrence Bender		

STRANGE BREW
Written and Directed by Allison Anders

Jezebel	Sammi Davis	**Diana**	Amanda de Cadenet
Athena	Valeria Golino	**Elspeth**	Madonna
Eva	Ione Skye	**Raven**	Lili Taylor
Kiva	Alicia Witt		
Director of Photography	Rodrigo Garcia	**Editor**	Margie Goodspeed

THE WRONG MAN
Written and Directed by Alexandre Rockwell

Angela	Jennifer Beals	**Sigfried**	David Proval
Director of Photography	Phil Parmet	**Editor**	Elena Maganini

THE MISBEHAVERS
Written and Directed by Robert Rodriguez

Man	Antonio Banderas	**Sarah**	Lana McKissack
Corpse	Patricia Vonne Rodriguez	**Wife**	Tamlyn Tomita

Juancho	Danny Verduzco	**TV Dancing Girl**	Salma Hayek
Director of Photography	Guillermo Navarro	**Editor**	Robert Rodriguez

THE MAN FROM HOLLYWOOD
Written and Directed by Quentin Tarantino

Angela	Jennifer Beals	**Norman**	Paul Calderon
Chester [Rush]	Quentin Tarantino		
Leo	Bruce Willis (uncredited)	**Director of Photography**	Andrzej Sekula
Steadicam Operator	Bob Gorelick	**Editor**	Sally Menke
Long Hair Yuppie-Scum	Lawrence Bender	**Betty**	Kathy Griffin
Taxi Driver	Paul Hellerman	**Baby Bellhop**	Quinn Thomas
Sam the Bellhop	Marc Lawrence	**Left Redhead**	Unruly Julie McClean
Right Redhead	Laura Rush	**Real Theadore**	Paul Skemp
Margaret	Marisa Tomei	**and Tim Roth as**	'Ted the Bellhop'
Stunt Players	Kane Hodder	**Production Manager**	Paul Hellerman
	Alan Marcus		
	Charles Belardinelli		
	Tom Bellissimo		
1st Assistant Director *The Wrong Man & The Man From Hollywood*	Fernando Altschul	**2nd Assistant Directors**	Brian Bettwy Louis Shaw Milito
Script Supervisor	Jayne-Ann Tenggren	**Camera Operator/ 1st Assistant Camera**	Ziad Doueiri
Production Sound Mixer	Pawel Wdowezack	**Key Hair/Make-Up Artist** *The Misbehavers & The Man From Hollywood*	Ermahn Ospina
Hairstylist for Bruce Willis	Pamela Priest	**Costume Supervisor** *The Wrong Man & The Man From Hollywood*	Jacqueline Aronson
Art Director	Mayne Schuyler Berke	**Set Director**	Sara Andrews
Unit Still Photographer	Claudette Barius	**Casting by**	Russell Gray
Extras Casting by	Rainbow Casting	**Special Mechanical Effects**	Bellisimo/ Bellardinelli
Special Make-Up	KNB EFX Group, Inc	**Supervising**	Bruce Fortune MPSE

Effects by	Effects, Inc	**Sound Editors**	Victor Iorillo MPSE
Re-Recording Mixers	Wayne Heitman	**Negative Cutter**	Theresa Repola
	Tom Dahl		Mohammed
Music Consultants	Karyn Rachtman		
	Mary Ramos		
	Kristen Becht		

Special Thanks To:	Agnes b	Stephanie Allain	Maureen Angelinetta
	Lola Babalon	Pamela Barish	Hugo Boss
	Zoe Cassavetes	Champagne Louis Roederer SA	Claire Chew
	Chris Connelly	Roald Dahl	Dolce & Gabbana
	Donna Karan Menswear	Emporio Armani	Giorgio Armani
	Guinness Distillers	Hama Design	Leland H Faust
	Jim Hannafin	Lisa Henson	Eddie Tishkoff, Hollywood Piano Co
	Jerry Lewis	Lawrence Lorre	Adam Lustig
	Gerald Martinez	Sean McCleese	Joel Millner
	Mike Simpson	Maya Montanez Smukler	Cindy Jo Stanberry
	Lee Stollman	Shelley Surpin	Frank Tashlin
	Jamie Toscas	United Inependent Taxi	Bumble Ward Kurt Voss
Animated Titles Created by	Bob Kurtz	**Animation Produced by**	Kurtz and Friends
Creative Consultant	Chuck Jones	**Animators**	Pam Cooke-Weiner Shane Zalvin Gary Mooney Dave Spafford

© 1995 Miramax Films

FROM DUSK TILL DAWN
produced 1995
US release 19 January 1996
UK release July 1996

Dimension Films presents
A Band Apart
in association with Los Hooligans Productions
A Robert Rodriguez Film

Salma Hayek overcame a phobia to win the part of Santanico Pandemonium in *From Dusk Till Dawn*. 'Robert [Rodriguez] told me "If you don't dance with the snake I'll give the part to Madonna."'

Directed by	Robert Rodriguez	**Produced by**	Gianni Nunnan
			Meir Teper
Screenplay by	Quentin Tarantino		
Based on an original story by	Robert Kurtzman	**Executive Producers**	Lawrence Bender
			Robert Rodriguez
			Quentin Tarantino
Co-producers	Elizabeth Avellan	**Director of Photography**	Guillermo Navarro
	Paul Hellerman		
	Robert Kurtzman		
	John Esposito		
Editor	Robert Rodriguez	**Production Designer**	Cecilia Montiel
Art Director	Marie Schuyler Burke	**Costume Designer**	Graciela Mazon
Music by	Graeme Revell	**Special Make-up Effects by**	Kurtzman, Nicotero & Berger EFX Group, Inc
Casting by	Johanna Ray, CSA & Elaine J Huzzar		

CAST

Jacob Fuller	Harvey Keitel	**Seth Gecko**	George Clooney
Richard Gecko	Quentin Tarantino	**Kate Fuller**	Juliette Lewis
Border Guard/ Chet Pussy/Carlos	Cheech Marin	**Frost**	Fred Williamson
Santanico Pandemonium	Salma Hayek	**Old Timer**	Marc Lawrence
Texas Ranger Earl McGraw	Michael Parks	**Newscaster Kelly Houge**	Kelly Preston
Sex Machine	Tom Savini	**FBI Agent Stanley Chase**	John Saxon
Razor Charlie	Danny Trejo	**Scott Fuller**	Ernest Liu
Pete Bottoms	John Hawkes	**Red-Headed Hostage**	Heidi McNeal
Blonde Hostage	Aimee Graham	**Hostage Gloria**	Brenda Hillhouse
Titty Twister Guitarist & Vocalist	Tito Larriva	**Titty Twister Saxophonist**	Pete Atsanoff
Titty Twister Drummer	Johnny 'Vatos' Hernandez	**Mouth Bitch Victim**	Gino Crognale
		Danny	Cristos
Santanico Victim	Greg Nicotero	**Big Emilio**	Ernest Garcia
Manny	Mike Moroff		
Danny the Wonder Pony	Danny the Wonder Pony	**Bar Dancers**	Michelle Beruba
Monsters	Jon Fidele		Neena Bidasha
	Michael McKay		Veena Bidasha
	Jake McKinnon		Ungela Brockman
	Josh Patton		Madison Clark
	Walter Phelan		Maria Diaz
	Wayne Toth		Rosalia Hayakawa
	Henrik Von Ryzin		Janine Jordae

Bar dancers	Jaque Lawson		
(continued)	Houston Leigh		
	Janine Liszewski		
	Tia Texada		
Production Co-ordinator	Dawn Todd	**Assistant Production Co-ordinator**	Cathy Agcayab
Production Manager	Paul Hellerman	**Unit Production Manager**	Luz Maria Rojas
Location Manager	Robert E Craft	**Post Production Supervisor**	Tamara Smith
1st Assistant Director	Douglas Aarniokski	**2nd Assistant Director**	Brian Bettwy
2nd 2nd Assistant Director	Dieter 'Dietman' Busch	**Script Supervisor**	Lou Ann Quast
Camera Operators	Robert Rodriguez	**Steadicam Operator**	Robert Rodriguez
	Guillermo Navarro		
Additional Steadicam Operator	Dave Chaneides	**Visual Effects Supervisors**	Daniel A Fort
			Diana Dru Botsford
Visual Effects Director	Diana Dru Botsford	**Visual Effects Producer**	Karen Skouras
Visual Effects Animators	Genevieve Yee	**Titty Twister Sign Design**	Jerry Martinez
	Julie Glazer		
	Gina Warr		
Set Designer	Colin de Rouen	**Set Decorator**	Felipe Fernandez del Paso
Costume Supervisor	Jacqueline Aronson	**Key Hair/Make-up Artist**	Ermahn Ospina
Tattoo Artist	Gil Montie	**Music Orchestrator/ Conductor**	Tim Simones
Music Consultants	Mary Ramos	**Music Editor**	Joshua Wingett
	Chuck Kelley		
Stunt Co-ordinator	Steve Davison		
Stunt Players	William Atwell	Robin Bonaccorsi	Robert F Brown
	Troy T Brown	Michele Burkett	William H Burton
	Jennifer J Caputo	Samuel D'Auria	Steve Davison
	Tim Davison	Ricardo Gaona	Lance Gilbert
	Troy Gilbert	Nadine Grycan	Randall J Hall
	Tom Harper	Anita Hartshorn	Ace Hatem
	Dana Hee	Freddie Hice	Steve Holladay
	Buddy Joe Hooker	Billy H Hooker	Thomas Huff
	Jeffrey Imada	Henry Kingi	Matt Johnston
	Billy (William) Lucas	Gary McLarty	Bennie Moore Jr
	Greg Nicotero	Hugh Aodh O'Brien	Marina A Oviedo
	Manny Perry	Chad Randall	Troy Robinson
	Danny Rogers	Erik L Rondell	Timothy P Trella
	Frank Torres	Scott Wilder	Spice Williams

Supervising Sound   Dean Beville
  Editor

Re-recording Mixers Sergio Royes
Tennyson Sebastian III
Robert Rodriguez
Thomas P Gerard

Animal Trainers   Reptile Rentals

Special Thanks to the Cities of Barstow and Lancaster and Scott Spiegel.

(c) Miramax Pictures 1995

BIBLIOGRAPHY

Additional sources are acknowledged within the main text.

ANDREW, GEOFF, 'Killing joke', *Time Out*, 21 September 1994, pp. 24, 26.

ARQUETTE, ROSANNA, 'We couldn't wait . . . ', *Interview*, August 1994, pp. 87-8.

BEELER, MICHAEL, 'From Dusk Till Dawn', *Cinefantastique*, January 1996, pp. 18-29, 125.

BERNARD, JAMI, *Quentin Tarantino: The Man And His Movies*, Harper Collins Publishers, 1995.

BISKIND, PETER, 'Four by Four', *Premiere*, November 1995, pp. 76-8.

BISKIND, PETER, 'Quentin 's Own', *Premiere*, October 1995, p.28.

BROWN, CORI, 'American maniacs', *Premiere*, October 1994, pp. 38-40.

CHARITY, TOM, 'Blood from a Stone', *Time Out*, 1 February 1995, pp. 18-21.

CHESHIRE, GODFREY, 'Hollywood's New Hit Men', *Interview*, September 1994, pp. 130-133,151.

CHUA, LAWRENCE, 'Woof', *Village Voice*, 20 October 1992, p. 60.

CLARKSON, WENSLEY, *Quentin Tarantino: Shooting From The Hip*, Judy Piatkus (Publishers) Ltd, 1995.

CLOVER, CAROL J., *Men, Women and Chain Saws: Gender in the Modern Horror Film*, British Film Institute, 1992.

DALLEY, ROBERT J., *Dick Dale - King of the Surf Guitar*, amateur publication, 1995.

DARGIS, MANOHLA, 'Pulp Instincts', *Sight And Sound*, May 1994, pp. 6-11.

DAWSON, JEFF, *Tarantino: Inside Story*, Cassell, 1995.

ELLIOTT, SUE, 'Watch Without Mother', *Q*, November 1994, p. 200.

FERRANTE, ANTHONY C., 'The Bad Boys of Horror', *Fangoria*, January 1996, pp. 32-7, 76.

FERRANTE, ANTHONY C., 'Reservoir Dead', *Fangoria*, November 1995, pp. 40-46, 81.

FLOYD, NIGEL, 'Quentin Tarantino: Blood Brother', *The Face*, June 1994, pp. 92-96.

FRIEND, TOM, 'Revenge of the Killer Tomato', *Premiere* (US), December 1995, pp. 86-92, 131.

GILBEY, RYAN, 'Overkill', *Premiere*, December 1994.

GILBEY, RYAN, 'From Dusk Till Dawn', *Premiere*, June 1996, pp. 12-12.

GILL, ANDY, 'Mr Nasty', *Q*, November 1994, pp. 196-197.

GORDINIER, JEFF, 'Nice Copy Nasty Copy', *Empire*, September 1995, pp. 94-101.

GUILLIATT, RICHARD, 'Quentin Tarantino', *Sunday Times Magazine*, 3 October 1993, pp. 56-61.

HATTENSTONE, SIMON, 'So you want to make a movie?', *Evening Standard*, 22 February 1996, p.25.

HAUT, WOODY, *Pulp Culture: Hardboiled Fiction and the Cold War*, Serpent 's Tail, 1995.

HIGGINBOTHAM, ADAM, 'Walken the Wild Side', *Premiere*, June 1996, pp. 62-70.

HINSON, HAL, 'Killer Instinct', *Washington Post*, 9 October 1994.

HOPPER, DENNIS, 'Theatre of Blood', *Loaded*, October 1994, pp. 48-52.

JACKSON, DEVON, 'Quentin Tarantino's negro problem - and Hollywood's', *Village Voice*, 28 March 1995, pp. 39-40.

KAEL, PAULINE, *Kiss Kiss Bang Bang: Film Writings 1965-1967*, Calder A Boyars, 1970.

KENNEDY, LISA, 'Natural born filmmaker', *Village Voice*, 25 October 1994, pp. 29-32.

KENNY, MARY, 'Sickening amorality masquerading as culture', *Daily Mail*, 22 October 1994, pp. 8-9.

KRIZANOVICH, KAREN, 'Hot shot part deux', *Sky Magazine*, August 1994, pp. 25-28.

MACAULAY, SCOTT, 'Producing Pulp', *FilmMaker*, Summer 1994, pp. 16, 61.

MALE, ANDREW, 'Dick Dale', *Select*, July 1996, p. 112.

MARTIN, JOHN, 'Tarantino Talks Trash', *Giallo Pages 3*, 1994, pp. 8-12.

MAXFORD, HOWARD, 'Stray Dogs', *What's On In London*, 10 January 1993, pp. 6,7.

McCABE, BOB, 'The Bodies Beautiful', *Empire*, July 1996, p. 18.

McCARTY, JOHN, *Hollywood Gangland: The Movies' Love Affair with the Mob*, St Martin's Press, 1993.

McCLELLAN, JIM, 'Tarantino: On the run', *The Observer Magazine*, 3 July 1994, pp. 26-30.

McGREGOR, ALEX, 'Reservoir Snogs', *Time Out*, 29 September 1993, pp. 32-33.

McKAY, PETER, 'A Western lesson in good old violence', *Evening Standard*, October 1994, pp. 26-27.

O'CARROLL, LISA, 'My robber son proves danger of video nasties', *Evening Standard*, 2 August 1995, p. 3.

O'HAGAN, SEAN, 'X Offender', *The Times Magazine*, 15 October 1994, pp. 12-14.

O'TOOLE, FINTAN, 'Bloody minded', *The Guardian 2*, 3 Februrary 1995, pp. 116-17.

PALMER, MARTYN, 'Four play', *Sky Magazine*, December 1995, pp. 38-45.

PORTMAN, JAMIE, 'Uncompromising Tarantino Does It All Himself', *Calgary Herald*, 9 October 1994.

PIZZELLO, STEVEN, 'From Rags to Reservoir Dogs', *American Cinematographer*, November 1992, pp. 62-8.

PULVERY, ANDREW, 'The art of darkness', *The Guardian 2*, 29 January 1996, pp. 4-5.

PULVER, ANDREW, 'The movie junkie', *The Guardian 2*, 19 September 1994, pp. 8-8.

ROTH, TIM, 'In pictures', *The Face*, December 1993, pp. 104-109.

RUBIN, MIKE, 'Hop on Cop', *Village Voice*, 16 February 1993, p. 62.

RYAN, JAMES, 'The Invisible Man', *The Face*, June 1995, pp. 110-4.

SASLAV, LEA, 'Pulp Fiction is out of control, but it works' *The Houston Post*, 9 October 1994.

SHONE, TOM, 'What makes Tarantino tick', *Premiere*, November 1994, pp. 48-56.

SIGAL, CLANCY, 'Killing Jokes?', *The Guardian Weekend*, 11 September 1993, pp. 24-5, 28-9.

SMITH, GAVIN, 'When you know you're in good hands', *Film Comment*, July/August 1994, pp. 32-43.

STEVENS, BRAD, 'Choice Cuts', *The Dark Side*, December 1995, pp. 47-50.

TARANTINO, QUENTIN et al, *Four Rooms*, Faber and Faber, 1996.

TARANTINO, QUENTIN et al, *From Dusk Till Dawn - The Graphic Novel*, Body Bag/Big Entertainment, 1996.

TARANTINO, QUENTIN, 'It's cool to be banned', *Index On Censorship*, November/December 1995, pp. 56-8. -

TARANTINO, QUENTIN, 'The Man From Hollywood', *Esquire*, December 1995/January 1996, pp. 102-108.

TARANTINO, QUENTIN, 'My heroes', *The Guardian*, 4 February 1995, p. 28.

TARANTINO, QUENTIN, *Natural Born Killers*, Faber and Faber, 1994.

TARANTINO, QUENTIN, *Pulp Fiction*, Faber and Faber, 1994.

TARANTINO, QUENTIN, 'Rebellious Jukebox', *Melody Maker*, 6 August 1994, p. 40.

TARANTINO, QUENTIN, *Reservoir Dogs*, Faber and Faber, 1994.

TARANTINO, QUENTIN, *True Romance*, Faber and Faber, 1995.

TAYLOR, DEREK, 'Real Gone . . . Harry Nilsson', *Mojo*, April 1994, pp. 122-123.

TAYLOR, ELLA, 'The Tarantino Gang', *Elle*, December 1995.

THOMAS, DAVID, 'It's an age old story. Young man in Hollywood meets with soaraway success', *Mail on Sunday: Night & Day*, 12 March 1995, pp. 36-40.

THOMPSON, ANDREW O. with ALTMAN, MARK A., 'Blood Brothers', *Sci-Fi Universe*, February 1996, pp. 48-61.

THOMPSON, DAVID, 'Tarantino, star of the show', *The Independent*, 17 October 1994, p. 22.

UNCREDITED, 'Fang Bangers', *Cinescape*, January 1996, pp. 18-24.

UNCREDITED, 'Production Hell', *SFX*, August 1996.

UNCREDITED, 'Reservoir Bunnies?', *Empire*, July 1995, p. 20.

WEBSTER, EMMA, 'Pulp Action', *The Face*, June 1994, p. 99.

WILLIAMS, DAVID E., 'It 's got To Go . . .', *Empire*, December 1994, p. 73.

WILLMAN, CHRIS, '. . . A Little Peace, A Little Menace', *Los Angeles Times*, 9 October 1994.

WOODS, PAUL A., *King Pulp: The Wild World of Quentin Tarantino*, Plexus Publishing Ltd, 1996.

WOOTTON, ADRIAN, 'Dazed and confused', *The Guardian*, 23 June 1994, pp. 12-13.

WRATHALL, JOHN, 'The Full Monte', *Premiere*, February 1995, p. 24.

I think about the audience all the time, but not a specific audience. Mostly I think in terms of *me*. I'm the eternal audience.

QUENTIN TARANTINO